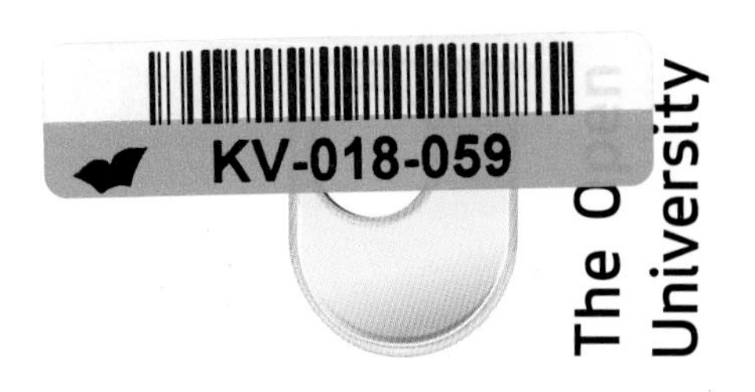

L192 *Bon départ:* beginners' French

Livre 3

This publication forms part of the Open University module L192 *Bon départ: beginners' French*. Details of this and other Open University modules can be obtained from the Student Recruitment, The Open University, PO Box 197, Milton Keynes MK7 6BJ, United Kingdom (tel. +44 (0)300 303 5303; email general-enquiries@open.ac.uk).

Alternatively, you may visit the Open University website at www.open.ac.uk where you can learn more about the wide range of modules and packs offered at all levels by The Open University.

To purchase a selection of Open University module materials visit www.ouw.co.uk, or contact Open University Worldwide, Walton Hall, Milton Keynes MK7 6AA, United Kingdom, for a catalogue (tel. +44 (0)1908 274066; fax +44 (0)1908 858787; email ouw-customer-services@open.ac.uk).

The Open University Walton Hall, Milton Keynes MK7 6AA

First published 2013, reprinted 2015

Edited, designed and typeset by The Open University

Printed and bound in the United Kingdom by Halstan Printing Group, Amersham

ISBN 978 1 7800 7781 9

2.1

Contents

L192 team

Module team

Uwe Baumann (academic)
Valérie Demouy (co-author and co-ordinator *Unité 10*)
Xavière Hassan (academic)
Sarah Heiser (academic)
Becky Jones (curriculum manager)
Tim Lewis (academic)
Jessica Podd (secretary)
Hélène Pulker (team chair; co-author and co-ordinator *Unité 9*)
Christine Sadler (curriculum manager)
Élodie Vialleton (author and co-ordinator *Unité 11*)
Chris Wrage (secretary)

Consultant authors

Bill Alder (co-author *Unité 9*)
Kate Fairbairn (co-author *Unité 10*)
Daniel Bosmans, Suzanne Trudeau and Véronique Grégo (for materials on francophone cultures)

Production team

Catherine Bedford (editorial media developer)
Michael Britton (editorial media developer)
Carole Brown (sound and vision assistant)
Kim Dulson (licensing and acquisitions assistant)
Cayra Goodyear (licensing and acquisitions assistant)
Elaine Haviland (editorial media developer)
Sarah Hofton (graphics media developer)
Lizzy Jones (sound and vision producer)
Alex Phillips (media assistant)
Sam Thorne (media project manager)
Andrew Whitehead (graphics media developer)
Perry Williams (learning delivery & technologies manager)

Critical readers

Arlette Child
Anne Verriès-Wade

External assessor

Dr Enda McCaffrey, Nottingham Trent University

Special thanks

The module team acknowledges the authors of and contributors to the first edition of this module.

The module team would also like to thank Sandrine Aguerre and Toan Nguyen for their contribution to the module materials and discussions at reviews.

Unité 9

ARTISAN BOULANGER
MAISON LANDEMAINE
Pâtissier
Chocolatier
Maison Rouyer
GLACES
BOUCHERIE
RÔTISSERIE
CHARCUTERIE
ARTISAN BOULANGER
FARINE MOULINS DE CHÉRISY

Unité 9 overview

Section	Language	Vocabulary	Skills	Cultural understanding
9.1 Talking about shopping habits	• Making comparisons using adjectives • The relative pronoun *où*	• Names of shops	• Organising vocabulary by topic • Organising vocabulary by grammatical term	• Sunday trading hours • *La pharmacie et la parapharmacie* • Wine consumption in France
9.2 Buying goods in shops	• Using *ce/cet/cette/ces* • Using *lequel, laquelle* to ask 'which one?' • Using *celui-ci, celle-ci…* • Using intonation to express surprise or disbelief	• Names of basic goods • Expressions of surprise and disbelief		• *La papeterie*
9.3 Ordering goods online	• Giving formal instructions to follow	• Words and expressions for ordering online		• Formal register
9.4 Paying for goods	• Paying in shops • Using the direct object pronouns *le*, *la* and *les* • Using *le*, *la* and *les* with the *passé composé*	• Paying vocabulary • Methods of payment		• *Les chèques-restaurants* • Paying by credit card in France
9.5 Making a complaint	• Making requests and complaints • Using *ça fait … que* + present tense • Using the pronouns *lui* and *leur*	• Expressions of request	• Understanding direct and indirect objects	
9.6 Negotiating in shops	• Using *il y a* and dans • Using *celui/celle qui, celui/celle que, celui/celle où*	• Vocabulary of special offers, freebies • Useful vocabulary for bargaining	• Making the most of your dictionary	

Section 9.1 Talking about shopping habits

In this section, you will learn about shops and shopping habits in France. You will learn the comparative using *plus/moins/aussi ... que* and the relative pronoun *où*. You will also develop further techniques to organise your vocabulary.

Activité 9.1.1

A

Perhaps you have had the opportunity to go to a French-speaking country and came across some shops. Can you remember the French words for any kinds of shops? Write them down.

Écrivez des noms de magasins en français.

B

Match each photo to the French word.

Associez les photos aux noms des magasins.

(a) une librairie-papeterie
(b) une charcuterie-traiteur
(c) une confiserie-chocolaterie
(d) un marchand de fruits et légumes
(e) une pâtisserie
(f) une quincaillerie
(g) une maroquinerie
(h) un magasin bio

C

Look at the photos and match the French words to their English equivalent.

Regardez les photos et faites correspondre les mots français à leur équivalent en anglais.

1 une épicerie fine	(a) shopping centre
2 une supérette	(b) delicatessen
3 un grand magasin	(c) supermarkets
4 un centre commercial	(d) takeaway
5 un supermarché	(e) small supermarket in town centre
6 un traiteur/plat à emporter	(f) department store

Activité 9.1.2

A

Look at the list of products below and place them in the appropriate column of the table according to which kind of shop they are sold in. Some items may be purchased in two different places.

Lisez la liste et classez les produits par magasins. Attention, il y a des produits que l'on peut acheter dans deux magasins différents.

des magazines • des produits de beauté et d'hygiène • des journaux • de la viande • des produits surgelés • des fruits et légumes • des produits laitiers • des plats cuisinés • des timbres • des cigarettes • des médicaments • de la charcuterie • du vin • des conserves

Au bureau de tabac, on achète...	**Dans une épicerie, il y a...**	**À la pharmacie, on vend...**	**À la boucherie, on peut acheter...**
des magazines			

B

Which items in the list do you think are **not** usually sold in French supermarkets?

À votre avis, quels sont les articles de la liste qu'on ne trouve pas dans un supermarché ?

Organising vocabulary by topic

There are many ways of organising and learning new vocabulary and expressions. For example, in Unit 8 you learned how to extend your vocabulary by looking for word families (*le travail, travailler, travailleur*). Another way of recalling more words and phrases you need more easily is to group them according to particular topic areas or situations. For example, you could start a list or a diagram, based on what was provided in *Activité 9.1.2*, to compile vocabulary related to the topic of shopping and add to this list or diagram every time you learn new vocabulary related to this topic. Other examples of groupings might be food and drink in Unit 2, modes of transport in Unit 4, work and studies in Units 5 and 8, or hobbies in Unit 6.

Activité 9.1.3

A

Read the following article about shopping habits and mark whether the statements are true or false. Correct the false answers.

Lisez l'article suivant et répondez aux questions par vrai ou faux. Corrigez les mauvaises réponses.

en période de fêtes *over Christmas*

PMU (pari mutuel urbain) *horse betting*

les habitudes (f.pl.) *habits*

aucun magasin ... ne *no shop ...*

En France, les magasins sont ouverts du lundi au samedi, en général de 9 h à midi et de 14 h à 19 h. Les petits commerçants ferment habituellement pendant environ deux heures au milieu de la journée (entre midi et 14 h). Toutefois, les habitudes changent en France et la pause traditionnelle de deux heures a tendance à disparaître, en particulier dans les grandes villes. Par exemple, beaucoup de magasins ne ferment pas entre 12 h et 14 h et certains réduisent leur période de fermeture de 12 h 30 à 13 h 45. D'habitude, les boulangeries restent ouvertes jusqu'à 12 h 30–13 h parce que les Français qui travaillent et qui terminent à midi aiment toujours (et veulent pouvoir) acheter leur pain frais tous les jours. La plupart des centres commerciaux et des grands magasins font de plus en plus souvent la « journée continue ». Quelques magasins dans les centres commerciaux et plusieurs supermarchés restent ouverts jusqu'à 20 h (ou 22 h en période de fêtes), mais aucun magasin ou grand magasin et aucune grande surface ne sont ouverts vingt-quatre heures sur vingt-quatre; seules les pharmacies (« de garde ») assurent une permanence dans les villes. Traditionnellement, les magasins sont fermés le dimanche à l'exception des petits commerces comme les boulangeries, les rôtisseries ou les bar-tabac-PMU et de quelques supérettes et supermarchés qui ouvrent le dimanche jusqu'à 12 h 30 ou 13 h. Il existe aussi des règlements spécifiques sur l'ouverture du dimanche pour les commerces des lieux très touristiques. Normalement, les commerces qui sont ouverts le dimanche matin n'ouvrent pas le lundi matin.

		True	False
1	Shops in France tend to close for a couple of hours over lunch time.	❑	❑
2	Small shops sometimes stay open in big towns.	❑	❑
3	Bakers always close at 12 noon.	❑	❑
4	More and more shopping centres and department stores close at lunch time.	❑	❑
5	No shops open 24/7.	❑	❑
6	Shops are normally closed on Sundays.	❑	❑

B

Now you are going to look at some adverbs. Go back to the text and find the French equivalent for the following words.

Trouvez l'équivalent des mots suivants dans le texte.

(a) generally
(b) usually (× 2)
(c) however
(d) particularly
(e) traditionally
(f) normally

C

Take the French adverbs from the *corrigé* of step B and classify them into the three categories below.

Classez les adverbes en trois catégories.

Describe a habit	**Introduce a contrast**	**Describe from generality to detail**

Organising vocabulary by grammatical term

Organising language in terms of its structure or use is another useful method of learning vocabulary. This might be particular verb types: for example, in Unit 1 you learned how to memorise verbs ending in *-er*, in Unit 2 verbs ending in *-dre*, and in Unit 5 verbs ending in *-ir*, etc. In Unit 4 you learned a group of discourse markers used when relating facts in a sequence (*d'abord, ensuite, après, enfin*). Here you have just worked with a list of adverbs. Making a list of all the adverbs you have learned so far can help you to recall this particular type of word whenever you need it. You may wish to list, for example, adverbs following the same pattern, or adverbs of frequency.

D

In this step, you will focus on the expressions of quantity in the text (of step A). Find the French equivalent for the following expressions.

Trouvez l'équivalent des expressions suivantes dans le texte.

1 a lot of shops
2 some shops
3 most shops
4 a few shops
5 several shops
6 no shop

E

Take the *corrigé* of step D and organise the expressions in increasing order (of the quantities they describe).

Classez les expressions par ordre croissant.

Activité 9.1.4

A

Below is an incomplete summary of the text on opening hours from step A of the previous activity. Fill in the gaps with the appropriate words from the box.

Complétez le résumé du texte avec les mots qui conviennent.

ferment • jusqu'à • sont fermés • matin • 24h/24 • ouvrent • ne ferment pas (x2) • dimanche • sont ouverts • toutefois • la journée continue • en général • sont ouvertes

En France, les magasins __________ du lundi au samedi et sont fermés le __________ __________ , ils __________ entre midi et 14 heures. __________ , les habitudes changent et de plus en plus de petits magasins __________ pendant deux heures et les grandes surfaces font __________. Habituellement, les boulangeries __________ à midi pile. Plusieurs supermarchés restent ouverts __________ 20 heures. Quelques magasins __________ le dimanche __________ et __________ le lundi matin. Les pharmacies de garde __________ la nuit, mais aucun supermarché n'est ouvert __________ .

B

Now, you are going to write about shopping hours in your country. First, make some notes of your own, following the model provided below for a large town in Switzerland.

Maintenant, vous allez écrire quelques lignes sur les habitudes d'achat dans votre pays. D'abord, prenez des notes suivant le modèle.

Exemple

Horaires d'ouverture et de fermeture	**Supérettes**	**Laiteries**	**Supermarchés**
en semaine	8 h – 12 h 14 h – 19 h	17 h – 19 h	8 h – 12 h 14 h – 19 h
le samedi	9 h – 12 h 14 h – 18 h	17 h – 19 h	9 h – 12 h 14 h – 18 h
le dimanche	Fermées	Fermées	Fermés

C

Write five complete sentences to describe shop opening hours in your country, based on the notes you have prepared. Use the vocabulary on opening hours which you have learned, as well as adverbs and expressions of quantity.

Écrivez cinq phrases en français pour décrire les horaires d'ouverture des magasins dans votre pays. Utilisez le vocabulaire que vous avez appris.

Sunday trading hours

The French constitution (through certain articles of the *Code du travail*) guarantees a mandatory day of rest for all employees – *le repos dominical*. Every employee must have a rest period of 24 hours in a row, mainly for health reasons, which must comprise at least part of Sunday. This legislation applies to all employees except self-employed workers, so in theory a shop owner can open shop on a Sunday as long as they do not employ any salaried workers. However, the law recognises that some flexibility is legitimate and necessary, so temporary and local exemptions may be granted by the local authorities through an *arrêt préfectoral* or *arrêt municipal*. As a result, there are many exceptions to the rules on Sunday opening hours, mainly in tourist areas and during the sales. Nonetheless, large companies and supporters of a relaxation of the existing law face a considerable challenge because the legislation on this matter is enshrined in the Constitution.

Activité 9.1.5

A

Track 9:1

Listen to Track 9:1, which is about shopping habits, and select the right answers.

Écoutez l'extrait et cochez les bonnes réponses.

1 La passante achète sa baguette:
   (a) à la boulangerie.
   (b) au supermarché.
   (c) au marché.
2 Elle achète ses fruits et légumes:
   (a) au marché.
   (b) dans les magasins.
   (c) chez le marchand de légumes.
3 Elle achète ses produits de beauté:
   (a) à la pharmacie.
   (b) à la parapharmacie.
   (c) au supermarché.
4 Elle achète sa viande: (cochez deux réponses)
   (a) au marché.
   (b) à la boucherie.
   (c) au supermarché.

B

Track 9:1

Listen to Track 9:1 again and answer the questions in English.

Écoutez à nouveau l'extrait et répondez aux questions en anglais.

1 Why does the woman interviewed buy her bread at the baker's?
2 Why does she buy organic bread from time to time?
3 Why does her husband buy fruit and vegetables from the market?
4 Why does she prefer the greengrocer's?
5 Why does she buy stamps at the tobacconist's/newsagent?
6 Why does she sometimes buy meat from the supermarket?

C

Now you are going to look at the expressions used to make comparisons. Look at the transcript of Track 9:1 and identify the French words for 'more', 'less' and 'as'.

Maintenant regardez la transcription et trouvez les mots français équivalents à 'more', 'less' *et* 'as'.

D

Now you have identified the words used for comparison, find the French terms in the transcript for the following words/expressions.

Trouvez la traduction des expressions suivantes.

1 more expensive
2 healthier
3 fresher
4 more varied
5 closer
6 less expensive (× 2)
7 more convenient
8 as good

E

Find the translation of the following sentence in the transcript of Track 9:1: 'I always buy my bread at the baker's, it's better.'

Trouvez dans la transcription la traduction de la phrase.

Making comparisons using adjectives

To compare different things or people you use *plus* (more), *aussi* (as) or *moins* (less) + adjective.

De temps en temps, j'achète du pain bio, mais c'est **plus cher**.
Occasionally I buy organic bread, but it's ***more expensive****.*

C'est **aussi bon**.
It's as good.

Je vais au supermarché, c'est **moins cher**.
I shop at the supermarket, it's ***less expensive****.*

To compare two objects or people, you use *plus/aussi/moins ... que*.

Le pain bio est **plus sain que** le pain blanc.
Organic bread is ***healthier than*** *white bread.*

C'est **aussi** bon **qu**'au restaurant.
It's ***as*** good ***as*** *at the restaurant.*

Son père est **aussi** jeune **que** sa mère.
Her/his father is ***as young as*** *her/his mother.*

Il est **moins** élégant **que** Pierre.
He is ***less*** *elegant* ***than*** *Pierre.*

Note the word *meilleur(e)*, meaning 'better'.

J'achète toujours ma baguette à la boulangerie ; elle est **meilleure** que la baguette du supermarché.
I always buy my baguette at the baker's; it's ***better*** *than the baguette from the supermarket.*

(Note: This could also have been said as: *J'achète toujours ma baguette à la boulangerie, c'est* ***meilleur*** (*meilleur* in its masculine form because an adjective agreeing with *ce* is always masculine.)

Le vin français est bon ; le vin italien est **meilleur**.
*French wine is good; Italian wine is **better**.*

To emphasise the comparison, you can use an adverb (*beaucoup, bien*).

Elle est **beaucoup** plus grande que son frère.
*She's **a lot** taller than her brother.*

Ils sont **bien** moins coûteux qu'à la pharmacie.
*They're **much** cheaper than at the chemist's.*

Note that *que* becomes *qu'* in front of a vowel.

Activité 9.1.6

Look at the information comparing products and complete the sentences below using *plus … que, moins … que* or *aussi … que.*

Complétez les phrases.

La baguette	À la boulangerie	1,20 €
	Au magasin bio	1,60 €
	Au supermarché	0,95 €

Les plats cuisinés	Au traiteur chinois	% de gras: 67%
	Au supermarché	% de gras: 48%

Les vins français	Qualité ****
Les vins étrangers	Qualité ****

Le shampooing	À la parapharmacie	5,80 €
	À la pharmacie	7,20 €

1 La baguette de la boulangerie est __________ chère __________ la baguette du magasin bio, mais elle est __________ chère __________ au supermarché.
2 Les plats cuisinés du traiteur chinois sont __________ gras __________ les plats du supermarché.
3 Les vins étrangers sont __________ bons __________ les vins français.
4 Le shampooing est __________ coûteux à la parapharmacie __________ à la pharmacie.

La pharmacie et la parapharmacie

You will have noticed people saying they buy their cosmetics from a *parapharmacie* because products are cheaper. A *parapharmacie* in France is a shop where you can buy a full range of cosmetics, over-the-counter medicines and other health and beauty products, whereas *les pharmacies* provide prescription medicines and sell dermo-cosmetics and cosmetic products. Cosmetics that can only be sold with the professional advice of a pharmacist are not found in *parapharmacies*. In a *pharmacie*, a qualified chemist needs to be on the premises at all times but a technician (*préparateur/préparatrice en pharmacie*) can also sell medicines in a *pharmacie* if under the supervision of the pharmacist in charge. In large *pharmacies*, the sales staff are rarely qualified chemists. *Une pharmacie* and *une parapharmacie* are often two distinct sections of one shop, with different staff.

Activité 9.1.7

A

Read the list of adjectives that can be used for describing wines and match them to their English equivalent. Use a dictionary if necessary.

Lisez les adjectifs qui décrivent des vins et faites correspondre chaque adjectif à son équivalent anglais.

1 corsé	(a) light
2 sec	(b) full-bodied
3 doux	(c) sweet
4 léger	(d) dry

B

Look at the information in the table and write a few sentences making comparisons between the French wines. Use adjectives such as: *cher*, *bon*, *coûteux*, *meilleur*, etc. and adjectives you've learned in step A as well as words of comparison you have learned in this section

Écrivez des phrases et faites des comparaisons entre les vins français.

Exemple

Le Sauterne est beaucoup plus vieux que le Côte de Beaune et il est plus cher, mais il est moins corsé.

Vins	**Année**	**Qualité**	**Prix**	**Teneur en alcool**	**Teneur en sucre**
Sauterne	1999	****	€€€€	✓✓	••••
Rosé de Provence	2009	**	€€	✓	•••
Château Chinon	2008	***	€€€	✓✓✓	••
Pouilly Fumé	2006	****	€€€	✓✓✓	•
Côte de Beaune	2010	****	€€	✓✓✓✓	•

Wine consumption in France

France is the world's largest producer of wine, and French people are still among the largest consumers of wine per inhabitant, but consumption has declined in the past few decades. Alcohol consumption went down by 10% in the 2000s and drinking habits have changed. Generally speaking, the older generation still consumes wine with meals while the younger generation tend to drink less wine at home on a daily basis but more beers and spirits when out, keeping wine for special occasions. In the 1980s, about 50% of the population were regular wine drinkers, as opposed to about 20% in the 2000s. Wines from all over the world are available in France but over 80% of imported wines come from EU countries.

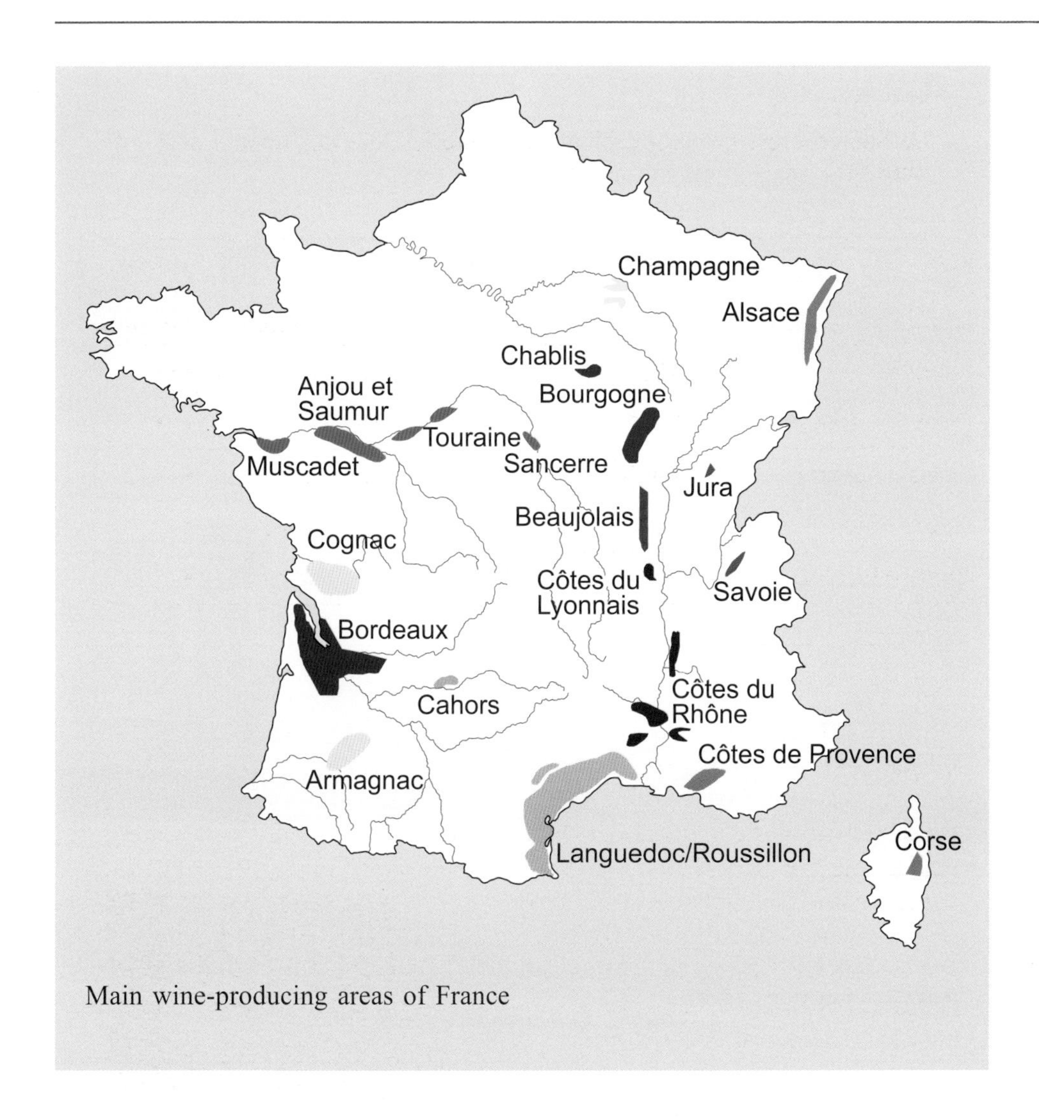

Main wine-producing areas of France

Activité 9.1.8

A

Track 9:2

Listen to Track 9:2, in which some people are being interviewed about their shopping habits, and match each person to the correct image (overleaf).

Nous avons interviewé des personnes sur leurs habitudes d'achat. Écoutez l'extrait et faites correspondre chaque personne à l'image qui convient.

1 Le premier monsieur
2 La demoiselle
3 Le deuxième monsieur
4 La dame

un micro-trottoir *a street interview*
gratuit *free*
produits (m.pl.) du terroir *regional/local products*
produits (m.pl.) saisonniers *seasonal products*
fait maison (adj.) *homemade*

(a) (b) (c) (d)

Track 9:2

B

Listen to Track 9:2 again and fill in the table. Who is buying what and where?

Écoutez et remplissez le tableau. Qui achète quoi et où ?

	Quels produits ?	**Où ?**
Le premier monsieur		
La demoiselle		
Le deuxième monsieur		
La dame		

Track 9:2

C

Listen to Track 9:2 again and answer the questions in English.

Écoutez à nouveau et répondez en anglais.

1 Why is the first man interviewed shopping at the supermarket?
2 How often does he go?
3 Why is the young woman shopping at a local small supermarket?
4 What are the advantages of shopping there?
5 What kind of products does the second man interviewed say he and his wife look for when they shop for food?
6 Why does the last woman interviewed buy fruit and vegetables at the market?

D

Look at the following extracts from the transcript of Track 9:2 and identify which word(s) in the sentence the pronoun *où* refers to.

Lisez ces phrases de la transcription et trouvez les mots que le pronom « où » remplace.

1 Ben le supermarché, c'est le magasin… euh… où j'achète presque tous mes produits alimentaires.
2 C'est un magasin où je trouve presque tout.
3 Nous faisons nos courses au marché et en particulier dans les petits commerces où nous achetons les produits du terroir.
4 Nous prenons notre viande chez le boucher où on trouve des morceaux de meilleure qualité.
5 De temps en temps, nous allons à l'épicerie où on vend des produits saisonniers.
6 Et bien sûr à la boulangerie où nous achetons notre pain fait maison.
7 Je préfère acheter mes fruits et légumes au marché où les produits sont plus frais.

Des produits du terroir

The relative pronoun *où*

You already know *où* used in a question to mean 'where?' *Où* is also used as a relative pronoun to add information about a location.

> Je vais à l'épicerie **où** on vend des produits saisonniers.
> *I shop at the grocer's **where** they sell seasonal products. / I shop at the grocer's that sells seasonal products.*
>
> Paris est la ville **où** je suis né(e).
> *Paris is the city **where** I was born.*

C'est la maison **où** ma tante habite.
*It's the house **where** my aunt lives.*

Grenoble 3, c'est l'université **où** j'ai étudié la géographie.
*Grenoble 3 is the university **where** I studied geography / is the university I studied geography at.*

Activité 9.1.9

Track 9:3

Now work with Track 9:3, speaking in the gaps.

Écoutez l'extrait et répondez dans les pauses.

Section 9.2 Buying goods in shops

In this section you will learn how to make a purchase in a shop. This will include using *ce/cet/cette/celui/celle*, etc. to point to items and using the question word *lequel/laquelle*, etc. to ask 'which one?' You will also practise intonation for expressing surprise.

Activité 9.2.1

You are going to use an audio recording in several activities to explore the language it contains. To prepare for your first listening activity, read the following words and match them to their French equivalent.

Lisez les mots et faites correspondre chaque mot à son équivalent français.

1	un adaptateur	(a)	size
2	une prise	(b)	which shows the dirt
3	une bouilloire sans fil	(c)	straps
4	un bas de jogging	(d)	checks
5	en nylon	(e)	a tracksuit bottom
6	salissant	(f)	shoe size
7	taille	(g)	a plug
8	pointure	(h)	bulky
9	les bretelles	(i)	adaptor
10	les carreaux	(j)	chic
11	classe	(k)	made of nylon
12	encombrant	(l)	a cordless kettle

Activité 9.2.2

A

Listen to the four short dialogues in Track 9:4 and match each dialogue to the correct shop.

Track 9:4

Écoutez l'extrait et faites correspondre chaque dialogue à la bonne image.

Dialogue 1: ______________

Dialogue 2: ______________

Dialogue 3: ______________

Dialogue 4: ______________

en vitrine *in the window*

facile d'entretien *easy-care*

ça sèche vite *it dries quickly*

jaune fluo *fluorescent yellow*

elles te plaisent ? *do you like them?*

la forme des coussins *the shape of the cushions*

(a) Un banc de vêtements

(b) Un magasin d'électro-ménager

(c) Un magasin de sport

(d) Un magasin de meubles

Track 9:4

B

Listen to Track 9:4 again and answer the questions.

Écoutez l'extrait à nouveau et répondez aux questions.

Dialogue 1

1 What is the customer buying?
2 What does he need the first item for?

Dialogue 2

1 What two items are the customers looking for?
2 What trouser size is needed?
3 What colour shoes does the boy prefer?
4 What's his shoe size?

Dialogue 3

1 What is the woman looking to buy?
2 What size is she?
3 In which colours is her first choice available?
4 What's the style of her second choice?

Dialogue 4

1 What are the two customers thinking of buying?
2 What model and colour are the first two they have picked?
3 What happens at the end of the dialogue?

C

You are now going to look at useful expressions for shopping. Read the transcript of Track 9:4 and identify:

1 the expressions used by sales assistants to approach customers;
2 the expressions used by customers to speak to sales assistants.

Lisez la transcription et trouvez les expressions.

D

Read the transcript again and identify the words used when showing an item. Complete the sentences.

Lisez la transcription et trouvez les mots utilisés pour désigner un objet ou une personne. Complétez les phrases.

1 J'ai __________ modèle qui contient 2 litres.
2 Alors, vous prenez __________ adaptateur et __________ bouilloire.
3 J'ai vu celles-là, en vitrine, __________ chaussures bleues.
4 Est-ce que vous avez __________ robe en rouge ?
5 J'aime bien __________ deux canapés.

Using *ce/cet/cette/ces*

You have already seen the words *ce/cet/cette/ces* in Unit 5, used to refer to a period of time:

ce soir **ce** matin **cet** été **cette** semaine **cette** année

When placed in front of a noun, *ce, cet, cette* or *ces* draws attention to specific people or things. The English translation would often be 'this/these' but can sometimes be 'that/those'. Note that *-là* is sometimes added for emphasis to point out where the thing is, e.g. *ce jogging-là*. In this case the translation is usually 'that', e.g. 'that tracksuit (over there)'.

Ce/cet/cette/ces are called demonstrative adjectives when used in this way and, like possessive adjectives or any other adjectives, their form changes to agree with the number and gender of the noun they are used with.

	Masculine	**Feminine**
Singular	**ce** modèle **cet** adaptateur **cet** homme **cet** hotel	**cette** robe **cette** école
Plural	**ces** canapés	**ces** chaussures

Activité 9.2.3

Read the following sentences and fill in the gaps with *ce*, *cet*, *cette* or *ces*.

Lisez et complétez les phrases avec « ce », « cet », « cette » ou « ces ».

1 __________ supérette est plus chère mais elle est plus pratique.
2 Je préfère __________ jupes; elles sont moins chères et elles sont plus faciles d'entretien.
3 Je vais réserver dans __________ hôtel; il est plus cher mais il est plus confortable.
4 __________ produits-là sont meilleurs parce qu'ils sont faits maison.
5 J'achète souvent des plats chez __________ traiteur. Il n'est pas trop cher et ses plats sont délicieux.

Activité 9.2.4

Look at the following extracts from the transcript of Track 9:4 and complete the sentences by identifying the question words used for asking a question related to a choice.

Relisez la transcription de l'extrait et trouvez les mots utilisés pour poser une question qui se rapporte à un choix. Complétez les phrases.

1 (Dialogue 1) Alors, __________ vous voulez ?
2 (Dialogue 2) J'aime bien celui-ci. – ______ ?
3 (Dialogue 3) Et celle-ci vous l'avez en 40 ? – ______ ?
4 (Dialogue 4) Tiens, regarde, j'aime bien ces deux canapés. Tu préfères __________ ?

Using *lequel/laquelle* to ask 'which one?'

To ask 'which one?', you use *lequel/laquelle/lesquels/lesquelles.*

These change their form according to the gender of the noun they refer to.

	Masculine	**Feminine**
Singular	Lequel... ?	Laquelle... ?
Plural	Lesquels... ?	Lesquelles... ?

J'ai acheté deux **robes**. **Laquelle** tu préfères ?
I've bought two dresses. Which (one) do you prefer?

Activité 9.2.5

Look at the transcript of Track 9:4 again and identify the missing words in the following sentences. They are words that refer to the underlined words in each sentence.

Trouvez les mots utilisés pour remplacer les mots soulignés dans les phrases suivantes.

1 J'ai ce modèle qui contient 2 litres ou __________, plus petit, de voyage.
2 Oui, vous cherchez un jogging en coton ou en nylon ? J'aime bien __________ .
3 J'ai vu ces chaussures bleues, __________ , en vitrine. Et __________ en noir, elles te plaisent ?
4 Vous avez cette robe en rouge ? __________ avec les bretelles.
5 J'aime bien ces deux canapés __________ , c'est un canapé-lit, c'est plus pratique et __________ est plus classe, mais plus encombrant.

Using *celui-ci/celle-ci*

To say 'this one / that one ...', you use *celui-ci/celui-là, celle-ci/celle-là, ceux-ci/ceux-là, celles-ci/celles-là.* (*-ci* means 'here' and *-là* means 'there'.) These demonstrative pronouns refer to specific people or things that have already been mentioned:

J'aime ces chaussures, mais celles-ci sont très jolies aussi.
I like those shoes but these ones are very nice too.

and change their form according to the gender of the noun they refer to:

	Masculine	**Feminine**
Singular	celui-ci celui-là	celle-ci celle-là
Plural	ceux-ci ceux-là	celles-ci celles-là

Activité 9.2.6

Now you're going to see how *lequel/laquelle* and *celui-ci/celle-ci* interrelate in sentences and practise using them. Complete the sentences with the appropriate words*: celui-ci/-là, celle-ci/-là, ceux-ci/-là, celles-ci/-là* and *lequel/laquelle/lesquels/lesquelles.*

Remplissez les blancs avec le mot qui convient.

Exemple

Ce modèle est classique. __________ est plus moderne, _____ est plus encombrant. __________ vous préférez ?

Ce modèle est classique. **Celui-ci** est plus moderne, **celui-là** est plus encombrant. **Lequel** vous préférez ?

les costumes *suits*

1 Ce canapé est en cuir. __________ est en tissu, __________ est en laine. Vous préférez __________ ?

2 Vous avez choisi vos chaussures ? __________ vous voulez essayer ? __________ ou __________ ?

3 Ces deux bouilloires sont très pratiques. __________ est de voyage, et __________ est sans fil. __________ vous voulez acheter ?

4 Voici les costumes de la dernière collection. __________ sont classiques et __________ sont plus modernes. __________ vous préférez ?

Activité 9.2.7

Track 9:5

A

Listen to Track 9:5 while looking at the drawing of stationery items below. Mark all the items in the picture that are mentioned in the dialogue.

Écoutez l'extrait et cochez sur l'image tous les articles qui sont mentionnés.

B

Find the English translation for each item in the drawing.

Cherchez la traduction des mots dans le dictionnaire.

C

Listen to Track 9:5 again and say whether the following statements are true or false. Correct the false answers.

Écoutez à nouveau l'extrait et cochez les bonnes réponses. Corrigez les réponses fausses.

	True	False
1 The scene takes place in a supermarket.	❑	❑
2 The customer is purchasing a number of stationery items.	❑	❑
3 He is buying a roller pen.	❑	❑
4 He is buying the pen for his nephew.	❑	❑
5 He is buying the pen as a birthday gift.	❑	❑
6 The total amount is 58 euros 80.	❑	❑

D

Write a short summary of the dialogue based on the answers from step B.

Écrivez un bref résumé du dialogue.

Exemple

Le client se trouve dans une papeterie. Il achète…

La papeterie

A *papeterie* is a store which sells stationery items, both general items for desk, office and school, and luxury goods such as leather diaries and expensive pens. There are numerous small, independent *papeteries* in French towns and luxury stationery departments in department stores and supermarkets. One reason for this is that schools in France do not provide pupils with stationery items but require families to buy their own. At the *rentrée des classes* (back-to-school time) in the autumn, teachers issue a long list of items to buy, which is followed by a rush to the *papeteries* and supermarkets.

Activité 9.2.8

Track 9:6

Listen to Track 9:6 and speak in the gaps following the prompts.

Écoutez l'extrait et répondez aux questions dans les pauses.

Activité 9.2.9

A

Read the extract from the cartoon *Joséphine est faible* (overleaf) and find the French for the words below.

Lisez la bande dessinée et trouvez les mots français.

1 to have a laugh
2 sweat
3 Is it the right size?
4 the minimum wage
5 the sales

B

Read the cartoon again and answer the questions in English.

Relisez la bande dessinée et répondez aux questions en anglais.

1 What is « Cher »?
2 What are Joséphine and her friend Chloé doing?
3 What are their initial reactions?
4 What does Joséphine want to do?
5 What's her friend advice?
6 What's the attitude of the sales assistant?
7 What does Joséphine ask the sales assistant?
8 What is the answer?

C

Identify the following three sets of expressions in the text of the cartoon.

Relisez la bande dessinée encore une fois et faites la liste des expressions.

1 All the expressions used by Joséphine and Chloé to express their **astonishment**.
2 All the expressions used by the sales assistant to show she is **helpful**.
3 All the expressions used by Chloé to **discourage** Joséphine.

Joséphine est faible

la p… (for *la perle*) *the unique item*

(Bagieu, P., 2009, *Joséphine 2. Même pas mal*, Paris, J.C. Gawsewitch)

Activité 9.2.10

A

Track 9:7

Listen to Track 9:7 and match each dialogue with the relevant image.

Écoutez l'extrait et faites correspondre chaque dialogue à l'image qui convient.

Dialogue 1: _______________

Dialogue 2: _______________

Dialogue 3: _______________

Dialogue 4: _______________

B

Track 9:7

Listen to Track 9:7 again and answer the questions.

Écoutez à nouveau l'extrait et répondez aux questions.

1 How much does the dress cost in Dialogue 1?
2 How much does the kilo of peaches cost in Dialogue 2?
3 How much does the watch cost in Dialogue 3?
4 What is the bill in Dialogue 4?

C

Track 9:7

Listen to Track 9:7 again and from the list below tick all the sentences you hear in the track. Don't worry if you do not understand all the vocabulary in each sentence. Concentrate on the sentences you can identify.

Écoutez à nouveau l'extrait et cochez toutes les phrases que vous entendez.

(a) Je n'y crois pas ! ❑

(b) C'est incroyable ! ❑

(c) Mais j'hallucine ! ❑

(d) Mais je rêve ! ❑

(e) C'est pas possible ! ❑

(f) Vous rigolez ! ❑

(g) Vous plaisantez ? ❑

(h) Ah bon ! ❑

(i) Ça alors ! ❑

(j) Ils sont fous ! ❑

(k) Tu rigoles ? ❑

(l) Tu plaisantes ! ❑

(m) Tu te moques de moi ! ❑

(n) C'est une plaisanterie ! ❑

Using intonation to express surprise or disbelief

You have already seen earlier in the module that intonation can change to convey a different type of message. For example, level intonation is used for a statement:

Tu viens de Paris. (*statement*)

and rising intonation is used when asking a question:

Tu viens de Paris ? (*question*)

Irony is often used to express surprise or disbelief, and the easiest way to spot irony is by observing the intonation. The sentence is pronounced in a descending voice and certain syllables are emphasised by lengthening a vowel, as you will have noticed in the previous activity.

C'est une plaisanterie ? (*question*)

C'est une plaisanterie ! (*disbelief*)

Tu rigoles ! (*disbelief*) [emphasis on -*goles*]

Here is a list of expressions which you can use when you want to express surprise or disbelief. These are informal and mainly used in spoken situations.

Expressing surprise	**Expressing disbelief**
Je n'y crois pas ! C'est incroyable ! Mais j'hallucine ! Mais je rêve ! Ce n'est pas possible ! Ah bon ! Ça alors ! Ils sont fous !	Vous rigolez ! Vous plaisantez ! Tu rigoles ! Tu plaisantes ! Tu te moques de moi ! Vous vous moquez de moi ! C'est une plaisanterie !

Track 9:8

Activité 9.2.11

Listen to Track 9:8 and repeat each sentence. Pay particular attention to the descending intonation and the syllables which are particularly emphasised.

Écoutez l'extrait et répétez chaque phrase.

Track 9:9

Activité 9.2.12

Listen to Track 9:9 and speak in the gaps following the prompts.

Écoutez l'extrait et répondez dans les pauses.

Section 9.3 Ordering goods online

In this section you will learn how to order online from a French website. This will include understanding written instructions and formal language.

Activité 9.3.1

A

Look at the graphic showing the homepage of a fictitious French website called www.LCJS.fr Loisirs et Culture pour Jeunesse et Seniors and find the French words for the English terms in the list.

Observez la page d'accueil du site internet www.LCJS.fr et trouvez les mots français.

1 Help
2 My account
3 My basket
4 Search site
5 Gift vouchers
6 Free delivery
7 Best sellers
8 Recently viewed items
9 Store finder
10 Subscribe
11 Customer services
12 Terms and conditions

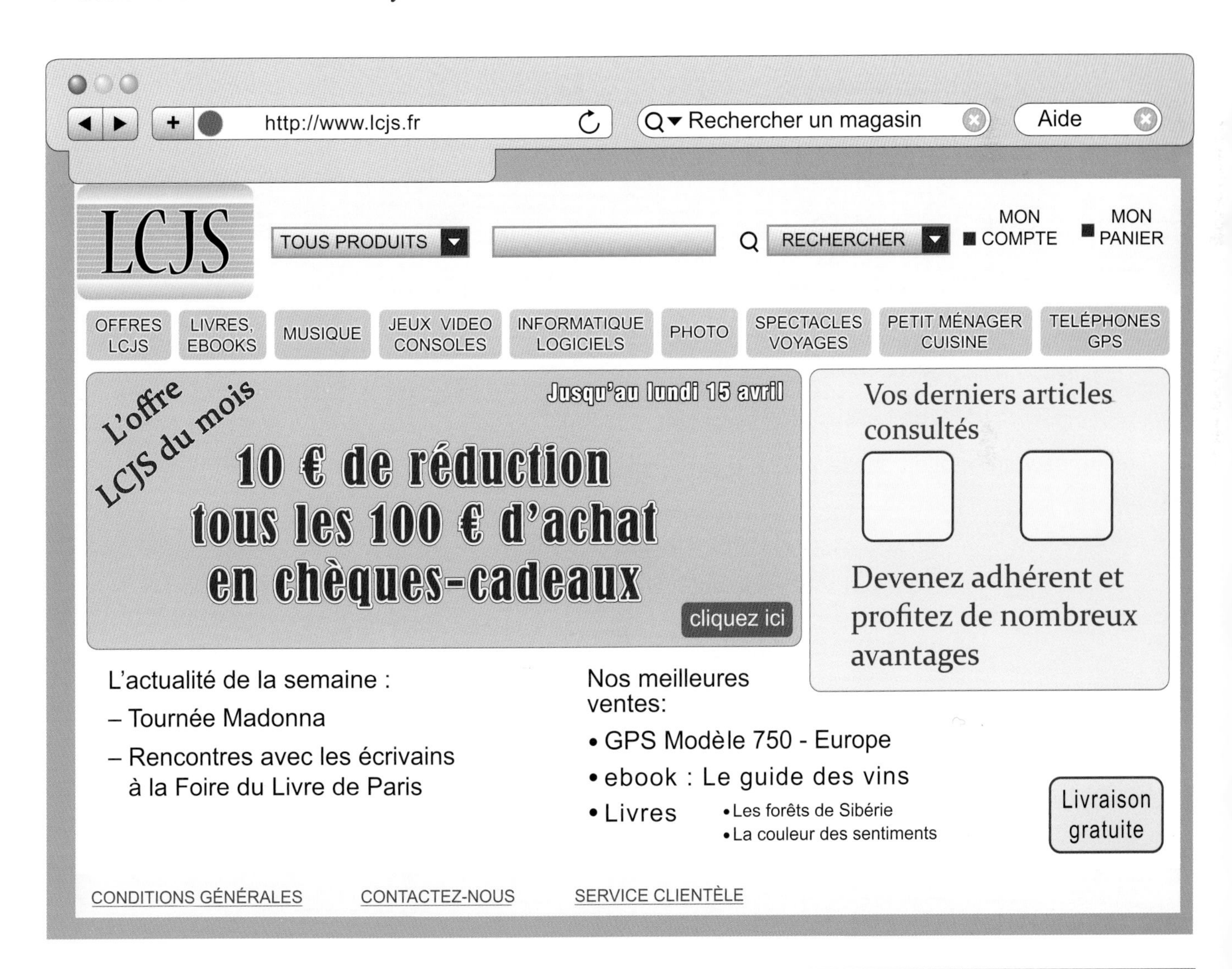

B

You are a new customer at www.LCJS.fr. You want to place an order and need to create an account first and register. Fill in the form as if you were doing so online. You do not wish to receive any mailing from them.

What does *champs obligatoires* mean?

Remplissez le formulaire en ligne.

LCJS

Complétez votre inscription * Champs obligatoires

Pays de résidence * Choisissez votre pays de livraison

Civilité * M. Mme Mlle

Prénom *

Nom *

Date de naissance *

Profession *

Code postal *

Ville de résidence *

E-mail *

Confirmez votre e-mail *

Mot de passe *

Confirmez votre mot de passe *

J'accepte sans réserve les conditions générales de vente du site LCJS.fr

Je souhaite recevoir par e-mail les offres et cadeaux

S'inscrire

C

Imagine you are Gisèle Tronche and you are looking for two books to give to a friend as a gift. You have looked at the best-sellers and made your choice. Look at the next screenshot, which gives information about your order and indicate whether the statements are true or false.

Regardez l'écran et répondez aux questions par vrai ou faux.

	True	False
1 You've ordered two items.	❑	❑
2 One of the two items is not available.	❑	❑
3 The total cost of the order includes free delivery.	❑	❑
4 You could use an online voucher with this order.	❑	❑

D

Look at the screen again and answer the following questions in English.

1 What are the different steps you need to go through to place your order?
2 Which items are you ordering?
3 If you have a problem and want to contact the company by phone, when can you do it?
4 How do you use e-vouchers?
5 What is the total amount of the order?
6 Which button do you have to press to place your order?

Activité 9.3.2

A

a été envoyé *has been sent*

Read the following email you have received from www.LCJS.fr and choose the right answer. Is it:

1 an email to confirm the order?
2 an email to confirm the dispatch of the order?
3 an electronic bill?

B

Read the email again and find the French for the following expressions.

Lisez et trouvez les mots ou expressions équivalents en français.

1 order
2 Thank you for your custom. (×2)
3 your order details
4 enter your customer number
5 manage your account
6 cancellation policy
7 cancel
8 your personal details
9 billing address
10 print

C

Read the email again and answer the following questions in English.

1 What are the two clues which indicate the order is for a gift?
2 When is the delivery expected?
3 How can you trace or modify your order?
4 What can you do if you have any questions regarding your order?
5 What do you need to do to cancel the order?
6 What are you supposed to do with this email?

Madame,

Nous avons bien enregistré votre commande sur LCJS.com et nous vous remercions de votre confiance.

Récapitulatif de votre commande du 5 janvier

Référence: P000LI/0112
La couleur des sentiments .... 22,61 €
Dans les forêts de Sibérie .... 17,01 €
Papier cadeau .... 2,70 €
Livraison gratuite prévue le 11 janvier
Montant total de la commande .... 42,32 €
Mode de paiement carte bancaire

Pour suivre votre commande

Pour consulter l'état de votre commande, il vous suffit de vous identifier sur la page d'accueil, et de cliquer sur 'mon compte' et puis 'suivi de commandes en ligne'.

Pour toute question concernant le suivi de votre commande, vos garanties et votre droit de rétractation, consultez nos pages 'aide en ligne' ou envoyez-nous un e-mail.
Vous pouvez également contacter notre service clientèle au 0 800 000 111 du lundi au samedi de 9 h 00 à 19 h 30 (coût d'une communication locale depuis un poste fixe depuis la France métropolitaine).
Pour annuler cette commande, vous devez nous prévenir par e-mail avant le 8 janvier.

Vos coordonnées

Veuillez nous signaler tout changement éventuel le plus vite possible.

Adresse de facturation	Adresse de livraison
Gisèle Tronche	Karine Guérin
56 bd de la Mer	Appt 6, 4e étage
34000 Montpellier	89 rue des Mimosas
	75013 Paris

Nous vous conseillons d'imprimer cette page afin de conserver les différentes références de votre commande.
Veuillez noter que cet e-mail de confirmation a été envoyé depuis une adresse qui ne peut recevoir de réponse. Merci de ne pas répondre à ce message.
Nous vous remercions de votre fidélité à LCJS.com.

À très bientôt.

L'équipe de LCJS.com

D

You may have noticed that the confirmation email received from www.LCJS.com, although automatically generated, is written in very formal language. Can you identify at least three expressions used for giving an instruction.

Trouvez au moins trois expressions pour donner une instruction.

Giving formal instructions to follow

You saw in Unit 4 that *il faut* and *vous devez* can be used to give instructions.

Il faut voyager avant le 10 décembre.
You must / have to / need to travel before 10 December.

Vous devez tourner à gauche.
You need to turn left.

Some other expressions used to give formal instructions in writing are:

Vous pouvez + infinitive

Vous pouvez consulter notre site internet.
You can consult our website.

Nous vous conseillons de + infinitive

Nous vous conseillons d'imprimer ce mail.
We advise you to print this email.

Merci de + *(ne pas)* + infinitive

Merci de ne pas répondre à ce mail.
Please do not reply to this email.

Il (vous) suffit de + infinitive is like *il faut*

Il vous suffit de vous identifier.
All you need to do is enter your customer number.

Imperative

Consultez nos pages « aide en ligne ».
Consult our Help pages.

Veuillez + infinitive

Veuillez nous signaler tout changement éventuel.
Would you please inform us of any changes.

(*Veuillez* is the imperative of *vouloir.*)

Activité 9.3.3

A

You are now going to practise all the different ways you have seen of giving instructions. Fill in the gaps with the correct expressions.

Remplissez les blancs avec les expressions qui conviennent.

veuillez • devez • conseillons • il vous suffit de • consultez • merci de • pouvez

1 Nous traitons votre commande. __________ ne pas répondre à ce mail.
2 Pour retirer votre passeport, vous __________ vous présenter avec une pièce d'identité.
3 Si vous voulez, vous __________ retirer votre billet sans faire de réservation.
4 En période de vacances scolaires, nous vous __________ de réserver à l'avance.
5 Pour le retrait de votre colis, __________ vous présenter au magasin le plus près.
6 Pour suivre l'évolution de votre commande, __________ notre suivi de commande en ligne.
7 Pour toute information supplémentaire, __________ consulter notre site.

B

Translate the following sentences using the phrases from step A.

Traduisez les phrases suivantes.

1 All you need to do is enter your customer number.
2 You must fill in all the boxes.
3 Please do not contact us by phone.
4 You must read and accept the terms and conditions.
5 Would you please inform us of any changes.
6 We advise you to enter your voucher reference number.

Formal register

You learned in Unit 8 that French correspondence may be very formal, and you can see here that administrative or business correspondence remains very formal even when online. The style of a business email, even if automatically generated, will use formal language with sophisticated expressions that may seem a little pompous. The choice of register and level of formality in French depends on the context rather than on the medium used.

Activité 9.3.4

You have to write some brief instructions for French speakers who have not ordered online before. Using the notes below, give step-by-step instructions to follow when placing an order online on LCJS. Use some verbs in the imperative and each of the following expressions at least once.

Exemple

You could start like this: *Pour passer une commande en ligne, il faut tout d'abord aller sur la page d'accueil, et puis…*

il faut • vous pouvez • vous devez • il vous suffit de • nous vous conseillons de • merci de

- Go to homepage.
- Enter your customer number.
- Check for best-sellers/special offers.
- Select items and add to basket.
- Place your order.
- Enter billing address and delivery address (may be different if for a gift).
- Enter your bank details.
- Confirm the order.
- We advise that you print the confirmation email.
- Do not respond to the confirmation email.
- Click on 'my account' to check order.

Section 9.4 Paying for goods

In this section you will learn how to pay for goods. You will practise the use of the direct object pronouns *le*, *la*, *les* and *l'* with the present tense and with the *passé composé*.

Activité 9.4.1

Read the words and match each word to its English equivalent.

Faites correspondre les mots à leur équivalent en anglais.

un billet • une carte de fidélité • un chèque • un chèque-restaurant • la monnaie • une carte bancaire • du liquide • un bon de réduction • un distributeur • des pièces • un bon d'achat

1 coins
2 a note
3 a cheque
4 a credit card
5 a voucher
6 a loyalty card
7 cash
8 a coupon
9 a restaurant voucher
10 a cash point
11 change

Les chèques-restaurants

Chèques-restaurants, *chèques-déjeuners* and *tickets-restaurants* are meal vouchers provided by employers to employees through a tax-efficient salary sacrifice scheme, similar to the luncheon voucher system that used to be widespread in the United Kingdom. They can be used to pay for all or part of a meal at many restaurants and for items from a delicatessen at lunchtime. They are intended to help employees pay for lunch when the employer cannot provide a canteen or even a dining space. The vouchers have to be used in the *département* of the workplace or in neighbouring *départements*. Only one voucher can be used per meal, and restaurants are not allowed to give change for them. These vouchers cannot be used on Sundays or bank holidays, unless otherwise stated, and have to be used within a time limit.

Activité 9.4.2

A

Read the dialogues below describing several paying scenes in which a payment is being made and match each dialogue to the right picture.

Lisez les dialogues et faites correspondre chaque scène à la bonne image.

1

– Je vous dois combien ?
– Alors, ça fait 6 euros 60.
– Voici un billet de 20 euros.
– Excusez-moi, je n'ai pas de monnaie.

2

– Ça fait combien ?
– Alors, ça fait 10,80 euros, s'il vous plaît.
– Je peux régler par carte ?
– Ah, non, désolé. À la charcuterie nous n'acceptons pas les cartes de crédit pour un montant inférieur à 15 euros.

3

– Et voici votre monnaie.
– Merci bien. Au revoir.

4

– Comment ça marche ?
– Il faut insérer les pièces, là.
– C'est deux euros pour une heure. Tu as la monnaie ?
– Oui, heureusement, l'appareil ne prend pas les billets !

5

– Je peux vous faire un chèque ?
– Oui, si vous avez une pièce d'identité.
– Oui, voici ma carte d'identité.

6

– Alors, ça vous fait 90 euros 20.
– Oui, je paie par carte.

B

Read the dialogues again and indicate how the customers pay or wish to pay in each dialogue by ticking the appropriate box.

Relisez les dialogues et cochez les bonnes réponses.

	Cash	Cheque	Card
Dialogue 1			
Dialogue 2			
Dialogue 3			
Dialogue 4			
Dialogue 5			
Dialogue 6			

C

In Dialogue 2, is it possible to pay by credit card? Explain your answer.

Expliquez en anglais.

Paying by credit card in France

As you have seen in Unit 2, payment by credit card is common in France but is not usual for paying small amounts in most shops. There is no legal minimum amount that shops can refuse to be paid by credit card, but you would usually have to spend at least 15 to 20 euros before you can pay by credit card, especially in small towns and villages or in shops like the *boulangerie*, *tabac*, *épicerie* and some cafés. On the other hand, it is less common nowadays to pay for an amount above 50 euros in cash.

The *carte bleue* is the most widespread bank card in France. It is actually a trade mark but people use the term to refer to a credit card. People often talk about credit cards (*les cartes de crédit*) meaning bank cards (*carte bancaire* or *carte de paiement*), which are debit cards. A customer with one of these chooses to pay immediately on purchase (*carte à débit direct*), or have a *carte à débit différé*, whereby the bank waits until the end of the month to withdraw the money.

So bear in mind when travelling in France that you probably won't be able to pay for everything by credit card and that some shops may accept debit cards but not credit cards.

Activité 9.4.3

Look at the dialogues in *Activité 9.4.2* and identify all the expressions that are used to ask for the price or to indicate how the payment will be made.

Lisez les dialogues et soulignez toutes les phrases qui servent à demander le prix.

Paying in shops

In Unit 2, you learned several ways of asking how much things cost:

Ça **coûte/fait** combien ?   Combien ça coûte/fait ?   C'est combien ?

Je vous **dois** combien ?   Combien je vous dois ?

To ask what **method of payment someone would like to use**, people ask:

Vous payez/réglez comment ?
How would you like to pay?

To ask **how you may pay**, you can say:

Je peux payer/régler par chèque/carte/en liquide ?
Can I pay by cheque/card/cash?

Je peux vous faire un chèque ?
Can I write you a cheque?

Vous prenez/acceptez les chèques/les cartes ?
Do you accept cheques/cards?

Note that the word *monnaie* has different meanings:

Vous avez la monnaie ?
Do you have the ***right amount****? (you may hear this on a bus)*

Je n'ai pas de monnaie.
I don't have ***anything smaller/any coins****.*

Voici votre monnaie.
Here is your ***change****.*

La monnaie de la France est l'euro.
The ***currency*** *in France is the euro.*

Activité 9.4.4

Match each question to the appropriate answer.

Faites correspondre les questions aux réponses.

1	Je vous dois combien ?	(a)	Oui, avec une pièce d'identité.
2	Vous avez la monnaie ?	(b)	Non, je n'ai pas d'argent sur moi.
3	Vous payez en liquide ?	(c)	Ça fait 10 euros, s'il vous plaît.
4	Vous acceptez les chèques ?	(d)	Non, je n'ai qu'un billet de 20 euros.

Activité 9.4.5

Track 9:10

Now work with Track 9:10 to practise the vocabulary you have just learned. Listen to the questions and speak in the gaps following the prompts.

Écoutez l'extrait et parlez dans les pauses.

Activité 9.4.6

A

Track 9:11

You are now going to learn about the direct object pronouns *le*, *la*, *les* and *l'*. To start with, listen to Track 9:11 and answer the questions in English.

Écoutez l'extrait et répondez aux questions en anglais.

la lessive *washing powder*
périmé *out of date*
on me dit que... *I'm told (that) ... ; I gather ...*
erroné *invalid*

1 Where does the situation take place?
2 What is the amount of the shopping bill?
3 What does the customer want to use?
4 Can she use it? Why?
5 What does the cashier ask about?
6 How does the customer wish to pay?
7 Can she make the payment? Why?
8 Does she have other methods of payment?

B

In the following sentences, what do *l'*, *la*, and *les* correspond to?

À quoi correspondent les mots « l' », « la », et « les » dans les phrases suivantes ?

1 J'ai un bon de réduction pour la lessive.
– Désolée, madame, je ne peux pas **l'**accepter.

2 Vous avez une carte de fidélité ? Je peux **la** valider.

3 J'ai deux autres cartes, mais je ne **les** trouve pas.

Using the direct object pronouns *le, la* and *les*

The words *le*, *la* and *les* can be used as pronouns, that is words like 'it', 'him', 'her' and 'them'. These are called direct object pronouns, because they are used in place of the noun object of a sentence.

J'ai **un nouveau pull**. Je **l'**adore. Je **le** porte tous les jours.
*I have a new sweater. I love **it**. I wear **it** every day.*

These pronouns are also used for people:

– Je vais voir **Paul** ce soir. Tu **le** vois souvent ?
*– I'm going to see Paul this evening. Do you see **him** often?*

As you can see, these pronouns generally stand before the verb they relate to.

Here are some more examples, with the noun and the pronoun that relates to it highlighted in bold:

le J'ai **un bon de réduction** pour la lessive. Je ne peux pas **le** prendre, il est périmé.
I have a coupon for the washing powder. I can't use it, it's out of date.

Je rencontre **mon directeur**. Je **le** rencontre demain.
I am meeting my director. I'm meeting him tomorrow.

la Vous avez une carte de fidélité ? Je peux **la** valider.
*Do you have a loyalty card? I can swipe **it**.*

Elle voit **sa sœur**. Elle **la** voit tous les jours.
She meets her sister. She meets her every day.

les J'ai **deux cartes de crédit**, je **les** utilise en vacances.
I have two credit cards, I use them on holiday.

Vous invitez **vos amis** ? Vous **les** invitez au restaurant ?
You're inviting your friends? Are you inviting them to the restaurant?

In **negative sentences**, the word order is as follows: subject + *ne* + pronoun + verb + *pas*.

J'ai deux autres cartes, mais je **ne les** trouve **pas**.
I have two other credit cards but I can't find them.

Tu as des nouveaux voisins et tu **ne les** invites **pas** à ta fête ?
You have some new neighbours and you're not inviting them to your party?

Here is the full range of forms:

Direct object pronouns	
elle **me** regarde	elle **nous** regarde
elle **te** regarde	elle **vous** regarde
elle **le/la** regarde	elle **les** regarde

Activité 9.4.7

A

Fill in the gaps with the correct pronoun: *le*, *la*, *les* or *l'*. Follow the example.

Remplacez les mots soulignés par « le », « la », « les » ou « l' » selon le modèle.

Exemple

Mon émission préférée c'est *Thalassa*. Je **la** regarde tous les vendredis à la télévision.

1 Anna adore les spaghettis, elle __________ cuisine surtout à la sauce tomate.
2 Ah, voici le musée de Normandie. Tu __________ vois, là, devant toi ?
3 Daniel et Nathalie ont deux enfants. C'est Daniel qui __________ conduit à l'école le matin.
4 Nous achetons ce jambon au supermarché ; nous __________ payons moins cher.
5 Il n'aime pas beaucoup sa cravate à rayures, mais il va __________ mettre pour son entretien d'embauche.
6 Vous parlez bien l'espagnol. Vous __________ étudiez à l'université ?

B

Answer each question using the prompt in brackets.

Répondez aux questions en utilisant les indices entre parenthèses.

Exemples

Tu achètes tes DVD ? (oui – en ligne)

→ Oui, je **les** achète en ligne.

Tu paies tes articles par carte ? (non – par chèque)

→ Non, je ne **les** paie pas par carte. Je **les** paie par chèque.

1 Tu passes tes commandes par catalogue ? (non – sur internet)
2 Tu regardes cette émission tous les jours ? (non – tous les lundis)
3 Tu aimes les plats cuisinés du traiteur chinois ? (oui – beaucoup)
4 Tu portes souvent le costume de ton mariage ? (non – seulement pour les grandes occasions)
5 Tu prends ton petit déjeuner à 8 heures ? (non – à 7 heures)
6 Tu écoutes la musique sur ton ordinateur ? (oui – toujours)
7 Tu fais tes exercises à la maison ? (non – à la gym)
8 Tu lis le journal dans le métro ? (oui – tous les jours)
9 Tu achètes tes fleurs au supermarché ? (non – chez le fleuriste)
10 Tu invites Isabelle samedi prochain ? (non – dimanche prochain)

Activité 9.4.8

A

Track 9:12

Now work with Track 9:12. Listen to the questions and answer in the gaps following the prompts, using a pronoun.

Écoutez l'extrait et répondez aux questions suivant les indications.

B

Track 9:13

Listen to Track 9:13. You will hear the same questions and no prompts. Provide your own answers.

Écoutez les questions de l'extrait et donnez vos propres réponses.

Activité 9.4.9

A

You have just placed an order online and are about to pay. Look at the screen and find the French words for the English items listed below.

Vous venez juste de commander sur internet et vous allez payer. Regardez l'écran et trouvez les mots français.

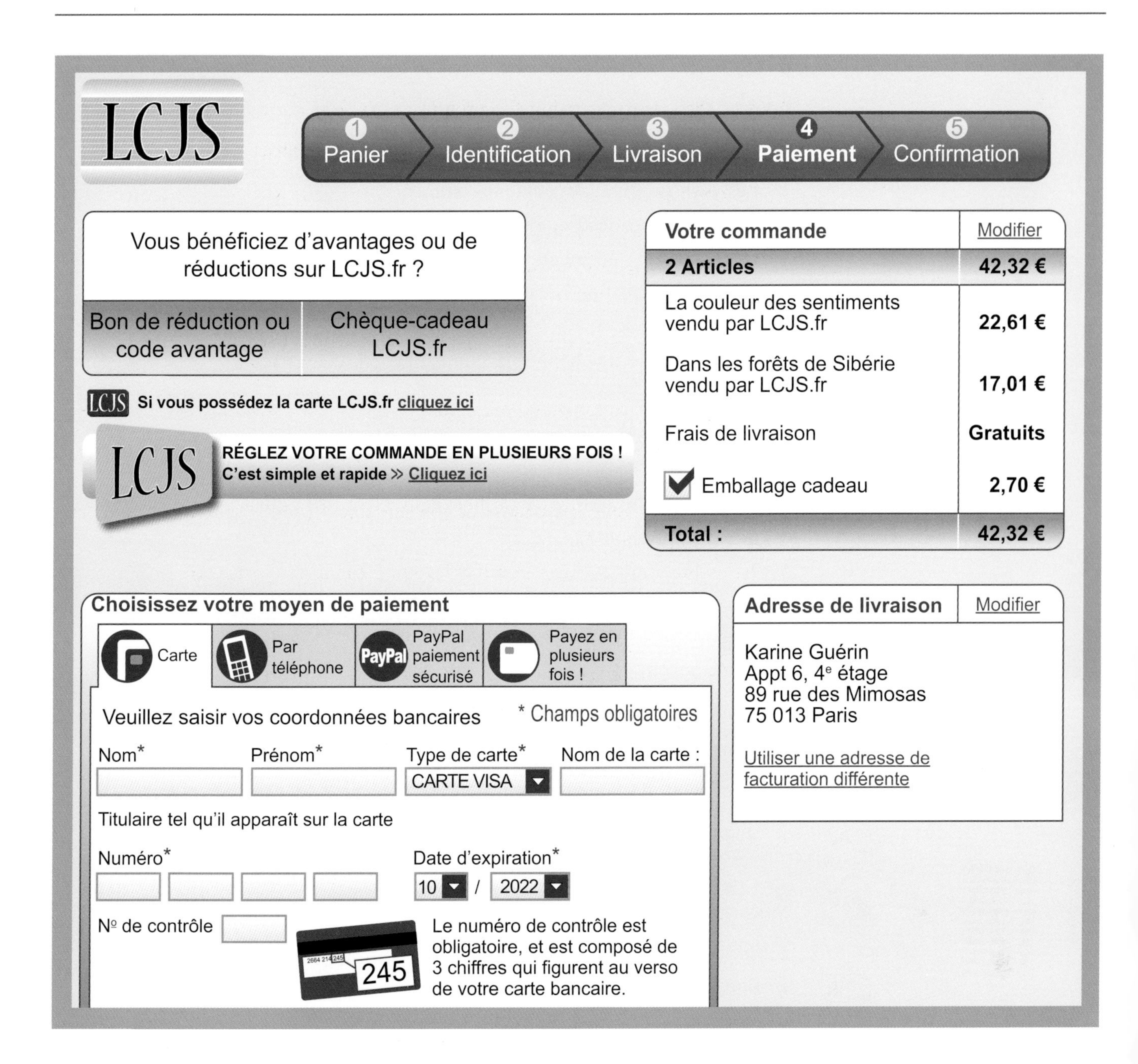

1 delivery costs
2 security code
3 expiry date
4 at the back of your bank card
5 Enter your bank details.
6 secure payment
7 method of payment
8 in several instalments

B

Look at the webpage graphic again and answer the questions in French.

Regardez à nouveau l'écran et répondez aux questions.

1 Les frais de livraison coûtent combien ?
2 L'emballage cadeau coûte combien ?
3 Quels sont les différents moyens de paiement ?
4 Quelles informations devez-vous saisir ?
5 Où se trouve le numéro de contrôle ?
6 Est-il possible de changer la commande sur cette page ?

Activité 9.4.10

A

Match each of the following to their equivalent in English.

Lisez et trouvez les synonymes.

1 au sujet de	(a) you should have received
2 vous avez dû recevoir	(b) when I ordered
3 effectivement	(c) about
4 toujours	(d) otherwise
5 reprendre	(e) indeed
6 au moment de la commande	(f) still
7 sinon	(g) take again

Track 9:14

B

Listen to Track 9:14 and tick the right answer.

Écoutez et cochez la bonne réponse.

The telephone call is to:

1 cancel an order ❑
2 enquire about an order ❑
3 place an order ❑

Track 9:14

C

Listen to Track 9:14 again and say whether the statements are true or false. Correct the false statements.

Réécoutez l'extrait et répondez par vrai ou faux. Corrigez les réponses fausses.

	Vrai	Faux
1 Le client a passé commande par internet.	❑	❑
2 Il ne trouve pas son numéro de référence de commande.	❑	❑
3 Il veut annuler sa commande.	❑	❑
4 Il a payé par carte bancaire.	❑	❑
5 Il n'a pas reçu ses billets.	❑	❑
6 Il a perdu sa carte bancaire.	❑	❑

D

Read the transcript and find the words that are replaced by *le, l'* and *les* in the following sentences. What do you notice about the past participle?

Observez ces phrases et trouvez dans la transcription les noms que les pronoms remplacent. Que remarquez-vous pour les participes passés ?

1 Je **l'**ai trouvé.
2 Vous **l'**avez confirmée.
3 Je **les** ai données.

Using *le, la* and *les* with the *passé composé*

Earlier in this section, you saw that direct object pronouns are placed in front of the verb.

J'aime beaucoup ce chapeau, mais je ne **le** porte pas souvent.
I like this hat but I don't wear it often.

When using these pronouns with the *passé composé*:

- the pronoun is placed immediately before *avoir*:
  Mon numéro de client ? Je **l'**ai perdu.
- the past participle agrees with the preceding *le*, *la*, *les*, *l'*:
  La commande, vous **l'**avez déjà confirmée.
  Mes coordonnées bancaires, mais je **les** ai déjà envoy**ées**.
  Les billets ? On ne **les** a pas reç**us**.

The word order is *ne* + pronoun + *pas* in a negative sentence:

- Je ne **l'**ai pas trouvé.

Note the **pronunciation** of past participles used with a verb in the *passé composé*. The *e* added to a past participle as a feminine ending alters the pronunciation if the past participle ends in a consonant. For example:

Le train, je l'ai **pris**. *(pronounced* [pʀi]*)*

La monnaie, je l'ai **prise**. *(pronounced* [pʀiz]*)*

Le travail, il l'a **fait**. *(pronounced* [fɛ]*)*

La vaisselle, il l'a **faite**. *(pronounced* [fɛt], *which sounds like* 'fête'*)*

Feminine plural endings such as *prises* and *faites* are pronounced the same as feminine singular endings, because the final *s* is silent.

Activité 9.4.11

A

Put the words into the right order to create sentences.

Remettez les phrases dans le bon ordre.

1 ai – dimanche – l' – pour – Je – prochain – invitée.
2 les – sur – commandés – internet – Nous – avons.
3 achetée – l' – en – solde – avez – Vous?
4 obtenus – a – les – gratuitement – Il.
5 la – Elle – l' – retrouvé – à – poste – a.

B

Now you have put the words in order, choose the correct answer from the words in the box, following the example.

Les phrases sont maintenent dans le bon ordre. Choisissez la (ou les) bonne(s) réponse(s) pour chaque phrase comme dans l'exemple.

Exemple

__________ ? Oui, je l'ai invitée pour dimanche prochain.
(Annie – Paul – mon collègue)

Answer: *Annie* (because the past participle *invitée* refers to a feminine noun).

1 __________ ? Oui, nous les avons commandés sur internet.
(les vêtements – les assiettes – les tables)

2 __________ , vous l'avez achetée en solde ?
(ces chaussures – cette robe – ce jogging)

3 __________ , il les a obtenus gratuitement ?
(les tickets de concert – la livraison – les entrées)

4 __________ ? Oui, elle l'a retrouvé à la poste.
(ses gants – sa bague – son chien)

C

Choose the correct answer.

Choisissez la bonne réponse.

1 Le café, Olivier l'a (bu/bue/bus) tout à l'heure.
2 La directrice, je l'ai (vu/vues/vue) trois fois aujourd'hui.
3 Les tomates, tu les as (prise/prises/pris) au rayon fruits et légumes ?
4 Les baguettes, vous les avez (acheté/achetée/achetées) à la boulangerie ?
5 Votre parapluie, vous l'avez (perdu/perdus/perdue) quand ?
6 Tes amis, tu les as (invité/invitée/invités) hier soir ?

rayon (m.) *section, counter*

Activité 9.4.12

A

Replace the words in bold with the correct pronoun: *le*, *la*, *les* or *l'*.

Remplacez les mots en gras par le pronom qui convient.

Regarde **ce stylo plume**.

Il est beau. Tu (1) __________as acheté dans une papeterie ?

Oui, je (2) __________ai acheté aux Galeries Lafayette. Et, j'ai **cette écharpe** aussi.

Elle est magnifique. Tu (3) __________as achetée aux Galeries Lafayette aussi ?

Non, je ne (4) __________ai pas achetée là-bas. Je (5) __________ ai achetée dans une petite maroquinerie.

Ils sont beaux **ces cadeaux**. Ils sont pour toi ?

Non, je (6) __________ ai achetés pour **mes amis Maurice et Elisabeth**.

Tu (7) __________ as invités à ta fête?

Non, toute la famille est partie en week-end. Tu sais, ils ont acheté **une maison de campagne**.

Ah, oui ! Tu (8) __________as visitée ?

Oui, elle est superbe. Regarde, j'ai **des photos**.

Ah, tu (9) __________ as prises quand ?

Cet été. Et tu vois **la piscine**, c'est Maurice qui (10) __________ a faite lui-même.

Maurice (11) __________a faite lui-même ! Mais c'est incroyable !

B

Track 9:15

Listen to Track 9:15 and speak in the gaps following the prompts.

Écoutez l'extrait et parlez dans les pauses.

Section 9.5 Making a complaint

In this section you will learn how to express dissatisfaction and make a complaint. You will also learn about the indirect object pronouns *lui* and *leur*.

Activité 9.5.1

A

Read the short email extracts below and match each email to the phrase that best describes the purpose of the message.

Lisez les extraits des trois courriels et faites correspondre chaque courriel à son titre.

je devais recevoir *I was meant to receive, I should have received*

la somme versée *the amount paid*

1

J'ai commandé récemment des articles dans votre catalogue, notamment des bols en porcelaine et une cafetière. Un des bols est arrivé cassé et la cafetière est endommagée. Je suis très déçue. Pourriez-vous remplacer ces articles dans les plus brefs délais, s'il vous plaît ?

2

J'ai passé une commande par internet il y a trois semaines. Selon les informations mentionnées dans votre courriel de confirmation de commande, je devais recevoir les articles sous un délai de 15 jours, mais jusqu'ici je n'ai rien reçu. Je voudrais faire une réclamation et annuler ma commande. Je dois vous dire que je ne suis pas du tout satisfaite de votre service.

3

J'ai récemment commandé un pantalon et un pull par téléphone. Le pantalon n'est pas le modèle que j'ai commandé et le pull n'est pas à la bonne taille. J'ai renvoyé les articles. Je vous ai envoyé deux courriels pour annuler ma commande mais vous ne m'avez pas répondu, et je n'ai toujours pas reçu mon remboursement. C'est vraiment inacceptable ! Je vous demande de me rembourser immédiatement la somme versée par carte bancaire.

(a) Articles non livrés : demande d'annulation de commande

(b) Annulation de commande : demande de remboursement

(c) Articles endommagés : demande d'échange des articles

B

Read the emails of step A again and answer the questions in English.

Relisez les courriels et répondez aux questions en anglais.

Email 1

1 What was ordered and how was the order placed?

2 What was the problem on delivery?

3 What is the customer requesting?

Email 2

4 How was the order placed?

5 What was the customer expecting?

6 What happened?

7 What does the customer want to do?

Email 3

8 What was ordered and how?

9 What happened to the order?

10 What did the customer do?

11 Did anything happen?

12 What is the customer requesting now?

C

Read the emails again, underline the three sentences which express a request and translate those sentences.

Soulignez les trois phrases qui expriment une demande et traduisez ces phrases.

D

Highlight the three sentences in the emails which express dissatisfaction, and translate those sentences.

Soulignez les trois phrases qui expriment le mécontentement et traduisez ces phrases.

Making requests and complaints

In Unit 8 you learned how to make requests using **pourriez-vous** + *verb in the infinitive* and **je voudrais/veux** + *verb in the infinitive.*

Pourriez-vous me dire si...

Je voudrais savoir si...

These two structures are also used for making a complaint:

Pourriez-vous remplacer ces articles dans les plus brefs délais, s'il vous plaît ?
Could you replace these items as soon as possible, please?

Je voudrais faire une réclamation.
I would like to lodge a complaint.

Some other, more direct or forceful expressions for complaining are:

- **je vous demande de** + *verb in the infinitive*

  Je vous demande de me rembourser immédiatement.
  I request an immediate reimbursement.

- **je veux / j'exige** + *noun*

  Je veux / J'exige le remboursement immédiat de ma commande.
  I demand the immediate reimbursement of my order.

Activité 9.5.2

A

Track 9:16

Listen to Track 9:16, in which a customer is complaining about an order. Can you tell if she is a satisfied customer at the end of the telephone call? Explain your answer in English.

Écoutez l'extrait. Est-ce que la cliente est satisfaite à la fin de la conversation téléphonique ? Expliquez votre réponse en anglais.

très occupés *very busy*
beaucoup d'appels *a lot of calls*
expédier *to send*
voyons *let's see*
un exemplaire *a copy*

B

To go into more detail, listen to Track 9:16 again and answer the questions in English.

Track 9:16

Réécoutez l'extrait et répondez aux questions en anglais.

1 When did she place the order?
2 What did she order?
3 What happened to the order?
4 What is the problem with one of the items she ordered?
5 What is she asked to do?

6 What does she request?
7 Will she remain a customer with that company?

C

Track 9:16

Now you will concentrate on the expression *ça fait ... que*. Listen to Track 9:16 again and tick the correct ending of each sentence.

Réécoutez l'extrait et cochez les bonnes réponses.

1 La cliente patiente au téléphone depuis :

(a) cinq minutes. ❑
(b) quinze minutes. ❑
(c) cent minutes. ❑

2 Elle attend sa commande depuis :

(a) trois semaines. ❑
(b) treize semaines. ❑
(c) trente semaines. ❑

3 Elle est cliente depuis :

(a) deux ans. ❑
(b) dix ans. ❑
(c) douze ans. ❑

Using *ça fait ... que* + present tense

In Unit 8, you learned to use the present tense + *depuis* to talk about something which started in the past but is still going on.

Je suis cadre **depuis** dix ans.
I have been *a manager* ***for*** *ten years.*

J'attends le bus **depuis** un quart d'heure.
I have been waiting *for the bus* ***for*** *a quarter of an hour.*

Ça fait ... que + present tense is used in similar circumstances but is more emphatic.

Ça fait dix minutes **que** je patiente.
I've been waiting for ten minutes.

Ça fait quinze ans **qu**'elle habite à Londres.
She's been living in London for fifteen years.

The present tense is always used in French if an action or a situation is still going on.

Activité 9.5.3

Read the following sentences and transform them according to the model.

Transformez les phrases selon l'exemple.

Exemple

Elle demande une promotion **depuis trois ans.**

→ **Ça fait** trois ans **qu**'elle demande une promotion.

1 Il est facteur depuis trente ans.
2 J'attends le colis depuis une dizaine de jours.
3 On fait la queue à la caisse depuis un quart d'heure.
4 Il patiente depuis dix minutes et le poste est toujours occupé !
5 Vous attendez votre remboursement depuis une semaine ?

Activité 9.5.4

Track 9:17

Now work with Track 9:17. Listen to the questions and speak in the pauses, following the prompts, using the expression *ça fait ... que.*

Écoutez l'extrait et parlez dans les pauses en utilisant l'expression « ça fait ... que ».

Activité 9.5.5

Track 9:18

Work with Track 9:18 to practise what you have learned so far in this section. Listen to the telephone conversation and speak in the gaps, following the prompts.

Écoutez et parlez dans les pauses.

Activité 9.5.6

A

You are going to work with the pronouns *lui* and *leur.* Read Dialogue 1 and answer the questions.

Lisez le dialogue et répondez aux questions.

Dialogue 1

Client Allô, oui bonjour. Je voudrais savoir si vous avez envoyé mes billets. Le numéro de référence de ma commande est le RBL009.

Employée Oui, un instant s'il vous plaît... [RBL009] Alors... C'est Monsieur Lemoine ? Euh, non, je suis vraiment désolé.

Client Mais c'est inadmissible. Ça fait un mois que j'attends. Le match est samedi. Je veux résoudre ce problème immédiatement. Je voudrais parler au directeur !

Employée Oui. Un instant. Je vais contacter ma responsable. Ne quittez pas, s'il vous plaît, je lui téléphone tout de suite.

Employée Allô Sylvie ? J'ai Monsieur Lemoine en ligne, c'est au sujet de ses billets du match de rugby Brive-Leicester.

Cadre Ah, oui. Je viens de recevoir une note des collègues de Brive. Les billets sont enfin arrivés. Je vais leur envoyer un courriel d'urgence. Ils vont expédier les billets de Monsieur Lemoine immédiatement. Tu peux lui dire qu'il va les recevoir après-demain au plus tard.

1 What is the dialogue about?
2 Why does the customer need to solve the problem immediately?
3 Can the problem be solved and how?

B

Read this dialogue, which is a continuation of the context above, and answer the questions.

Lisez le dialogue et répondez aux questions.

une lettre recommandée *a letter sent recorded delivery*
des dommages et intérêts *compensation*

Dialogue 2

Ami Ah, salut. Ça va?

Client Pas vraiment. Ça fait un mois que j'attends mes billets pour le match Brive-Leicester, je n'ai toujours rien reçu et le match est demain.

Ami Mais c'est inadmissible ! Tu as contacté les services ?

Client Oui, je leur ai envoyé un courriel, puis je leur ai téléphoné deux fois. Je devais les recevoir ce matin.

Ami Mais alors, tu les as reçus finalement ?

Client Non. J'ai parlé à la responsable ce matin. Je lui ai téléphoné, je lui ai demandé de résoudre mon problème immédiatement mais malheureusement, c'est trop tard, elle ne peut rien faire. Alors, j'ai écrit au directeur général, je lui ai envoyé une lettre recommandée pour demander des dommages et intérêts, mais je ne vais pas pouvoir aller voir le match, c'est sûr !

1 Has the problem been solved?
2 What did the customer do in the first instance?
3 When was the order due?
4 What did the customer do this morning?

C

Underline the phrases in the two dialogues which correspond to the following sentences.

Lisez les dialogues et soulignez les phrases qui correspondent aux phrases suivantes.

1 Je téléphone tout de suite à ma responsable.
2 Je vais envoyer un courriel d'urgence aux collègues de Brive.
3 Tu peux dire à Monsieur Lemoine qu'il va les recevoir après-demain au plus tard.
4 J'ai envoyé un courriel aux services.
5 J'ai téléphoné deux fois aux services.
6 J'ai téléphoné à la responsable.
7 J'ai demandé à la responsable de résoudre mon problème immédiatement.
8 J'ai envoyé une lettre recommandée à ma collègue.

Using the pronouns *lui* and *leur*

In Section 9.4 you learned about the direct object pronouns *le*, *la*, *les* and *l'*. *Lui* and *leur* are also pronouns. They are used when verbs are followed by *à* and so are called indirect object pronouns.

– Tu as téléphoné **à ta directrice** ?
– Non, je **lui** ai envoyé un courriel.
– *Did you phone* ***your manager****?*
– *No, I sent* ***her*** *an email. (= I sent an email* ***to her****)*

– Vous avez parlé **aux enfants** ?
– Non, nous **leur** avons envoyé un message.
– *Did you speak* ***to the children****?*
– *No, we sent* ***them*** *a text. (= we sent a text* ***to them****)*

Many verbs followed by the preposition *à* are verbs for expressing communication or giving something to someone.

parler à	écrire à	téléphoner à	proposer à
donner à	montrer à	demander à	conseiller à
offrir à	dire à	répondre à	prêter à

In the following sentence:

Je **lui** ai donné le livre hier.
I gave the book ***to him/her*** *yesterday.*

the thing given is 'the book', so that is the object of the verb 'give', and the person to whom it is given, 'to him/her', is the indirect object pronoun.

lui/leur (3rd person indirect object pronouns)	
Masculine	lui
Feminine	lui
Plural	leur

Lui and *leur* are always placed before the verb, whether the verb is in the present tense or the *passé composé*.

Je **leur** ai proposé une tasse de thé.
I offered them a cup of tea.

Nous **lui** conseillons d'arriver tôt.
We advise him/her to arrive early.

Elle **lui** a envoyé un courriel.
She sent him/her an email.

In **negative sentences** in the present, the word order is: subject + *ne* + pronoun + verb + *pas*.

Elle **ne lui téléphone pas** le dimanche.
She doesn't ring him/her on Sundays.

In negative sentences in the *passé composé*, the word order is: subject + *ne* + pronoun + *avoir* + *pas* + past participle.

Vous **ne leur avez pas répondu**.
You didn't reply to them.

When *lui* and *leur* are used with two verbs, they are placed in front of the second verb.

Je veux parler au directeur. Je **veux lui parler** tout de suite.
I want to speak to the manager. I want to speak to him straight away.

Here is the full range of forms of indirect object pronouns:

Indirect object pronouns	
elle **me** téléphone	elle **nous** téléphone
elle **te** téléphone	elle **vous** téléphone
elle **lui** téléphone	elle **leur** téléphone

Il leur dit bonjour.

Il lui raconte une blague.

Elle lui téléphone.

Il lui parle.

Activité 9.5.7

Rewrite the following sentences, replacing the indirect object words with *lui* or *leur*.

Transformez les phrases ci-dessous en utilisant « lui » ou « leur ».

> Exemples
>
> Il téléphone à sa mère ? (oui – souvent) → Oui, il **lui** téléphone souvent.
>
> Tu as donné la clé à tes amis. (oui – ce matin) → Je **leur** ai donné la clé ce matin.

1 Tu écris à ton correspondant américain ? (oui – de temps en temps)
2 Elle a téléphoné à Éric ? (non)
3 Paul, tu as parlé au patron au sujet de ta promotion ? (oui – hier)

4 Vous envoyez des courriels à vos collègues ? (oui – tous les jours)
5 Colette a montré son album de photos à sa voisine ? (non)
6 Tu as demandé ton remboursement à la directrice. (oui – par téléphone)
7 Joséphine, vous avez répondu à vos parents ? (oui – il y a deux jours)
8 Tu as dit bonjour à la voisine ? (non)

Understanding direct and indirect objects

Here are a couple of examples to illustrate direct and indirect objects further.

Martine achète une nouvelle voiture. Elle **la** paye à crédit.

In this sentence, the object (*une nouvelle voiture*) follows the verb directly (there is no preposition between the verb and the object). The object is therefore called a 'direct object', and it can be replaced by a direct object pronoun (which in this case is *la*).

Martine parle à sa tante. Elle **lui** téléphone tous les jours.

In this sentence, the object (*sa tante*) does not follow the verb directly. There is a preposition (*à*) between the verb and the object: they are **indirectly** linked. The object is therefore called an 'indirect object', and it can be replaced by an indirect object pronoun (*lui*, in this sentence).

Be aware that verbs may be constructed differently in English and French. Sometimes the English verb takes a preposition when the equivalent verb translation in French does not:

I am **listening to** audio CDs. I am listening **to them** in the car.
J'écoute ***des CD audio****. Je* ***les*** *écoute dans la voiture.*

But sometimes the French verb is followed by a preposition while the English verb is not.

Tu as téléphoné **à tes parents** ? Non, je ne **leur** ai pas téléphoné.
Did you phone ***your parents****? No, I didn't phone* ***them****.*

So you need to look at the direct/indirect object relationship within the French words and try not to be influenced by the English translation of them.

One way of memorising direct and indirect verbs in French is to classify them into two categories and fill in the table as you come across new verbs, as shown in the example overleaf.

Verbes directs	Verbes indirects
aimer acheter vendre commander prendre connaître inviter voir	parler à donner à envoyer à téléphoner à

Activité 9.5.8

You are going to translate some sentences from English into French in order to help your understanding of direct and indirect objects.

- First decide **which verb** to use and write it down in the infinitive.
- This will give you a clue for the **pronouns** which you might need.
- Then work out **which tense** you need.
- Find the **right form of the verb** according to the subject.

Traduisez les phrases suivantes.

Exemple

I told them.

- The verb to use to translate 'to tell' is *dire à.*
- Likely pronouns are *lui* or *leur.*
- 'told' is in the past tense (*passé composé = ai dit*).
- Translation: *Je leur ai dit.*

1 She invited them.
2 We phone her twice a day.
3 Henri and Sophie speak to him every day.
4 They saw him last week.
5 The books, they ordered them by phone.
6 His car, he bought it two days ago.
7 She showed them her dress in the shop.
8 He didn't say hello to her.
9 We didn't give her the flowers.

Activité 9.5.9

You have had a problem with an order you placed recently, so you write a letter of complaint to the managing director of the company. Write about 120 words based on the following notes, using expressions of dissatisfaction, requests, *ça fait … que*, and the pronouns *lui* and *leur*.

- Give details about your order.
- Give the delivery due date.
- Explain the problem.
- Say what you've done to address the problem.
- Say what responses you got from the company.
- Express your dissatisfaction.
- Make a complaint and explain your request.

Écrivez environ 120 mots.

Section 9.6 Negotiating in shops

In this section, you will learn how to negotiate in order to get the best deal. You will practise the structures *il y a + passé composé* and *dans* + present tense. You will also learn to use *celui* and *celle* combined with *qui*, *que* and *où*.

Activité 9.6.1

A

Look closely at these three advertisements and find the words for:

1 low prices
2 special deals
3 instant discount

Observez ces trois publicités et trouvez les mots français.

50%
de remise immédiate
sur tous les smartphones

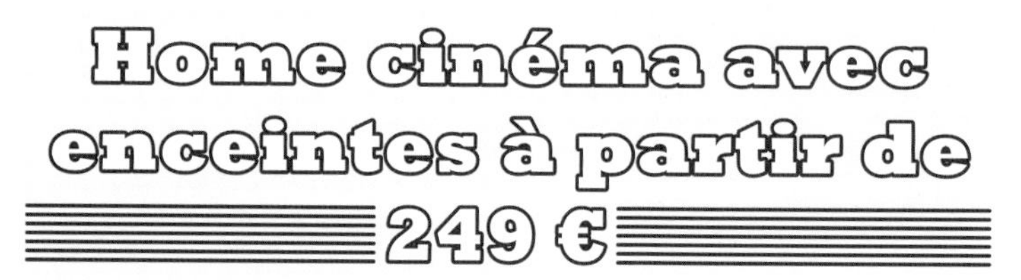

B

Match the following expressions to their French equivalent.

Faites correspondre les synonymes.

1 compris	(a) moins cher
2 rembourser	(b) réduire
3 baisser	(c) inclus
4 meilleur marché	(d) régler en une seule fois
5 payer comptant	(e) rendre l'argent

Activité 9.6.2

A

Track 9:19

Listen to Track 9:19 and tick the right answers.

Écoutez l'extrait et cochez les bonnes réponses.

1 Le client achète :
- (a) un téléviseur HD à écran plat. ❑
- (b) une tablette tactile. ❑
- (c) un appareil photo numérique. ❑

2 Les modèles avec wifi et Bluetooth et capacité standard coûtent :
- (a) 409 euros. ❑
- (b) 419 euros. ❑
- (c) 489 euros. ❑

3 Les modèles à 529 euros ont :
- (a) une garantie de 5 ans. ❑
- (b) un GPS intégré. ❑
- (c) un étui. ❑

4 Si le client trouve la même tablette tactile moins cher, le magasin :
- (a) rembourse la différence. ❑
- (b) offre une garantie plus longue. ❑
- (c) offre une remise. ❑

5 Le magasin fait des remises de 30 à 60% :
- (a) pendant l'été. ❑
- (b) pendant la rentrée scolaire. ❑
- (c) pendant les soldes. ❑

6 Le magasin ne propose pas le service gratuit suivant :
- (a) livraison gratuite. ❑
- (b) garantie pendant 5 ans. ❑
- (c) échange ou remboursement. ❑

7 Le client achète :
- (a) une tablette à 489 euros en blanc. ❑
- (b) une tablette à 529 euros en noir. ❑
- (c) une tablette à 489 euros en noir. ❑

B

Using information from step A, explain to a friend about your recent purchase and say what the terms and conditions are. Write about 100 words.

Utilisez les informations de l'extrait et expliquez à un ami ce que vous avez acheté et les conditions de vente. Écrivez environ 100 mots.

Activité 9.6.3

A

Track 9:20

Listen to Track 9:20 and answer the questions.

Écoutez l'extrait et répondez aux questions.

1 Where does the dialogue take place?
2 What did the customer purchase and where from?
3 What does the customer want to do?
4 What's the model of the item?
5 What were the terms and conditions of purchase and is the customer's request possible?
6 How can the customer get what he is asking for?

B

What words can you hear in the following sentences? What do they mean?

Quels mots entendez-vous dans les phrases suivantes? Traduisez ces mots.

1 J'ai acheté une tablette tactile __________ une semaine.
2 J'en ai besoin __________ une semaine absolument.
3 Vous pouvez aller la chercher en magasin __________ trois jours.

Using *il y a* and *dans* with expressions of time

As you saw in Unit 8, you use *il y a* + *passé composé* to talk about how long ago something happened in the past.

J'ai obtenu mon bac **il y a** 20 ans.
I got my *baccalaureat* 20 years **ago**.

J'ai acheté une tablette tactile **il y a** une semaine.
I bought an iPad a week **ago**.

To talk about something that is going to happen a certain amount of time in the future, you use *dans* + present.

Je reviens **dans** une demi-heure.
*I'll be back **in** half an hour or **in** half an hour**'s time**.*

Vous pouvez aller la chercher en magasin **dans** trois jours.
*You can go and collect it from the shop **in** three days**' time** or **in** three days.*

Activité 9.6.4

A

Fill in the gaps in the following sentences with *il y a* or *dans*.

Remplissez les blancs dans les phrases suivantes avec 'il y a' ou 'dans'.

1 Mes parents sont partis au Maroc __________ dix jours. Ils rentrent __________ une semaine.
2 J'ai passé ma commande __________ deux jours ; je la reçois __________ trois jours.
3 Elle a commencé ses études __________ un an, et elle finit __________ deux ans.
4 Il est arrivé __________ une heure. Il part __________ cinq minutes.
5 On s'est rencontrés __________ six mois, et on se marie __________ un an.
6 Elles ont vu une robe dans un magasin __________ dix minutes ; elles vont l'essayer __________ cinq minutes.

B

Track 9:21

To practise the use of *il y a* and *dans*, work with Track 9:21. Listen and speak in the pauses, following the prompts.

Écoutez l'extrait et répondez dans les pauses en suivant les indications.

Activité 9.6.5

A

Track 9:22

Listen to Track 9:22 and indicate whether the statements are true or false.

Écoutez l'extrait et répondez par vrai ou faux. Corrigez les réponses fausses.

		Vrai	Faux
1	Le modèle qu'on solde est un vieux modèle.	❑	❑
2	Le modèle préféré de la cliente est l'appareil rouge.	❑	❑
3	Le modèle rouge a un grand angle.	❑	❑
4	Le modèle rouge se trouve dans la vitrine.	❑	❑
5	Le modèle noir a un grand angle.	❑	❑
6	Le vendeur conseille le modèle noir.	❑	❑
7	La cliente va acheter un appareil avec un grand angle.	❑	❑
8	Un étui rigide est compris dans le prix.	❑	❑
9	Le modèle est disponible sur internet.	❑	❑
10	Le modèle est moins cher en magasin.	❑	❑

appareil (m.) photo numérique *digital camera*
un grand angle *wide angle*
qu'on solde *which is in the sales*
offres promotionnelles *special offers*
est livré avec *comes with*

B

Match the following sentences. Try to do this exercise without listening to the audio extract or reading the transcript.

Faites correspondre les phrases. Essayez de faire l'exercice sans écouter l'extrait ni lire la transcription.

1	Vous avez plusieurs appareils : vous avez ceux	(a)	qui se trouve dans la vitrine, a un grand angle.
2	et ceux	(b)	que je préfère.
3	Le modèle plus vieux est celui	(c)	qu'on solde.
4	Cet appareil rouge, là, c'est celui	(d)	que vous pouvez acheter sur internet.
5	Et ce noir, là, celui	(e)	qui est livré avec un étui.
6	L'appareil avec un grand angle : c'est celui	(f)	qui ont un zoom numérique,
7	et c'est celui	(g)	que je vous conseille,
8	Et c'est aussi celui	(h)	qui ont un zoom optique.

Using *celui/celle qui, celui/celle que, celui/celle où*

You have already seen the following demonstrative pronouns:

	Masculine	**Feminine**
Singular	celui	celle
Plural	ceux	celles

You combine these with *qui*, *que* or *où* when you want to express the idea of 'the one (which/that)', 'the one who' or 'the one where'.

Ce magasin d'appareil électroménager est **celui que** je préfère.
This electrical appliances shop is the one (that) I prefer.

Ce magasin d'appareil électroménager est **celui qui** se trouve au centre-ville.
This electrical appliances shop is the one which/that is situated in the town centre.

Ce magasin d'appareil électroménager est **celui où** j'ai acheté mon téléviseur.
This electrical appliances shop is (the one) where I bought my television.

Cette fille-là, c'est **celle qui** habite près de chez moi.
That girl is the one who lives near me.

Cette maîtresse, c'est **celle que** je rencontre tous les jours à l'école.
That's the teacher I see at school every day. / That teacher is the one I see at school every day.

Activité 9.6.6

A

Fill in the gaps in the following sentences with the appropriate words.

Complétez les phrases avec les mots qui conviennent.

celui qu' • celles que • celui que • ceux qui • celle qui • celles qui

1 Il y a plusieurs musées dans la ville. __________ nous avons visité hier n'était pas intéressant.
2 Elle cherche un appartement. __________ elle va voir aujourd'hui est à deux minutes du centre-ville.
3 Il y a des serveuses de toutes les nationalités dans ce restaurant. __________ travaille ce soir est italienne.
4 On trouve des cathédrales magnifiques dans toute la France. __________ je préfère sont à Reims et à Amiens.
5 J'ai trouvé plusieurs tablettes tactiles. __________ sont sur internet sont meilleur marché.
6 J'adore les grands magasins à Paris. __________ se trouvent sur le boulevard Haussmann sont mes préférés.

B

You are showing your friends a few photos. Imagine what they mean to you and write two or three sentences to describe each photo. Use demonstrative adjectives and pronouns.

Écrivez deux ou trois phrases pour chaque photo.

Photo 1: Ce restaurant, c'est __________ .

Photo 2: Cette petite ville, c'est __________ .

Photo 3: Ce village, c'est __________ .

Photo 4: Ces amis, ce sont __________ .

1 2 3 4

Track 9:23

Activité 9.6.7

To practise what you have learned so far in this section, listen to Track 9:23 and answer the questions in the pauses, following the prompts.

Écoutez l'extrait et parlez dans les pauses.

Activité 9.6.8

A

Now you are going to work on useful vocabulary for bargaining. Read the messages posted in a forum and answer the questions.

Lisez les messages et répondez aux questions.

1 What is the discussion about?

2 Find a short phrase in the forum which could be the title of the thread of this discussion.

14 mai 2012 à 10:30 **Répondre**

hamlet19

Salut,
Je pars bientôt à Marrakech et je voudrais savoir plusieurs choses sur la négociation. Je sais que c'est un sport national mais peut-on négocier partout, aussi bien dans les souks que dans les "vrais" magasins ? En général, on doit diviser le premier prix par combien ? 4 ? 10 ? Quelles sont les arnaques à éviter ? Enfin, je sais bien que c'est normal là-bas, mais comment bien négocier à Marrakech ? En France, un type qui négocie, c'est très mal vu donc je ne suis pas vraiment habitué…
Merci.

16 mai 2012 à 18:45 **Répondre**

mmaaaarrrccc

Ma technique personnelle est la suivante : tu divises le prix par 2 ou 3 par rapport au prix que le vendeur te fixe et tu lui offres un prix inférieur à celui que tu veux réellement obtenir. Comme ça, la négociation commence, le vendeur baisse le prix et toi, tu peux monter jusqu'à ta limite. Le tout avec un grand sourire et surtout, il ne faut pas refuser un petit verre de thé si on te le propose !

23 mai 2012 à 07:58 **Répondre**

fleur38

Il y a une règle élémentaire dans la négociation, c'est qu'il faut se fixer un prix maximum que l'on ne veut pas dépasser et proposer un prix minimum au vendeur. L'objectif est d'arriver à un consensus où chacun trouve son compte et, si possible, faire une bonne affaire !
Bonne négociation !

28 mai 2012 à 15:00 **Répondre**

cha-cha-cha

Si tu n'aimes pas marchander, je te conseille le centre artisanal près de la place Djama el Fna où les prix sont quasiment fixes et affichés, les artisans te laissent regarder, la qualité est très bonne et les prix sont souvent plus bas que dans les souks. Et en plus, le cadre est magnifique ! Moi, personnellement, j'achète mes bricoles à Essaouira à 2h de route de Marrakech, tu te promènes tranquille dans les souks sans être abordé.

30 mai 2012 à 19:43 **Répondre**

potter000

Tous ces conseils sont bons pour ta question. Mais, pour moi, le principe de base c'est d'être courtois et avenant, les Marocains sont en général très gentils, le marchandage est une coutume, voire une tradition. Il faut savoir le prix que tu veux dépenser et ne jamais changer d'avis. Et même si tu paies une marchandise plus cher que sa valeur réelle, considère que tu as eu le plaisir de converser, de rire, et que tu reviendras avec un souvenir que tu as ramené de là-bas. Ne t'inquiète pas, reviens avec des images, des odeurs, des parfums et des couleurs plein la tête, cela n'a pas de prix.

B

Read the forum again and answer the following questions by true, false or can't tell.

Répondez aux questions par vrai, faux ou je ne sais pas.

		True	False	Can't tell
1	The person who asks the question is going to Marrakech on business.	❑	❑	❑
2	He has a lot of experience of dealing with situations in Morocco.	❑	❑	❑
3	It may be that you will be offered a cup of tea while purchasing something on the market in Marrakech.	❑	❑	❑
4	When purchasing in Marrakech, the idea is that the seller and the vendor reach a compromise.	❑	❑	❑
5	There aren't any shops offering fixed prices in Marrakech.	❑	❑	❑
6	It is possible to wander in some markets without being approached.	❑	❑	❑
7	Haggling is highly unusual in Morocco.	❑	❑	❑
8	The important thing is the exotic sensations and memories you bring back with you.	❑	❑	❑

C

Make a list of all the recommendations given in the discussion.

Faites la liste des recommandations.

D

Look up the following expressions in a dictionary.

Cherchez les expressions suivantes dans un dictionnaire.

1 diviser le prix par
2 les arnaques
3 baisser le prix
4 monter le prix
5 une règle élémentaire
6 dépasser un prix
7 marchander
8 affiché

9 être abordé
10 avenant
11 le marchandage
12 faire une bonne affaire

E

Now find the different meanings of the following words in your dictionary and choose the correct meaning of each for this context.

Cherchez ces mots dans un dictionnaire et trouvez le sens dans ce contexte.

1 le cadre
2 les bricoles
3 un souvenir

F

Find a translation for the following expressions. How would you find them in the dictionary?

Traduisez les expressions en anglais.

1 C'est très mal vu.
2 Je ne suis pas vraiment habitué.
3 Chacun y trouve son compte.
4 Cela n'a pas de prix.

Making the most of your dictionary

Using the various features of your dictionary will help you to improve your language overall, not just your vocabulary. Here are a few tips to make the most of this useful tool.

- Read through the introduction to your dictionary as a quick route to understanding the conventions adopted.
- Use your dictionary to extend your vocabulary a little. Read around the word you are looking up and you will find not only the straightforward translation but expressions and idioms contained in that headword.
- When searching for a word in the target language, check its entry in the other half of the dictionary. This way, you can make sure that you have chosen the most appropriate word for your needs.
- Note down related words/expressions which are of interest to you. It is much easier to remember things you are interested in.

Activité 9.6.9

Imagine you are 'Hamlet19' (from the forum of the last activity). Write an email thanking the others for their advice and telling about your experience of haggling in Marrakech. Write about 120 words, using as much language from this section as possible.

Écrivez un message d'environ 120 mots dans le forum.

Unité 10

demandez conseil
Maalox
Rennie
Imodium
Drill
Sédatif PC
douleur et fièvre
stress sommeil
forme vitalité
médicaments libre accès

Unité 10 overview

Section	Language	Vocabulary	Skills	Cultural understanding
10.1 Saying what you do to stay healthy	• Forming and using adverbs ending in *-ment* • Using *ne ... jamais, ne ... plus* and *ne ... rien*	• Healthy lifestyles		• Anti-smoking laws in France
10.2 Talking about illnesses and injuries	• Saying how you are feeling • Using the pronouns *moi, toi, lui*, etc. • Pronouncing the sounds [ɥ] and [w] • Talking about injuries	• Illnesses and injuries • Parts of the body	• Using bilingual dictionaries	
10.3 Understanding the French health system	• The simple future tense			• *La Sécurité sociale* • Health care in Belgium and Quebec
10.4 Talking about treatment	• Further uses of the imperative • Using the pronoun *en* • Giving advice	• Medicines and treatment	• The importance of repetition	• Medicine consumption in France
10.5 Talking about alternative medicine	• Expressing opinions	• Alternative medicine	• Writing skills	• Alternative medicine

Section 10.1 Saying what you do to stay healthy

In this section you will learn how to say what to do to stay healthy. You will learn how to form and use adverbs, and will practise negative structures.

Activité 10.1.1

A

Read the statements below, which were used as part of a survey on staying healthy, and match each to its equivalent in English.

Faites correspondre les informations en français à leur équivalent en anglais.

1	Vous mangez équilibré.	(a)	You take a course of vitamins.
2	Vous faites du sport.	(b)	You go outside for fresh air.
3	Vous allez chercher le soleil pendant vos vacances.	(c)	You go and have a beauty treatment in a salon.
4	Vous faites une cure de thalassothérapie.	(d)	You have a thalassotherapy spa treatment.
5	Vous faites une cure de vitamines.	(e)	You eat a balanced diet.
6	Vous vous amusez et sortez avec vos amis.	(f)	You sleep a lot.
7	Vous gardez le sourire et vous restez toujours positif/ve.	(g)	You do sport.
8	Vous dormez beaucoup.	(h)	You have a holiday in the sun.
9	Vous vous détendez devant la télé, au cinéma ou au théâtre.	(i)	You try to keep calm, to live your life to the full.
10	Vous sortez prendre l'air.	(j)	You keep smiling and stay positive.
11	Vous allez faire un soin dans un institut de beauté.	(k)	You relax in front of the television, at the cinema or the theatre.
12	Vous essayez de rester zen pour profiter de la vie au maximum.	(l)	You have fun and go out with your friends.

B

Now do the questionnaire yourself. What do you do to stay healthy?

Faites le sondage « Que faites-vous pour garder la forme ? ».

Activité 10.1.2

A

1 Read the posts below, taken from a student forum, and answer questions (a) and (b).

Lisez les messages et répondez aux questions.

(a) What does Pixel want to know?

(b) What general advice is she given?

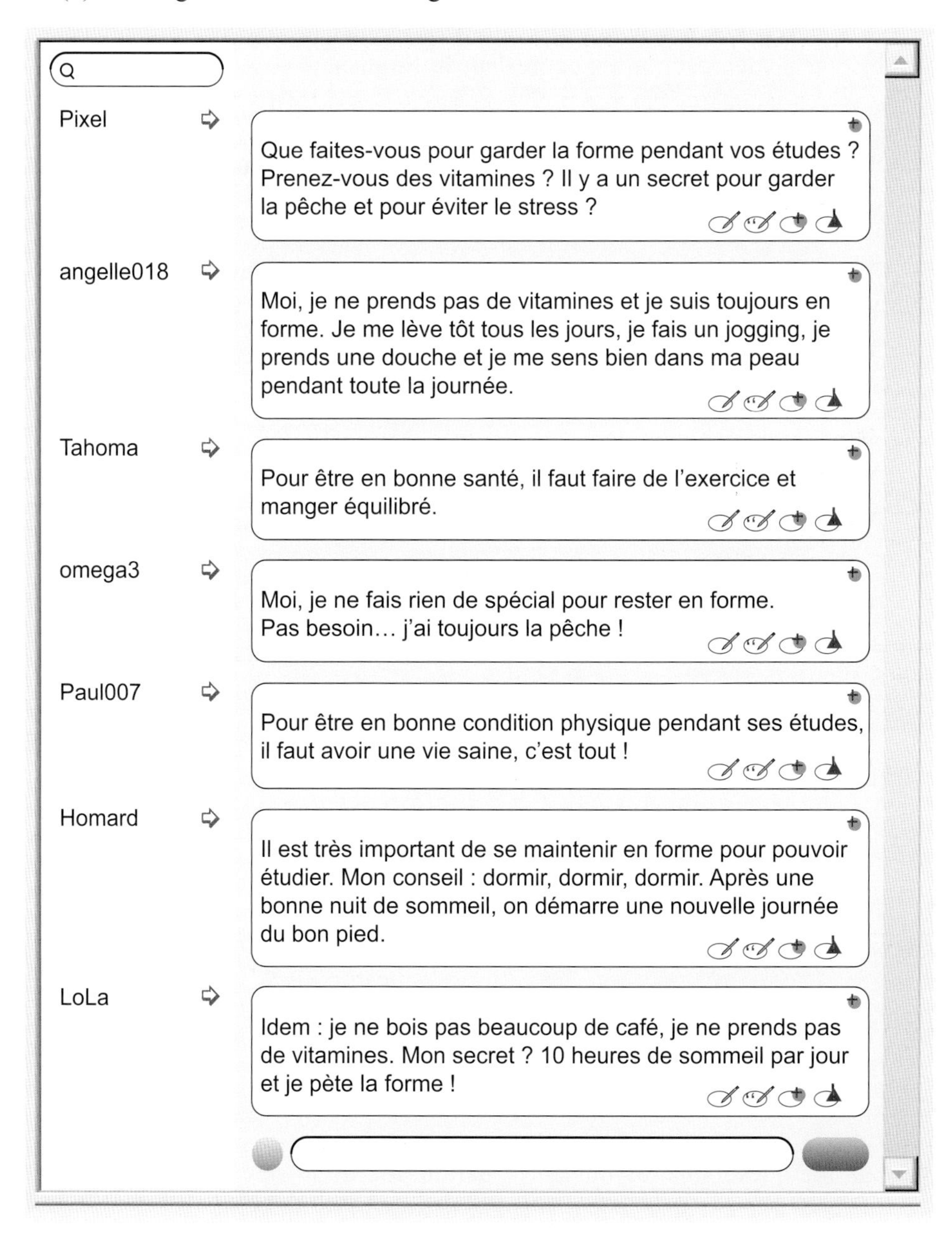

2 Identify all the expressions that are used in the posts to say how to stay or be healthy.

Relisez les messages et trouvez toutes les expressions synonymes de « garder la forme » ou « être en forme ».

démarre du bon pied *get off to a good start*

idem *Latin expression meaning 'ditto'*

B

Listen to Track 10:1, where people say what they think you should do to stay healthy, and fill in the table below. Some answers have been given for you.

Écoutez l'extrait 10:1 et remplissez le tableau.

Track 10:1

	Pour être en bonne santé, il faut...
Agnès	• bien dormir • •
Philippe	• • •
Pascaline	• •
Jean-Claude	• • avoir un bon métier •
Leïla	• •
Sandrine	• éviter le stress •
Ahmed	• •
Céline	• •

C

Listen to Track 10:1 again and fill in the gaps with the correct adverb from the box.

Écoutez l'extrait 10:1 et complétez les phrases.

suffisamment • beaucoup • positivement • bien • régulièrement • sainement • bien

1 Il faut __________ dormir.
2 Il faut manger __________.
3 Il faut dormir __________.
4 Il faut __________ manger.
5 Il faut penser __________.
6 Il faut se détendre __________.
7 Il faut faire de l'exercice __________.

Forming and using adverbs ending in *-ment*

You have already come across adverbs in previous units. You used *beaucoup*, *bien* and *assez* in Unit 2 to say how much you like or dislike something:

J'aime **bien** le poisson. *I like fish a lot.*

Je n'aime pas **beaucoup** les légumes. *I don't like vegetables much.*

You also practised using adverbs and learned about adverbs of frequency in Unit 6:

Je fais du sport **de temps en temps**.
I play sport from time to time.

Je vais **souvent** à la piscine.
I often go to the swimming pool.

In the last activity, you used a new type of adverb (known as adverbs of manner), which end in *-ment.* Most of this type of adverb are formed by adding *-ment* to the **feminine** form of an adjective:

Masculine adjective	Feminine adjective	Adverb
régulier *(regular)*	régulière	**régulièrement** *(regularly)*
sain *(healthy)*	saine	**sainement** *(healthily)*
positif *(positive)*	positive	**positivement** *(positively)*

For adjectives that end in a vowel, *-ment* is added to the **masculine** form:

Masculine adjective	**Adverb**
poli *(polite)*	**poliment** *(politely)*
vrai *(true)*	**vraiment** *(truly)*

To form adverbs from adjectives ending in *-ant* or *-ent*, add ***-amment*** or ***-emment***:

Adjective	**Adverb**
suffisant *(sufficient)*	**suffisamment** *(sufficiently)*
différent *(different)*	**différemment** *(differently)*

In most cases, adverbs are placed after the verb they relate to:

Il mange **sainement**. — *He eats healthily.*

Elle dort **beaucoup**. — *She sleeps a lot.*

Je fais de l'exercice **régulièrement**. — *I exercise regularly.*

Je me suis reposé(e) **suffisamment**. — *I rested enough/ sufficiently.*

Elles ne mangent pas **assez**. — *They don't eat enough.*

But you may sometimes come across examples where the adverb is positioned differently:

Il faut **bien** dormir. — *One must sleep well.*

On a **mal** mangé dans ce restaurant. — *We ate badly in that restaurant.*

Il s'est **suffisamment** détendu. — *He relaxed sufficiently.*

You can use *bien, très, plutôt* or *assez* before adverbs to emphasise them:

Nous avons mangé **très sainement**. — *We ate very healthily.*

Il fait de l'exercice **assez régulièrement**. — *He exercises quite regularly.*

Elle se sent **plutôt bien** dans sa peau. — *She feels mostly happy with herself.*

Activité 10.1.3

A

Form the adverbs derived from the following adjectives.

Trouvez les adverbes correspondants.

1 long
2 ancien
3 constant
4 dur
5 généreux
6 prudent
7 faible
8 franc

B

Match each of the following adverbs to its opposite. The first one has been done for you.

Faites correspondre les adverbes à leur contraire.

Exemple

1 (b)

1	fortement	(a)	irrégulièrement
2	rarement	(b)	doucement
3	intelligemment	(c)	désagréablement
4	heureusement	(d)	rapidement
5	régulièrement	(e)	dernièrement
6	premièrement	(f)	fréquemment
7	aimablement	(g)	malheureusement
8	lentement	(h)	bêtement

Activité 10.1.4

A

Read the comments from the following people. Who has a healthy lifestyle and who doesn't?

Qui vit sainement ?

un pousse-café *a liqueur (familiar)*

Qui vit sainement ?	Qui ne vit pas sainement ?
Frédérique	Arlette

B

Reread the comments in step A and answer the following questions in English.

Relisez les messages et répondez aux questions.

1 What does Thierry do to allow him to sleep for up to 10 hours a night?
2 According to Thierry, why is running so good for you?
3 Why doesn't Grégoire like sport?
4 What is the only 'sport' Grégoire does?

5 What is Joseph's 'bad' habit?

6 What are the two reasons Farad gives for not doing any sport?

C

Reread the comments and for each of the people interviewed, write one or two sentences to say whether they have a healthy lifestyle. Make sure you use an adverb in each sentence.

Faites des phrases suivant le modèle.

Exemple

Frédérique mange **sainement**.

Arlette ne fait pas **suffisamment** d'exercice.

Activité 10.1.5

A

Track 10:2

Listen to Track 10:2, in which six people are asked whether they smoke, and indicate which of the following statements are true or false.

nocif/ve *harmful*

je suis tombée enceinte *I became pregnant*

un tabacologue *tobacco addiction specialist*

Écoutez et cochez vrai ou faux.

		Vrai	Faux
1	Nathan fume.	❑	❑
2	Lionel ne fume plus.	❑	❑
3	Vanessa a arrêté de fumer.	❑	❑
4	Marine n'a jamais fumé.	❑	❑
5	Medhi fume.	❑	❑
6	Véronique veut arrêter de fumer.	❑	❑

B

Track 10:2

Listen to Track 10:2 again and answer the following questions in English.

Répondez aux questions.

1 Why did Nathan, Vanessa and Marine stop smoking?

2 How long has Lionel smoked?

3 How many cigarettes did Marine smoke per day?

4 What is Medhi's attitude to smoking?

5 What is Véronique considering to help her give up smoking?

C

Read the transcript of Track 10:2 and note down the French for the following expressions.

Trouvez les expressions en français.

1 never
2 no longer
3 nothing

Using *ne ... jamais, ne ... plus* and *ne ... rien*

Jamais, *plus* and *rien* are words to express negations. They work like *pas* and are generally used with *ne*. Like *ne ... pas*:

- *ne ... jamais/plus/rien* are positioned on either side of the verb in the present tense.

Elle **ne** fait **jamais** de sport.	*She never plays sport.*
Je **ne** fume **plus**.	*I no longer smoke.*
Il **ne** fait **rien** pour sa santé.	*He does nothing for his health.*

- In the *passé composé, ne ... jamais/plus/rien* are positioned on either side of the auxiliary verb *être* or *avoir*:

Il **n'**a **jamais** fumé.	*He has never smoked.*
Anna **n'**a **rien** mangé.	*Anna has eaten nothing.*

Note that *ne ... personne* (nobody/anybody) is an exception to this rule, as *personne* is placed **after** the past participle in the *passé composé*:

Elle **ne** voit **personne**.	*She doesn't see anybody.*
Elle **n'**a vu **personne**.	*She didn't see anybody.*

With pronominal verbs, *ne* comes before the reflexive pronoun:

Ils **ne** se sont **jamais** reposés.	*They never rested.*

Activité 10.1.6

Put the following words into the correct order to form sentences.

Mettez les mots dans l'ordre.

1 ne / je / jamais / bois
2 n' / fumé / je / dans / ai / chambre / jamais / ma
3 au / il / joue / tennis / ne / plus
4 ils / rien / sont / dit / se / ne
5 plus / voient / elles / ne / se
6 veux / je / rien / ne
7 ne / personne / il / à / parle
8 personne / nous / avons / consulté / n'

Track 10:3

Activité 10.1.7

Listen to Track 10:3, which is about smoking, and answer the questions following the prompts.

Répondez aux questions en suivant les indications.

Anti-smoking laws in France

Smoking in enclosed public places has been banned in France since January 2008. Even though it took several months for the ban to be enforced properly, on the whole it seems to be working. However, it is difficult to assess precisely the effect the law has had on smoking in France. Overall, surveys reveal that the ban has not persuaded French people to give up smoking. Some bar and restaurant owners claim that they have had to close their business as a result of the law but the consumption of tobacco products does not seem to have decreased. As a result of the ban, increasing numbers of people gather to smoke under canopied areas of bars and restaurant terraces.

If France's anti-smoking laws have failed to reduce the number of smokers, they have, on the other hand, changed attitudes towards smoking. Most people now seem to agree that it is not acceptable to be exposed to second-hand smoke in public places.

Activité 10.1.8

A

Read the text and match the correct subheadings (a)–(d) to the paragraphs numbered 1 to 4.

Associez les sous-titres aux paragraphes.

(a) Maintenir une bonne hygiène de vie
(b) Surveiller son alimentation est primordial
(c) Savoir profiter de la vie au maximum
(d) Bouger devient essentiel pour se sentir bien

primordial *essential*
bouger *to move*
sans ... ni *without ... or*
OGM (organisme génétiquement modifié) *GMOs (genetically modified organisms)*
ne pas en abuser *not to overdo it (drink excessively)*
la clé de *the key to*
qui fait que *which means that*
s'en priver *to go without it*

Quatre astuces pour rester en bonne santé

1 Le surpoids et l'obésité sont à l'origine de diverses maladies comme l'hypertension, le diabète ou les maladies cardio-vasculaires. Il faut donc bien faire attention à ce qu'on mange pour rester en bonne santé. Il est recommandé de consommer une nourriture saine et équilibrée, ni trop grasse, ni trop salée. Consommez des aliments frais, sans colorant, ni conservateur, ni OGM. Achetez des fruits bio si possible, et préférez les poissons ou les viandes blanches. Enfin, il faut absolument éviter le grignotage d'aliments riches en graisses et en sucres entre les repas.

2 Faites du sport. L'activité physique entraîne de nombreux bienfaits pour le cœur. Pratiquée régulièrement, elle contribue au bon fonctionnement de votre système cardiovasculaire. Sans devenir un grand sportif, il suffit de faire une activité physique pendant au moins 20 minutes par jour, ou au moins 3 fois par semaine. Laissez votre voiture au parking et partez au travail à vélo. Prenez les escaliers et montez les marches deux par deux. L'exercice physique permet de s'oxygéner, de se muscler et de se détendre.

3 Pour être en forme, c'est simple, il faut vivre sainement. Le tabagisme et l'abus d'alcool sont fortement déconseillés. Il n'est pas interdit de boire un verre de bon vin de temps en temps, mais il faut rester prudent et ne pas en abuser. Manger à des heures régulières est aussi essentiel pour la santé, c'est mieux pour la digestion. Il est conseillé de boire 1,5 litres d'eau par jour, cela permet de bien hydrater le corps. Et enfin, dormez et récupérez. Le sommeil est la clé d'une bonne forme. Ainsi, il faut se coucher à des heures régulières pour être en forme le lendemain.

4 Avoir la forme, c'est d'abord avoir le moral. Sortir, aller boire un café avec un copain ou une copine, et rire le plus possible sont des remèdes pour retrouver son énergie. Le plaisir est primordial pour rester en bonne santé, il favorise la sécrétion d'endorphines, qui fait que l'on se sent bien, alors il ne faut pas s'en priver !

B

Read the title of the text in step A. What do you think the word *astuces* means? Can you think of another French word that means something similar?

À votre avis, que veut dire le mot « astuces » ? Répondez à la question.

C

Read the text again and find the French for the following words and expressions.

Trouvez les équivalents français dans le texte.

1 overweight
2 high blood pressure
3 diabetes
4 heart
5 smoking
6 heavy drinking
7 colouring
8 preservatives
9 snacking
10 to be in a good mood/to feel happy

D

Read the text again and answer the following questions based on the information given in the text.

Lisez et répondez aux questions selon les informations du texte.

1 Why is it important to have a healthy and balanced diet?
2 What are the main benefits of regular exercise?
3 What recommendations for maintaining a healthy lifestyle are given in the third paragraph?
4 How are health and being in a good mood related?
5 According to the text, what three things should be avoided?

Activité 10.1.9

Based on what you have learned in this section, write around 120 words to say what you do to stay healthy. You should use:

- vocabulary and expressions about healthy living
- at least three adverbs ending in *-ment*
- at least two negative expressions.

Écrivez 120 mots.

Section 10.2 Talking about illnesses and injuries

In this section you will learn how to talk about illnesses and injuries. You will learn how to say how you feel, use pronominal verbs to describe injuries and practise the sounds [w] as in *toi*, and [ɥ] as in *lui*.

Activité 10.2.1

A

Track 10:4

Listen to Track 10:4, where some people are discussing health issues, and select the correct answers.

Et ben dis donc *an expression of surprise which is roughly equivalent to 'oh dear' or 'you don't say'*

souffre de *suffers from (from* souffrir de*)*

Écoutez et choisissez les bonnes réponses.

1 Sandra téléphone à son travail pour dire qu'elle ne va pas venir au bureau parce que...

(a) Elle est malade. ❑

(b) Elle veut prendre un jour de congé. ❑

(c) Sa voiture est en panne. ❑

2 Nathalie est inquiète parce que...

(a) Le père de Nathalie à des problèmes d'argent. ❑

(b) Le père de Nathalie mange très mal. ❑

(c) Le père de Nathalie a des problèmes de santé. ❑

3 Laurent n'est pas en forme parce que...

(a) Il vient de manquer une promotion. ❑

(b) Il vient de perdre son emploi. ❑

(c) Il est toujours stressé. ❑

B

Track 10:4

Listen to Track 10:4 again and tick all the expressions that you hear from the list below.

Réécoutez l'extrait 10:4 et cochez les expressions que vous entendez.

1 Je ne me sens pas très bien. ❑

2 Je me sens bien dans ma peau. ❑

3 Ce n'est vraiment pas la forme. ❑

4 Je n'ai vraiment pas la pêche. ❑

5 Ça va mieux ? ❑

6 Il est toujours en bonne santé. ❑

7 Il est toujours aussi fatigué. ❑

8 Oui, en pleine forme. ❑

9 Je fais attention à ma forme. ❑

10 Bof, ça va, sans plus. ❑

11 Ça ne va plus. ❑

12 Je suis un peu déprimé. ❑

C

Read the transcript of Track 10:4 and note the French equivalent for the following words and expressions.

Écoutez et notez les expressions en français.

1 I have a headache.
2 I feel hot and cold.
3 Flu
4 I've caught a bad cold.
5 He is always tired.
6 He feels dizzy.
7 He has stomach ache.
8 He suffers from rheumatism.
9 He is always stressed.

Saying how you are feeling

You can describe how you are feeling in a variety of ways. You have already used *ça va*. Here are a few more expressions with *ça* or *ce*:

C'est la forme ?	*How are you feeling? (familiar)*
Ça va bien/mal.	*I'm well/unwell.*
Ça ne va pas très bien.	*I'm not very well.*
Ça ne va pas mal.	*I'm not too bad.*
Ça va mieux.	*I'm better.*
Ce n'est pas la forme.	*I'm not feeling too good.*
Bof, ça va, sans plus.	*So-so. (familiar)*

You can also use *se sentir bien/mal*:

Je me sens très bien/mal.	*I feel really well/bad.*
Elle ne se sent pas bien en ce moment.	*She isn't feeling too good at the moment.*

You can say you have or have caught an illness using *avoir* or *attraper* + *un/une* + name of illness:

J'**ai** un rhume.	*I have a cold.*
Mon fils **a attrapé** une bronchite.	*My son has caught bronchitis.*

With some illnesses, the definite article (*le/la,* etc.) normally has to be used in French:

Elle a **la** grippe.	*She has (the) flu.*
Nous avons attrapé **la** varicelle.	*We caught chickenpox.*

To describe a pain in a part of your body, you can use *avoir mal à* + part of the body:

J'**ai mal** au genou.	*My knee aches.*
Elle **a mal** à la tête.	*She has a headache.*
Il **a mal** aux dents.	*He has toothache.*

Activité 10.2.2

Track 10:5

A

Listen to the dialogue in Track 10:5, in which you meet a friend who asks how you are. Take part in the dialogue following the prompts, speaking in the pauses.

Parlez dans les pauses en suivant les indications.

Track 10:6

B

A few weeks later you meet the same friend. Listen to Track 10:6 and take part in the dialogue following the prompts.

Parlez dans les pauses en suivant les indications.

Activité 10.2.3

A

Look at the transcript for Track 10:4, and find two words for 'tired' in Dialogue 2.

Cherchez deux mots pour tired *dans le dialogue 2.*

B

Look up the word *crevé* in your bilingual/English–French dictionary. How many meanings of the word can you find?

Cherchez le mot « crevé » dans votre dictionnaire. Combien de traductions possibles trouvez-vous ?

C

Look at the dictionary entries for *crevé* below and translate the following sentences.

Traduisez ces phrases.

crevé, e /kʀəve/ (ptp de **crever**) ADJ [1] *[pneu]* burst, punctured ◆ **j'ai un pneu (de)** ~ I've got a puncture *(Brit)*, I've got a flat tyre *(Brit) ou* tire *(US)*, I've got a flat * [2] ⁑ *(= mort)* dead; *(= fatigué)* dead beat *, bushed *, exhausted, knackered ⁑ *(Brit)* NM *(Couture)* slash ◆ **des manches à ~s** slashed sleeves

(From *Collins Robert French Dictionary,* HarperCollins, 2010)

1 J'ai crevé sur l'autoroute.

2 Elle travaille trop, elle est crevée.

3 Il y a un mouton crevé dans le champ.

Using bilingual dictionaries

Looking up words in a bilingual dictionary may not always be an easy task. A word may have several possible meanings and may belong to more than one category: it may be a noun and a verb, be part of an idiomatic expression or even technical jargon.

You may not know what category the word you are looking up belongs to. However, dictionaries are structured and use abbreviations to help you find what you are looking for without having to read sometimes very lengthy entries. Bear in mind, however, that the number of definitions and examples of different contexts given will depend on the size of your dictionary.

It is a good idea to familiarise yourself with the way your dictionary is organised and classified by reading its introduction. Different types of words have different labels to show what category they belong to. If a word is both a noun and a verb, for example, the entry will be split accordingly with definitions for the noun labelled with 'N' (+ 'F' or 'M' to show the gender), and meanings for the verb labelled with 'V' (+ another letter/abbreviation, such as 'B', 'I', 'PR', 'T', 'TI', depending on the type of verb).

When considering the range of definitions offered for a word (for example, for *crever*, which can mean a number of different things from *percer* to *mourir*), use the information the dictionary gives about the context in which this meaning is likely. This information is normally in brackets, for example for *percer*, which reads '[+ *pneu*]' and '[+ *ballon*]'.

Dictionaries also provide information about what categories of vocabulary a word belongs to, for example 'Admin' for administrative words, and 'Zool' for zoological entries. The recommended dictionaries for L192 *Bon départ* use a system of stars to indicate whether words are informal language (*), ranging to offensive language (three asterisks/*), so you should familiarise yourself with the list of abbrevations and symbols at the front of your dictionary.

Before you decide to open your dictionary, ask yourself the following question. Can you guess the meaning of the word or expression from the context? If you need to use your dictionary, knowing the context will help you know which definition to look at. Finally, remember that you should try to use the vocabulary and structures you have learned in the module so far to express what you want to say.

Activité 10.2.4

A

Look at the dictionary entry for *forme* below. For each of the following sentences, say which definition they correspond to (1, 2, 4 or 6).

Choissiez la bonne définition.

forme /fɔʀm/ NF [1] (*= contour, apparence*) shape, form ◆ **cet objet est de ~ ronde/carrée** this object is round/square (in shape) ◆ **en ~ de poire/cloche** pear-/bell-shaped ◆ **elle a des ~s gracieuses** she has a graceful figure ◆ **elle prend des ~s** she's filling out ◆ **vêtement qui moule les ~s** clinging *ou* figure-hugging garment ◆ **une ~ apparut dans la nuit** a form *ou* figure *ou* shape appeared out of the darkness ◆ **n'avoir plus ~ humaine** to be unrecognizable ◆ **sans ~** *[chapeau]* shapeless; *[pensée]* formless ◆ **prendre la ~ d'un rectangle** to take the form *ou* shape of a rectangle ◆ **prendre la ~ d'un entretien** to take the form of an interview ◆ **prendre ~** *[statue, projet]* to take shape ◆ **sous ~ de comprimés** in tablet form ◆ **sous la ~ d'un vieillard** in the guise of *ou* as an old man ◆ **sous toutes ses ~s** in all its forms

[2] (*= genre*) *[de civilisation, gouvernement]* form ◆ **~ d'énergie** form of energy ◆ **~ de vie** (*= présence effective*) form of life, life form; (*= coutumes*) way of life ◆ **une ~ de pensée différente de la nôtre** a way of thinking different from our own ◆ **les animaux ont-ils une ~ d'intelligence ?** do animals have a form of intelligence?

[4] (*Ling*) form ◆ **mettre à la ~ passive** to put in the passive ◆ **~ contractée** contracted form ◆ **~ de base** base form

[6] (*gén, Sport*) ◆ **~ (physique)** form, fitness ◆ **être en (pleine** *ou* **grande) ~, tenir la ~** * (*gén*) to be in (great) form, to be in *ou* on top form; (*physiquement*) to be very fit ◆ **il n'est pas en ~, il n'a pas la ~** * (*gén*) he's not on form, he's off form; (*physiquement*) he's not very fit, he's unfit ◆ **il est en petite ~** he's not in great shape ◆ **baisse de ~** loss of form ◆ **retrouver la ~** to get back into shape, to get fit again ◆ **ce n'est pas la grande ~** * I'm (*ou* he's *etc*) not feeling too good * ◆ **centre de remise en ~** ≃ health spa; → **péter**

(From *Collins Robert French Dictionary,* HarperCollins, 2010)

(a) Ce vase a la forme d'une bouteille.

(b) Ce n'est pas la même forme du verbe.

(c) J'ai commencé la Zumba il y a un mois et depuis je suis en super forme.

B

Translate the sentences from step A.

Traduisez les phrases.

Activité 10.2.5

Look at the transcript of Dialogue 3 in Track 10:4 and answer the following questions.

Trouvez les mots utilisés par Laurent.

1 What word does Laurent use to stress the fact that he's addressing Nadja?
2 What word does he use to indicate that he's talking about himself?
3 What word does he use to stress the fact that he's talking about his brother?

Using the pronouns *moi, toi, lui,* etc.

You have already come across *moi* and *toi* in previous units:

Moi, je m'appelle Jean. Et **toi** ? — *I'm Jean. What about you?*

The pronouns *moi, toi, lui, elle, nous, vous, eux, elles* are used a lot in spoken French. You use them in the following instances.

- When you want to put the emphasis on the subject of a sentence:

Oh **moi**, ça va, sans plus.	*Oh, I'm sort of alright.*
Mon frère, **lui,** va très bien.	*My brother is very well.*
Ma mère, **elle**, ne dort pas.	*My mother doesn't sleep.*

- After *c'est*:

C'est Pierre ? Oui, c'est **lui**.	*Is it/that Pierre? Yes, it's him.*

- After words such as *à, et, chez, avec, pour, sans, de, par ...*

Et **vous**, vous vous sentez bien ?	*What about you? How are you feeling?*
Il rentre chez **lui** demain.	*He's going home tomorrow.*
Partez sans **eux**.	*Go without them.*
Pour **moi,** un steak frites.	*I'll have steak and chips.*

Note that when the subject of a sentence is *on*, ***soi*** is used:

> Si on se sent malade, on doit rester chez **soi**.
> *If you feel ill you must stay at home (literally 'if one feels ill, one must stay at home').*

You may also want to remember the following expressions:

Moi aussi.	*Me too.*
Moi non plus.	*Me neither.*

Activité 10.2.6

A

Change the following sentences using *moi*, *toi,* etc. to put emphasis on the subject.

Transformez les phrases.

Exemple

Je suis en pleine forme. → **Moi**, je suis en pleine forme.

1 Et tu as mal au ventre ?
2 Ils ont faim.
3 Elles n'ont pas la grippe.
4 Il est souvent malade.
5 Tu souffres de diabète ?
6 Et vous surveillez votre poids ?

B

Fill in the gaps in the following sentences with the correct pronoun.

Complétez les phrases suivantes avec le pronom qui convient.

1 __________ , je suis en pleine forme. Paul, je vais venir avec __________ au tennis. *(informal)*
2 Mon père, __________ , il est très fatigué, il reste toujours chez __________ .
3 Ah, oui, j'ai commandé un coca, oui, c'est pour __________ .
4 Attendez ! Ne partez pas sans __________ , ils arrivent dans deux minutes.
5 Martine ne fait pas assez d'activité physique, va marcher avec ________ .

Activité 10.2.7

A

Track 10:7

Listen to Track 10:7 and repeat each word.

Écoutez et répétez.

B

Track 10:8

Listen to Track 10:8 and repeat each word.

Écoutez et répétez.

Pronouncing the sounds [ɥ] and [w]

Several of the pronouns you have just learned contain semivowels, for example, [w] in *moi* and [ɥ] in *lui*. There are only three semivowels in the French language and the third one is the sound [j], as in *yaourt,* which you practised in Unit 8. Semivowels are always followed by another vowel (such as [i] or [a]), and they combine with that vowel to make a single sound.

Although [ɥ] can be followed by other vowel sounds, for example, [ɛ̃] as in *juin*, it is most frequently combined with [i] (in words such as *nuit, huit,* etc.). To make the sound, start with the [y] (as in *tu*) and very quickly change to [i] by spreading your lips.

Common [w]/vowel combinations include [w] + [i], as in *Louis,* or [w] + [e] as in *louer* or [w] + [ɛ] as in *ouest.* It is very frequently found followed by [a] as in *moi*, *Guadeloupe*, or *dois*. To make the sound, start with the [u] sound and quickly change to [a]. In both cases, be careful to make just one syllable/sound.

Activité 10.2.8

A

Track 10:9

Listen to Track 10:9 and repeat the words you hear.

Écoutez et répétez.

B

Track 10:10

Listen to Track 10:10 and repeat each sentence to practise the sounds [ɥ] and [w].

Écoutez et répétez.

Track 10:11

C

You are now going to practise using pronouns *moi, toi, lui*, etc. for emphasis. Listen to the questions on Track 10:11 and answer in the gaps following the prompts.

Parlez, en suivant les indications.

Activité 10.2.9

A

Look at the drawing and label each body part correctly, using the vocabulary below.

Trouvez les parties du corps qui correspondent aux numéros du dessin.

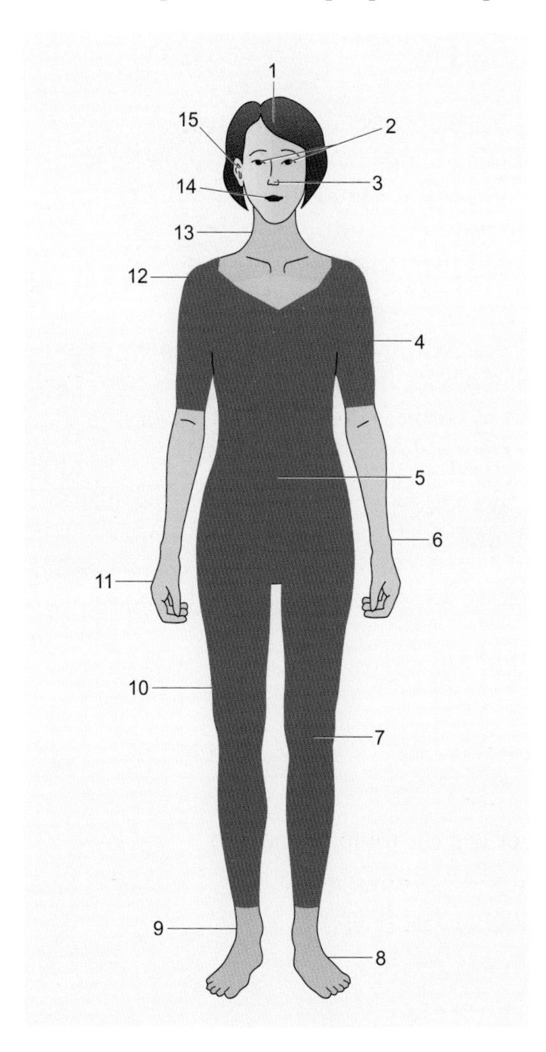

l'oreille • le genou • la tête • le nez • le bras • le cou • la bouche • le pied • la cheville • le poignet • les yeux • l'épaule • la main • la jambe • le ventre

B

Look at the drawings (1–6) and match each one to the correct description below (a–f).

Associez les dessins aux légendes.

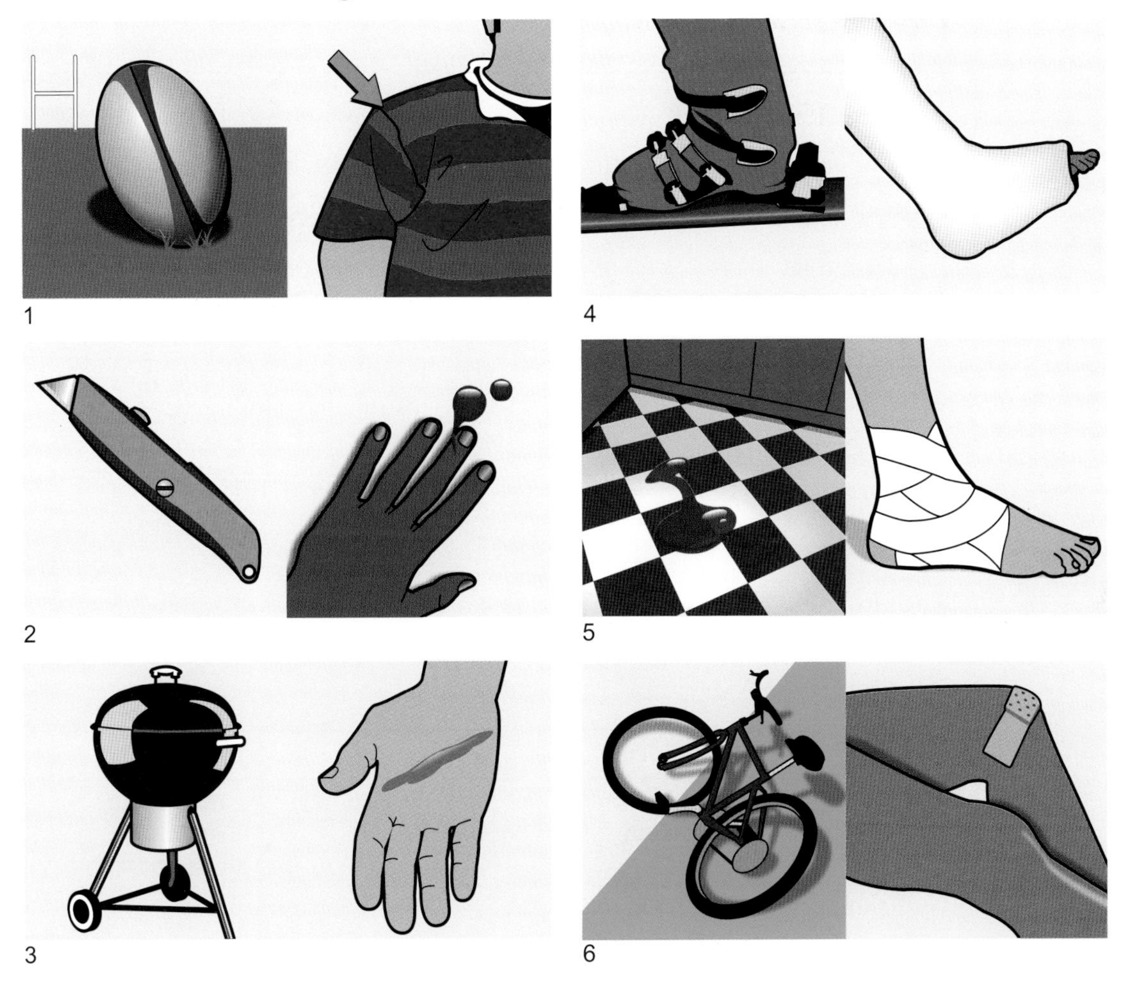

(a) Marion faisait du ski, elle est tombée et elle s'est cassé la jambe.
(b) Elle est tombée de son vélo et elle s'est fait mal au genou.
(c) Fabien a glissé sur le carrelage et il s'est foulé la cheville.
(d) Mon cousin jouait au rugby et il s'est déboîté une épaule.
(e) Mon voisin a fait un barbecue hier et il s'est brûlé la main.
(f) Pauline a fait du bricolage avec un cutter et elle s'est coupée.

glissé *slipped (from* glisser)
s'est foulé *sprained (from* se fouler)
s'est déboîté *dislocated (from* se déboîter)
un cutter *Stanley knife*

Activité 10.2.10

A

je boite *I have a limp*
allumettes (f.pl.) *matches*

In this activity, you are going to listen to five people talking about accidents and injuries they had in the past. Below is a list of expressions you will encounter in the recording. Match each to its English equivalent.

Faites correspondre les expressions en français à leur équivalent anglais.

1	J'ai fait de la rééducation.	(a)	I slipped in the snow.
2	J'ai eu des séances de kiné.	(b)	I played with matches.
3	J'ai glissé dans la neige.	(c)	I had to have a skin graft.
4	J'ai eu un plâtre.	(d)	I had physiotherapy.
5	Je jouais avec des allumettes.	(e)	I had physiotherapy.
6	J'ai dû avoir une greffe.	(f)	I don't work with sharp instruments any more.
7	Je ne travaille plus avec des objets coupants.	(g)	I had a cast.

Track 10:12

B

Listen to Track 10:12, in which five people talk about accidents they have had in the past. Complete the table in English. The first row has been done for you.

Complétez le tableau.

Name	Accident	Injury	Treatment
Jacques	serious motorbike accident	broken arm, leg and pelvis	2 months in hospital, physiotherapy
Guillaume			
Margaux			
Annie			
Raoul			

Track 10:12

C

Listen to Track 10:12 again and say whether the following statements are true or false. Correct the false statements.

Vrai ou faux ?

		True	False
1	Jacques has fully recovered.	❑	❑
2	Jacques still rides a motorbike.	❑	❑

3	Guillaume has put on a lot of weight.	❑	❑
4	Guillaume still plays rugby.	❑	❑
5	Margaux's ankle hurts from time to time.	❑	❑
6	Margaux has bad memories of her accident.	❑	❑
7	Raoul has changed his job since the accident.	❑	❑

D

Look at the transcript of Track 10:12 and identify the five different expressions used to ask if someone has fully recovered.

Lisez la transcription et trouvez les cinq phrases.

Talking about injuries

You can say you have sustained an injury using a variety of expressions.

To talk generally, use *se faire mal* + *au/à la/aux* + part of the body:

Je **me suis fait mal au dos.** — *I **hurt my back**.*

To be more precise, use *se fracturer/se casser/se brûler/se fouler* + *le/la/les* + part of the body:

Annie **s'est brûlé la main**. — *Annie **burned her hand**.*

Elle **s'est foulé la cheville**. — *She **sprained her ankle**.*

(In Track 10:12 you heard: '*Je me suis cassé **une** jambe et **un** bras*', but the use of *le/la/les* is generally more common.)

You have learned to make the past participle agree with the subject when using pronominal verbs, for example:

Elle **s**'est lav**ée**. — *She **washed** (herself).*

Il **s**'est coup**é**. — *He **cut himself**.*

When a pronominal verb is used with a body part, as in the following examples, there is no agreement of the past participle:

Elle **s'est lavé les mains**. — *She **washed her hands**.*

Elle **s'est coupé la main**. — *She **cut her hand**.*

You can also describe having an injury using *avoir* + *le/la/les* or *un/une/des* + part of the body + past participle:

J'**ai le poignet foulé**. — *I **have a sprained wrist**.*

Elle **a la moitié du visage brûlé**. — ***Half of her face is burnt**.*

Elle **a une jambe cassée**. — *She **has a broken leg**.*

Activité 10.2.11

Read the following scenarios and describe the resulting injuries, based on the indication about the body part involved.

Lisez et décrivez la blessure.

Exemple

Jean a eu un accident de vélo. (pied)

→ Il s'est fracturé le pied.

1 Henri faisait de l'escalade, il est tombé. (jambe)
2 Jean-Pierre faisait de la boxe. (nez)
3 Cécile a eu un accident pendant le barbecue hier. (main)
4 François faisait du bricolage avec un marteau. (doigt)
5 Martine est tombée dans les escaliers. (genou)

Activité 10.2.12

A

A friend of yours posted the following message on a social network recently. Read it and tick the correct answers.

Lisez le message et cochez les bonnes réponses.

à l'improviste *unexpectedly, without warning*

je me suis coincé le doigt *I caught my finger (from* se coincer)

la portière *car door*

L'autre jour j'ai décidé d'aller voir ma copine, à l'improviste. Je sortais de la maison quand j'ai laissé tomber mes clés. Je les ai rattrapées mais je me suis cogné la tête contre la porte d'entrée. Pressée de partir j'ai descendu la marche trop vite et je me suis foulé la cheville. Je suis montée dans ma voiture mais j'ai fermé la portière trop vite et je me suis coincé le doigt ! Finalement, j'ai décidé d'abandonner ma visite et je suis remontée dans mon appartement. Un peu plus tard, j'ai reçu un coup de téléphone de ma copine. Elle était à l'hôpital. Vous ne devinerez jamais ce qui lui est arrivé ! Elle venait me voir à l'improviste, elle est tombée dans les escaliers, elle a une jambe cassée !

Hier 14:35

1 Your friend was on her way to …
   (a) school. ❑
   (b) work. ❑
   (c) see a friend. ❑
2 As she left the house she …
   (a) dropped her keys. ❑
   (b) let go of her dog's lead. ❑
   (c) poured coffee over her clothes. ❑

3 In haste, she hurt her … (tick as many as appropriate)

(a) face. ❑
(b) head. ❑
(c) ankle. ❑
(d) knee. ❑
(e) elbow. ❑
(f) finger. ❑

4 In the end, she decided to …

(a) go back home. ❑
(b) go to the hospital. ❑
(c) go to her friend's. ❑

5 Her friend has a broken leg because …

(a) she had a car accident. ❑
(b) she fell down the stairs. ❑
(c) she slipped on an icy pavement. ❑

B

Read the message again and find the French equivalents for the following English expressions.

Trouvez l'équivalent des expressions dans le texte.

1 I caught my finger.
2 I bumped my head.
3 I sprained my ankle.
4 She has a broken leg.

Activité 10.2.13

A

You are about to take part in three dialogues. In order to prepare what you will say, read the following sentences and translate them into French. Try to rely on what you have learned so far in this and other units before using a dictionary.

Traduisez les phrases suivantes.

1 I have a crooked nose.
2 I fell down the stairs two years ago.
3 I hurt my back.
4 My back hurt for six months.
5 I put on a lot of weight.

le nez tordu *crooked nose*
l'échelle (f.) *ladder*
le bassin *pelvis*

6 My back still hurts from time to time.
7 I fell off a ladder.
8 I fractured my pelvis.
9 I had a cast.
10 I had physiotherapy for six months.

Track 10:13

B

Listen to Track 10:13, which features three dialogues. Listen to the questions and answer in the gaps following the prompts.

Écoutez et répondez aux questions.

C

Now write a brief account of an accident that you have had. The information you provide can be real or imaginary. Remember to use the past tense(s).

Écrivez des phrases.

Section 10.3 Understanding the French health system

In this section you will learn how the French health system works and what you should do if you are taken ill in France. You will also learn a new tense: the simple future.

Activité 10.3.1

A

The article below, taken from a French website for foreign students, explains some basic facts about the health service in France. Read the first section and say if the following statements are true or false.

Lisez l'article et dites si les informations sont vraies ou fausses.

Médecin, pharmacie... Qui consulter ?

Vous êtes malade : qui consulter ?

En cas de maladie pendant votre séjour, vous pouvez consulter un médecin traitant pour obtenir des médicaments.

Le médecin traitant

Lorsque vous serez malade pour la première fois en France, vous choisirez un médecin qui deviendra votre médecin traitant pour toute la durée de votre séjour. Cela signifie que vous irez toujours le voir en premier avant de consulter un spécialiste, d'aller chez le kinésithérapeute ou de passer une radio.

Qu'est-ce qu'un médecin traitant et quel est son rôle ?

C'est le médecin généraliste ou spécialiste que vous choisissez comme médecin référent. Lorsque vous tombez malade, c'est lui que vous consultez en premier. Si votre état nécessite l'intervention d'un spécialiste, il vous oriente vers le professionnel de santé le plus compétent puis centralise toutes les informations de votre dossier.

...

Vous pouvez aussi bien choisir un médecin généraliste ou un spécialiste, sans contrainte géographique particulière. Choisissez le médecin qui vous connaît le mieux et ce qui est le plus pratique pour vous. ...

...

Vous êtes également libre de changer à tout moment de médecin traitant sans vous justifier.

(Adapted from www.smeno.com/etudiants/1431_qui-consulter.html and www.smeno.com/etudiants/428_medecin-traitant.html, last accessed 27 November 2012)

des médicaments (m.pl.) *medicine*

le kinésithérapeute *physiotherapist*

passer une radio *to have an X-ray*

		True	False
1	If you are ill in France, the doctor you choose to see as your first port of call is called a *médecin traitant* or a *médecin référent.*	❑	❑
2	A *médecin traitant/référent* has to be a general practitioner.	❑	❑
3	It is easy to change doctors.	❑	❑
4	You cannot see a doctor who is not geographically close to where you live.	❑	❑

B

Now read the next section below and find the French equivalent for the words and expressions in the passage.

Trouvez les mots et les expressions en français dans le passage.

Le médecin :

- vous ausculte : il vous demande d'expliquer ce qui ne va pas, écoute votre cœur, prend votre tension artérielle, cherche des symptômes pour identifier votre mal ;
- rédige une ordonnance en fonction de son diagnostic : il vous prescrit des médicaments que vous trouverez en pharmacie ou bien il vous prescrit d'autres soins médicaux (analyse de sang, kinésithérapie, radiologie, etc.).

votre mal (m.) *pain/ache/illness*
la kinésithérapie *physiotherapy*

Le médecin traitant est la personne centrale dans le système de soins français :

- vous ne pouvez pas acheter certains médicaments sans ordonnance ;
- si vous consultez un spécialiste sans son avis, vous êtes moins bien remboursé par la Sécurité sociale.

(www.smeno.com/etudiants/1431_qui-consulter.html, last accessed 27 November 2012)

1 prescribes medicines to you
2 examines you (with a stethoscope)
3 listens to your heart
4 a prescription
5 blood test
6 takes your blood pressure

C

Read the rest of the text below and answer the following questions in English.

Répondez aux questions.

La pharmacie

C'est l'endroit où l'on achète les médicaments. Certains sont **en vente libre**, ce qui veut dire que vous pouvez les acheter **sans ordonnance**. C'est le cas pour l'aspirine, certains sirops pour la toux, médicaments contre le rhume, etc. Lorsque vous achetez des médicaments en vente libre mais sans ordonnance, vous ne pouvez pas être remboursé par la Sécurité sociale.

Les médicaments sur ordonnance sont vendus uniquement sur autorisation du médecin traitant. C'est le cas des antibiotiques, des pilules contraceptives, en général de tous les médicaments puissants.

Les urgences

En cas de problème grave qui nécessite une intervention rapide, vous devez vous rendre directement aux urgences hospitalières les plus proches de chez vous. Ces services sont ouverts 24h sur 24.

Si vous ne pouvez pas vous déplacer, appelez **les pompiers** en composant **le 18 d'un téléphone fixe** ou **le 112 à partir d'un téléphone portable**.

(www.smeno.com/etudiants/1431_qui-consulter.html, last accessed 27 November 2012)

1 What are *médicaments en vente libre*?
2 What are *médicaments sur ordonnance*?
3 What medicines are not reimbursed by the French health service?
4 What do you need to do if you have a serious health problem that needs urgent intervention?
5 In case of emergency, if you can't get yourself to casualty what should you do?

D

Find the French for the following English expressions in the text in step C.

Trouvez les expressions en français.

1 a landline
2 cold medicines
3 the Pill
4 a mobile phone
5 cough syrup

La Sécurité sociale

Created in 1945, *la Sécurité sociale*, often referred to simply as *la Sécu*, is the name of the French welfare system. It is divided into four distinct branches, which are public health; pensions; family (i.e. child, housing and disability benefits); and occupational health. Each branch is governed by a different administrative body.

In terms of health care, the principle behind *la Sécu* is to provide this for all. Since the year 2000, all legal French residents are covered for medical treatment, whether they pay into the system or not. This is funded by compulsory salary contributions paid by both employers and workers.

In most cases, *la Sécu* covers about 70% of health costs, the remainder being charged to the patient. However, those who are most in need, i.e. patients suffering from long-term or severe illnesses or needing expensive treatment, are fully covered. There are varying rates of cover for prescription medicines.

Traditionally the system worked on the principle of reimbursement: patients paid for their treatment and prescriptions and then claimed money back from the *Sécu*. This has been simplified thanks to the introduction of a health care smart card, *la carte vitale*. Private additional health insurance, to cover the 30% of costs which are not covered by the state, can be purchased from private health companies; they are usually not-for-profit cooperative organisations called *mutuelles*.

Most doctors work for private practices but receive payments (not a salary) from the *Sécu*. The fees that the *Sécu* will cover are regulated, and these are called *honoraires conventionnés*, but some doctors set their own fees (known as *honoraires libres*) so patients who consult the latter must pay the difference in fees. Patients need to choose a main doctor (*médecin traitant*) to qualify for full levels of reimbursement for medical expenses. To see most specialists, patients need to be referred by their *médecin traitant*. However, patients can get direct appointments with eye doctors, dentists or gynaecologists without being referred.

Activité 10.3.2

A

Read the following sentences from the text in *Activité 10.3.1* and underline the verbs.

Soulignez les verbes dans les phrases.

> Lorsque vous serez malade pour la première fois en France, vous choisirez un médecin qui deviendra votre médecin traitant pour toute la durée de votre séjour.
>
> Vous irez toujours le voir en premier.

B

Give the infinitive form of the verbs you have underlined in step A.

Donnez l'infinitif des verbes.

The simple future tense

You have already learned one way to express actions you are about to do using *aller* + infinitive:

> Je **vais partir** en vacances. *I **am going to go** on holiday.*

In the text you have just studied, you have come across another way to express the future: the simple future tense. It is used when you want to talk about something that will take place or happen in the future:

> Vous **choisirez** un médecin. *You **will choose** a doctor.*

To form the simple future tense, take the infinitive of the verb and add the following endings:

je	donner**ai**
tu	donner**as**
il/elle/on	donner**a**
nous	donner**ons**
vous	donner**ez**
ils/elles	donner**ont**

Note the following exceptions.

Verbs ending in *-re* in the infinitive drop the final *-e* before adding the appropriate future tense ending:

vendre → **vendr** → vendra

Le pharmacien vous **vendr**a des médicaments.
*The pharmacist **will sell** you some medicine.*

Note that *-er* verbs preceded by the letter **e** + a **consonant** change to reflect their pronunciation:

acheter → j'ach**è**terai

Vous **achèterez** les médicaments en pharmacie.
*You **will buy** the medicine at the pharmacy.*

appeler → j'appe**ll**erai

Elle **appellera** le médecin demain.
*She **will call** the doctor tomorrow.*

With irregular verbs, you use the same endings as for regular verbs but you do not use the infinitive of the verb to form the stem. Irregular verbs use the same stem in the future and in the conditional tense, so you will need to learn this for each irregular verb:

pouvoir → pou**rr-**

Vous **pourrez** avoir accès aux soins.
*You **will be able to** have treatment.*

devoir → de**vr-**

Vous **devrez** vous rendre aux services des urgences hospitalières.
*You **will need to go** to A & E/casualty.*

être → **ser-**

Vous ne **serez** pas remboursés.
*You **will not be** reimbursed.*

devenir→ dev**iendr-**

Il **deviendra** votre médecin.
*He **will become** your doctor.*

Note that in French, the simple future tense is used with *quand* or *lorsque* ('when') whereas English uses the present tense:

Quand/lorsque vous **serez** malade, vous **choisirez** un médecin traitant.
*When **you are** ill, you **will choose** a doctor.*

Activité 10.3.3

To help you to learn the future tense form of the most common irregular verbs, complete the tables below.

Complétez les tableaux.

	être	**avoir**	**aller**	**faire**	**prendre**
je/j'			irai		
tu		auras			
il/elle/on	sera				prendra
nous				ferons	
vous					
ils/elles					

	venir	**pouvoir**	**devoir**	**vouloir**	**voir**
je	viendrai			voudrai	verrai
tu					
il/elle/on					
nous					
vous			devrez		
ils/elles		pourront			

Activité 10.3.4

Put the verbs in brackets into the simple future tense.

Mettez les verbes au futur simple.

1 Je __________ au pharmacien la semaine prochaine. (parler)
2 Les enfants __________ les comprimés avant d'aller se coucher. (prendre)
3 Nous __________ le formulaire pour demander une carte européenne de santé. (remplir)
4 Est-ce que tu __________ les médicaments à la pharmacie ? (acheter)
5 M. Claveau, est-ce que vous __________ le médecin ? (appeler)
6 Je me sens toujours malade, j'__________ consulter le médecin demain. (aller)
7 Je suis sûre que tu __________ mieux très bientôt. (se sentir)
8 Vous __________ payer vos médicaments à la pharmacie. (devoir)
9 Les laboratoires d'analyses __________ fermés à partir de 18 heures demain. (être)
10 Il __________ plus d'exercice quand il __________ en meilleure forme. (faire – être)

11 Les amis de mon mari __________ nous voir l'été prochain. (venir)

12 Nous avons mangé trop de chocolat, nous __________ mal au ventre demain. (avoir)

Activité 10.3.5

A

Read the following account of a real story and fill in the blanks with the right verbs from the box below.

Complétez les blancs avec les verbes qui conviennent.

sera • accouchera • paiera • devra • aura droit

enceinte *pregnant*
accoucher *to give birth*
la grossesse *pregnancy*
l'accouchement (m.) *birth/delivery/labour*
comme si elle y était assurée *as if she was insured there*
frais d'accouchement (m.pl.) *costs associated with the birth*

Sécurité sociale à l'étranger : bien se renseigner avant de partir

Lucia est couverte par l'assurance maladie obligatoire en Italie et passe quelque mois en France pour terminer ses études. Elle possède une carte européenne d'assurance maladie, qu'elle a obtenue en Italie. Elle est enceinte et __________ (1) en France. La grossesse et l'accouchement demandent des soins médicaux urgents, donc Lucia __________ (2) aux soins médicaux nécessaires en France en présentant sa carte européenne d'assurance maladie.

Lucia __________ (3) traitée en France comme si elle y était assurée. Lucia __________ (4) les frais d'accouchement et elle __________ (5) ensuite demander un remboursement.

B

Translate the following sentences to prepare for the next step.

Traduisez ces phrases pour préparer l'étape suivante.

1 I will give birth in France.
2 I will have to request a European health insurance card.
3 With my European health insurance card I will be entitled to medical treatment.
4 I will be treated as if I was insured in France.
5 I will pay for the costs associated with the birth and I will have to claim the money back.

Track 10:14

C

Listen to Track 10:14. Lucia, who you have just read about, is answering some questions about what she will have to do while she is abroad. Answer the questions as if you are Lucia.

Écoutez et répondez aux questions.

Activité 10.3.6

A

Imagine you are going to be interviewed about the health care system in your own country. In order to prepare for the interview, read the following questions and make notes to prepare your answers.

Lisez les questions et préparez vos réponses.

Comment s'appelle le système de santé dans votre pays ?

Comment ça marche ?

Est-ce que l'équivalent de la carte vitale existe dans votre pays ?

Devez-vous payer les consultations chez le médecin traitant, ou chez les spécialistes comme les dentistes, les ophtalmologistes et les gynécologues, etc. ?

Est-ce que le système des mutuelles existe ?

Faut-il payer les médicaments chez le pharmacien et les frais à l'hôpital ?

B

Track 10:15

Now listen to the questions in Track 10:15 and provide your own answers, based on the system in your country, or use the *corrigé* from step A. You may want to pause the track to give yourself time to answer.

Écoutez les questions de l'extrait 10:15 et donnez les réponses sur le système de santé de votre pays.

Health care in Belgium and Quebec

Health care in Belgium is of a very high standard and is funded partly by social security contributions and partly by private health organisations. Residents have to join a *mutuelle* (private health insurance company) which reimburses most of the costs, such as doctors' fees, but they may or may not opt for further private insurance cover. Belgian pensioners get free health care. There is no equivalent of the *carte vitale* and residents pay doctors' fees up front. As in France, doctors' fees vary.

The health care system in Quebec is called the RAMQ *(la Régie de l'assurance maladie du Québec*). Under the RAMQ, all legal residents of Quebec have access to free basic medical care, which includes seeing doctors and hospital visits as well as medicine, and are issued with a *carte d'assurance maladie* (health insurance card). Most doctors are part of the Quebec Health Insurance Plan and, as with the *carte vitale*, this health insurance card can be used to pay their fees. However, those doctors who are not part of the system will not accept the health insurance card and will charge fees.

Activité 10.3.7

Track 10:16

This final activity is an optional listening activity, in which two people are talking about health care in Belgium and Quebec. It is quite challenging, so you are not expected to understand everything, and you may want to listen and read the transcript at the same time. Much of the information contained in the recording is explained in English in the box above.

Écoutez.

Section 10.4 Talking about treatment

In this section you will learn how to talk about and give advice about treatment for illnesses and health problems. You will revise the imperative and use it with pronouns, you will learn a set of expressions for giving advice and you will find out about French people's attitudes towards medication.

Activité 10.4.1

A

Read the following words and expressions and match them to their English equivalent.

Faites correspondre les mots et expressions à leur équivalent anglais.

1	des douleurs	(a)	if it's not getting any better
2	une fièvre	(b)	a tablet
3	ausculter	(c)	allergic reaction
4	un comprimé	(d)	a temperature
5	ça ira mieux	(e)	it will get better
6	mal soigné	(f)	examine with a stethoscope
7	une réaction allergique	(g)	not properly treated
8	si ça ne va pas mieux	(h)	aches and pains

B

Track 10:17

Listen to Track 10:17, in which three people visit health professionals, and match each dialogue to the right health problem.

Écoutez et répondez aux questions.

1	Dialogue 1	(a)	tonsillitis
2	Dialogue 2	(b)	an allergic reaction
3	Dialogue 3	(c)	flu

une épidémie *an epidemic*
une angine *tonsillitis*
prescrire *prescribe*
une rougeur *a rash*
j'ai mal au cœur *I feel sick*
à jeun *on an empty stomach*
la nourriture épicée *spicy food*

C

Track 10:17

Listen to Track 10:17 again and tick the symptoms you hear in each dialogue.

Réécoutez et cochez les bons symptomes.

	Dialogue 1	**Dialogue 2**	**Dialogue 3**
J'ai une rougeur.	❑	❑	❑
J'ai chaud, j'ai froid.	❑	❑	❑
J'ai mal au cœur.	❑	❑	❑
J'ai très mal à la gorge.	❑	❑	❑

J'ai des vertiges.	❑	❑	❑
J'ai un peu mal à la tête.	❑	❑	❑
J'ai des douleurs.	❑	❑	❑
Je ne mange pas beaucoup.	❑	❑	❑
Je suis très fatigué(e).	❑	❑	❑
J'ai un peu de fièvre.	❑	❑	❑
Je suis épuisé(e).	❑	❑	❑

D

Track 10:17

Listen to Track 10:17 again and select the right answers for each dialogue.

Écoutez et choisissez les bonnes réponses.

1 Dans le dialogue 1, le docteur donne au patient le choix entre :

(a) de l'ibuprofène ❑

(b) de l'aspirine ❑

(c) du paracétamol ❑

(d) des antibiotiques ❑

2 Le patient doit prendre ses médicaments :

(a) une fois par jour ❑

(b) trois fois par jour ❑

(c) deux fois par jour ❑

3 Dans le dialogue 2, le docteur prescrit :

(a) des antibiotiques ❑

(b) du paracétamol ❑

(c) de la codéine ❑

4 Le patient doit prendre ses médicaments :

(a) une fois par jour ❑

(b) quatre fois par jour ❑

(c) deux fois par jour (matin et soir) ❑

5 Dans le dialogue 3, la pharmacienne conseille au patient de prendre :

(a) des comprimés antidépresseurs ❑

(b) des comprimés anti-inflammatoires ❑

(c) des comprimés antihistaminiques ❑

6 Le patient doit prendre ses medicaments :

(a) à jeun ❑

(b) avec ses repas ❑

E

Look at the transcript for Track 10:17 again. Identify all the verbs in the imperative and give their infinitive form.

Soulignez les verbes à l'impératif et donnez leur infinitif.

Exemple

Prenez du paracétamol... : **prendre**

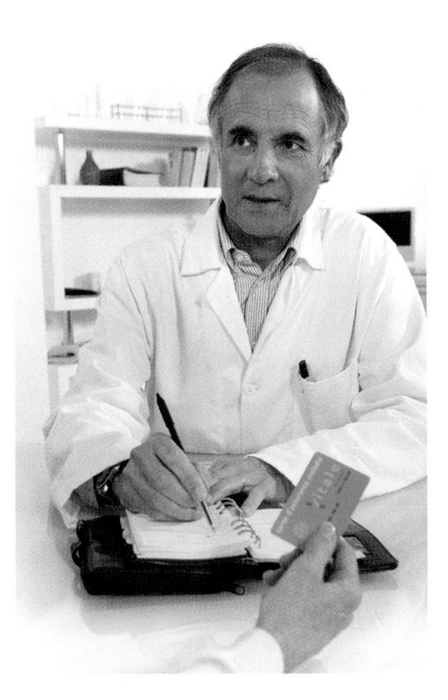

Further uses of the imperative

In Unit 4, you saw that the imperative was used to give directions. It can also be used to give instructions or advice:

Tournez à droite et **prenez** la première rue à gauche.
Turn right and take the first road on the left. (directions)

Arrêtez le traitement immédiatement.
Stop the treatment immediately. (instruction)

Faites plus de sport.
Play more sport. (advice)

You know how to form the *vous* form of the imperative, by using the *vous* form of the verb in the present tense, without the subject pronoun *vous*. The *tu* form of the imperative is formed by taking the *tu* form of the verb in the present tense without the subject pronoun *tu*. With *-er* verbs, you also need to take off the 's' at the end of the conjugated form of the verb as follows:

manger → tu manges → **mange** plus de fruits *(eat more fruit)*

Tourne à gauche.	*Turn left.*
Bois beaucoup d'eau.	*Drink a lot of water.*
Va voir le médecin.	*Go and see the doctor.*

In the negative form, the *ne … pas* is placed around the verb as usual:

Ne mangez pas de nourriture épicée.
Don't eat spicy food. (formal)

Ne bois pas d'alcool.
Don't drink alcohol. (informal)

With pronominal verbs used in the imperative, the pronoun is placed **after** the verb:

Reposez-**vous**.	*Have a rest. (formal)*
Repose-**toi**. (te *becomes* toi)	*Have a rest. (informal)*

This is the same for direct object pronouns:

Prenez **du paracétamol**. Prenez-**le** trois fois par jour.
(le = le paracétamol)
Take some paracetamol. Take it three times a day.

Prenez **deux comprimés**. Prenez-**les** au moment des repas.
(les = deux comprimés)
Take two tablets. Take them with your meals.

In the negative form, the pronoun is placed **before** the verb:

Ne **vous** fatiguez pas.	*Do not get tired.*
Ne **t'**inquiète pas.	*Do not worry.*

Ne **le** prenez pas pendant plus d'une semaine.
Do not take it for more than a week.

Ne **les** prenez pas à jeun.
Do not take them on an empty stomach.

Activité 10.4.2

Practise using the imperative to give one or two pieces of advice about how to treat the following conditions, using either your own ideas or suggestions from the box below. Try to include some negative as well as positive advice. Use the *vous* and *tu* forms of the imperative, as indicated.

Donnez des conseils.

1 J'ai mal à la tête. (tu)
2 J'ai beaucoup grossi ! (vous)
3 J'ai des douleurs dans une jambe. (tu)
4 J'ai de la fièvre. (vous)
5 J'ai la grippe. (tu)
6 J'ai mal aux dents. (tu)
7 Je suis fatigué(e). (vous)
8 J'ai des rougeurs partout sur le ventre et j'ai des vertiges. (vous)

se coucher • aller chez le dentiste • manger équilibré • prendre des anti-inflammatoires • se reposer un moment • téléphoner au médecin • prendre du paracétamol • arrêter de fumer • faire de l'exercice • boire beaucoup

Activité 10.4.3

Reply to the following statements using the verbs in brackets in the imperative (positive or negative) with the information provided and the direct object pronouns *le*, *la*, *les*. Take care with word order and check for specific cases where you need to use the *tu* or the *vous* form of the verb.

Répondez en utilisant l'impératif et les pronoms « le, la, les ».

Exemple

J'ai des comprimés pour mon rhume. (prendre – quatre fois par jour) (tu)

→ Prends-les quatre fois par jour.

1 Les antibiotiques me donnent mal à l'estomac. (ne pas prendre – à jeun) (tu)
2 Ce café est brûlant ! (boire – lentement) (vous)
3 Ces comprimés sont pour les adultes. (ne pas donner – à ta fille) (tu)
4 Ce sirop est très fort. (ne pas prendre – plus de trois fois par jour) (vous)
5 Tu as besoin de prendre tes comprimés. (ne pas oublier – à midi) (tu)
6 Ces comprimés pour la sinusite me font dormir. (prendre – avant d'aller au lit) (tu)
7 Il y a des noix dans ta salade. (ne pas manger – tu es allergique) (tu)
8 Tu ne vas bien du tout. Tu dois appeler le docteur. (appeler – le plus tôt possible) (tu)

Track 10:18

Activité 10.4.4

Listen to Track 10:18 where you are talking to Marie-Claude, a friend of yours who has not been well recently. Speak in the pauses following the prompts.

Écoutez et parlez dans les pauses.

Activité 10.4.5

A

Match each of the items below with its English equivalent. Some you will be able to guess easily, but others may require you to use your dictionary.

Associez les expressions françaises à leur équivalent anglais.

sparadraps (m.pl.) *plasters*
les coups *knocks, bumps*
tout un tas de choses *loads of things*
crème au propolis (f.) *propolis cream (propolis is a resin collected by bees)*

1	des brûlures d'estomac	(a)	to disinfect wounds
2	l'alcool à 90 degrés	(b)	heartburn
3	de l'eau oxygénée	(c)	very dry skin
4	désinfecter les plaies	(d)	cream to relieve insect bites
5	soigner les petits bobos	(e)	surgical spirit
6	une crème pour les piqûres d'insectes	(f)	hydrogen peroxide
7	la peau très sèche	(g)	to treat little cuts

Track 10:19

B

Listen to Track 10:19, in which three people are interviewed. What question are they asked? Answer in English.

Écoutez l'extrait. Quelle est la question posée ?

Track 10:19

C

Listen to Track 10:19 again and fill in the gaps with the words you hear.

Écoutez et complétez les phrases avec les mots que vous entendez.

comprimés effervescents • pastilles • gélules • sachets • comprimés

1 **Pierre** : Alors, moi, j'ai de l'aspirine, des __________ d'ibuprofen, j'ai du bicarbonate de soude et des __________ pour le mal de gorge.

2 **Pierre** : Ça se vend en __________ . Il faut diluer un ou deux __________ dans un verre d'eau.

3 **Julien** : J'ai des __________ de paracétamol.

D

Now, using your French–English dictionary, look up the words featured in the box in step C and give an English equivalent for them.

Cherchez les mots dans le dictionnaire et donnez un équivalent en anglais.

E

Read the transcript for Track 10:19 and complete the table to match each person with the medicines or supplements they mention.

Faites correspondre la personne aux médicaments.

Une pharmacie

médicaments homéopathiques • aspirine • paracétamol • ibuprofen • crème au propolis • bicarbonate de soude • pommade à l'arnica • pastilles pour le mal de gorge • magnésium • somnifères

Pierre	**Julien**	**Marie**

Activité 10.4.6

Look at the following pairs of sentences in which *en* is used to avoid repetition in the second sentence. Identify the words this replaces.

Observez les phrases qui contiennent le pronom « en » et identifiez les mots qu'il remplace.

Exemple

J'ai du bicarbonate de soude. J'en prends régulièrement.

(en *replaces* bicarbonate de soude)

1 Moi, j'ai surtout des médicaments homéopathiques. J'en prends pour tout un tas de choses.
2 J'utilise de la crème au propolis. J'en passe tous les matins.
3 J'ai du magnésium. J'en fais des cures deux fois par mois.
4 Vous avez de l'aspirine ? Non, j'en utilise très peu.

Using the pronoun *en*

The pronoun *en* is used to avoid repetition of information previously given (usually a noun) as follows:

- To replace an indefinite quantity:

  Tu manges **du poisson** ?
  Do you eat fish?
  – Oui, j'**en** mange tous les vendredis.
  – *Yes, I eat some (fish) every Friday.*
- To replace a definite quantity:

  Il y a combien de **sachets** dans une boîte ?
  How many sachets in a box?
  – Il y **en** a dix.
  – *There are ten (of them).*
- When used with a verb + *de:*

  Vous faites **du sport** ?
  Do you play sport?
  – Oui, j'**en** fais beaucoup.
  – *Yes, I do a lot of sport.*
  J'ai **du magnésium**, j'**en** fais des cures deux fois par mois.
  I have some magnesium. I take a course of it twice a month.

Activité 10.4.7

Answer the questions using the pronoun *en* and the information given.

Répondez aux questions.

Exemple

Vous mangez des céréales ? (oui – tous les matins)

→ Oui, j'**en mange** tous les matins.

1 Vous avez des enfants ? (oui – quatre)
2 Elle fait assez de sport ? (oui – trois fois par semaine)
3 Katia mange de la salade ? (oui – tous les soirs)
4 Est-ce qu'il y a du paracétamol dans l'armoire à pharmacie ? (oui – deux boîtes)
5 Vous prenez du magnésium ? (oui – tous les mois)
6 Il parle de ses vacances en France ? (oui – tout le temps)

Medicine consumption in France

France is one of Europe's biggest consumers of medicines. This has forced the *Sécurité sociale* to take action by directing campaigns at health care professionals in order to cut expenditure on prescribed medicines. Doctors are now required to prescribe generic medicines whenever possible to help cut costs.

Self-medicating is on the increase in France, but is still relatively rare because fairly common medicines, such as paracetamol, are reimbursed by the *Sécu* if prescribed by a doctor. Increasingly, adults use the internet to find information about their health problems and medication, and many patients argue against generic medicines as they believe they are not as efficient. As with everywhere else in Europe and the West, stress-related illnesses are on the increase in France.

L'intérieur d'une pharmacie

Activité 10.4.8

A

Track 10:20

Listen to Track 10:20, in which several people are talking about health problems, and match each dialogue (1–3) to the health problem it discusses.

Faites correspondre le problème au dialogue.

Dialogue 1	(a) Les migraines
Dialogue 2	(b) La digestion
Dialogue 3	(c) Le stress

Track 10:20

B

Listen again to Track 10:20 and fill in the gaps with the missing information.

Trouvez les informations qui manquent.

décompresser *to relax*
une tisane *herbal tea*
déplacement d'affaires (m.) *business trip*

Dialogue 1

Amélie ne dort pas parce qu' __________.

Elle est __________.

Elle a besoin de __________.

Dialogue 2

Thierry n'est pas __________.

Il a souvent des __________.

Dialogue 3

Thomas a toujours des __________.

Il est souvent __________.

Il mange __________.

Track 10:20

C

Listen to Track 10:20 again, if necessary, and match up the sentences below, which are taken from the dialogues.

Complétez les phrases.

1	Vous devriez	(a)	bouillir 6 à 8 feuilles pour faire une tisane.
2	Je vous conseille de	(b)	manger plus lentement.
3	Je te recommande	(c)	éviter les nourritures trop grasses.
4	Fais-en	(d)	essayer le yoga.
5	Bois-en	(e)	la camomille.
6	Vous devriez	(f)	boire des tisanes.
7	Il faudrait	(g)	un verre tous les matins.
8	Je vous suggère de	(h)	faire une cure de magnésium.

D

Now look at the transcript for Track 10:20 and identify the expressions used to reassure people.

Trouvez les expressions pour rassurer.

Giving advice

To give advice you can use the following tenses and structures.

- The conditional:

  Tu **devrais**/vous **devriez** faire un régime.
  You should go on a diet.

  Il faudrait/il vaudrait mieux éviter les nourritures trop grasses.
  You'd better avoid fatty foods.

  Tu **pourrais**/vous **pourriez** essayer le yoga.
  You could try yoga.

- The imperative:

  Appelez le 15.
  Call the emergency services.
  N'attendez pas.
  Don't wait.

  Fais bouillir des feuilles de camomille.
  Boil up some camomile leaves.

- *Je te/vous conseille/recommande/suggère de* + infinitive:

  Je vous conseille de faire une cure de magnésium.
  I would advise you to take a course of magnesium.

  Je te recommande (**de prendre** de) la camomille.
  I recommend camomile.

  Je vous suggère de boire des tisanes.
  I suggest that you drink herbal tea.

As well as giving advice, you may want to give a few words of reassurance. You can use the following expressions:

Ce n'est pas grave. / C'est pas grave.
It's not serious.

Ce n'est rien. / C'est rien.
It's nothing.

Ne t'inquiète pas. / Ne vous inquiétez pas.
Don't worry.

Ne t'en fais pas. / Ne vous en faites pas.
Don't worry about it.

Rassure-toi. / Rassurez-vous.
Don't worry.

Activité 10.4.9

A

For each sentence below, give advice using *devoir* in the conditional. You can use your own ideas or the suggestions given in the box below.

Donnez des conseils avec « devoir ».

1 J'ai pris 5 kilos en 3 mois.
2 J'ai mal à la tête.
3 J'ai une rage de dents terrible !
4 Je me suis cassé le poignet au squash et foulé la cheville en montagne. Sans parler de mon genou tordu au ski !

prendre un rendez-vous chez le dentiste • faire du sport • utiliser de la pommade à l'arnica • aller au lit à la même heure tous les soirs • boire une tisane • manger plus équilibré • prendre de la camomille • se coucher • faire des bains de bouche • arrêter de faire du sport

Exemple

Je dors mal et je suis fatigué(e).

Tu devrais/vous devriez aller au lit à la même heure tous les soirs.

Tu devrais/vous devriez faire du yoga.

Tu devrais/vous devriez prendre du magnésium.

B

Repeat the exercise in step A, giving the same advice and using the imperative or any other structures.

Donnez les conseils avec l'impératif ou autres expressions.

Exemple

Je dors mal et je suis fatigué(e).

Va/allez au lit à la même heure tous les soirs.

Fais/faites du yoga.

Je te/vous recommande de prendre du magnésium.

C

Track 10:21

Now listen to Track 10:21, where you will give the advice you practised in step B orally. You may want to pause the track to give yourself time to answer. There are no prompts but you will be told to whom you are talking so that you can decide whether to use *tu* or *vous*. (The exercise assumes that you would use *vous* for a colleague.)

Écoutez et donnez des conseils.

The importance of repetition

You will have noticed that *Activité 10.4.9* involved repetition. Repetition is a key part of language learning, particularly for developing speaking skills, because once a language pattern becomes automatic your mind is freer for other tasks. This is why many exercises encourage some degree of repetition. The next step is to apply language patterns you know to different situations, for example, using the conditional in the negative, or the imperative with different verbs. The more you practise structures in different contexts, the more confident you will feel to apply familiar structures to different contexts.

Activité 10.4.10

Using the vocabulary provided in the box, give reassurance to the various people below.

Rassurez vos amis.

Exemple

Je me fais des soucis : Jean a l'air très fatigué.

Ne t'inquiète pas ! Il a sûrement trop de travail.

1 Je n'ai pas eu le temps d'acheter un cadeau à ma mère pour son anniversaire.

2 Je suis vraiment très inquiète. Marcel est en retard.

3 J'ai oublié de prendre mes médicaments à midi.
4 J'ai raté mon émission de télévision préférée hier soir.
5 Mon ordinateur est encore en panne.
6 Aïe ! Je me suis coupé le doigt.
7 Il n'y a plus de thé !
8 Je ne sais pas quoi préparer pour le dîner ce soir.

pouvoir le réparer • beaucoup de circulation • pouvoir les prendre ce soir • faire une omelette • un sparadrap • regarder en ligne sur l'ordinateur • envoyer des fleurs • paquet dans le placard

Section 10.5 Talking about alternative medicine

In this section you will learn about alternative medicine, and how to give an opinion in a discussion.

Activité 10.5.1

A

Look at the following questionnaire which was published in a French health magazine. What is the French for 'alternative medicine'?

Quelle est la phrase qui veut dire alternative medicine *?*

B

To complete the questionnaire, match the types of alternative medicine (1–7) to to the correct definition (a–g).

Faites correspondre le nom à sa définition.

Testez-vous : connaissez-vous les médecines douces ?

1 L'homéopathie	(a) Une technique de relaxation et de connaissance de soi.
2 La réflexologie	(b) Une médecine chinoise qui utilise des aiguilles.
3 La sophrologie	(c) Très populaire et repose sur l'absorption de substances naturelles et de minéraux fortement dilués.
4 L'acupuncture	(d) Une médecine manuelle qui consiste à faire des manipulations douces des muscles et du squelette.
5 L'ostéopathie	(e) Un massage des points réflexes situés sur les pieds ou les mains.
6 La phytothérapie	(f) Exploite les eaux de source qu'on boit ou qu'on utilise en application dans les cures thermales.
7 Le thermalisme	(g) Soigne par les plantes.

C

Can you guess the meaning of the following words and expressions used in the questionnaire?

Trouvez le sens des mots suivants.

1 la connaissance de soi
2 des aiguilles
3 repose sur
4 fortement dilués
5 des manipulations douces
6 soigne

Activité 10.5.2

A

Look at the following vocabulary and match up the pairs of synonyms. This will help you to understand the audio track used in the next step. Can you work out what each pair of synonyms means?

Faites correspondre les expressions avec leur synonyme.

1	ça marche vraiment	(a)	je ne souffre plus du tout
2	c'est du pipeau	(b)	c'est tout dans la tête
3	ça n'a pas du tout marché	(c)	c'est très efficace
4	il m'a complètement guéri	(d)	c'est déplorable
5	c'est scandaleux	(e)	ça n'a pas été du tout efficace
6	c'est contesté	(f)	ce n'est pas sérieux
7	c'est psychologique	(g)	c'est remis en question

B

Track 10:23

Listen to Track 10:23, which features a panel discussion (*table ronde)* on the radio in which five people (Nicolas, Alice, Isabelle, Martin and Philippe) discuss using alternative medicine. Select which type of alternative medicine each speaker mentions in the table below.

Écoutez et completez le tableau.

	Nicolas	**Isabelle**	**Alice**	**Martin**	**Philippe**
homéopathie	❑	❑	❑	❑	❑
acupuncture	❑	❑	❑	❑	❑
réflexologie	❑	❑	❑	❑	❑
ostéopathie	❑	❑	❑	❑	❑
cures	❑	❑	❑	❑	❑

débattre de *to debate*
des séances *treatments*
nocif *harmful*
un psoriasis *psoriasis*
une cure de jouvence *revitalising/anti-ageing treatment*

C

Track 10:23

1 Listen to Track 10:23 again. Who is for alternative medicine, who is against, and who has no opinion on the subject?

Écoutez et notez les opinions des participants.

(a) Nicolas
(b) Isabelle
(c) Alice
(d) Martin
(e) Philippe

2 Match the reasons that each of the speakers you have just heard give for their views.

Faites correspondre les raisons données aux participants.

Who…

(a) thinks it plays on people's naivety, that there is no proof it works and finds it scandalous that they are reimbursed by the French health service.

(b) used osteopathy to cure back and shoulder pain and thinks it's better to use natural ways to treat people.

(c) thinks there is no evidence they do or don't work and doesn't use any alternative medicine.

(d) tried to stop smoking with acupuncture but it did not work, so thinks it's all in the mind.

(e) uses arnica cream for bruises, has had reflexology, and has a mother who had spa treatment that cured her psoriasis.

D

Now look at the transcript of Track 10:23 and identify all the expressions used for giving an opinion.

Lisez la transcription de l'extrait 10:23 et trouvez les expressions utilisées pour donner une opinion.

Expressing opinions

You have already learned a few expressions for giving an opinion, for example:

Je trouve ça intéressant.	*I find that interesting.*
Il pense que c'est amusant.	*He thinks it's funny.*

You can also use *à mon avis* to introduce your opinion:

À mon avis, c'est efficace.	*In my opinion, it's effective.*

To express support, agreement or disagreement, you can say:

Je suis (tout à fait) pour/contre.	*I'm (absolutely) for/ against it.*
Je suis d'accord (avec toi/vous).	*I agree (with you).*
Je ne suis pas d'accord (avec toi/vous).	*I disagree (with you).*
J'y crois.	*I believe in it.*
Je n'y crois pas.	*I don't believe in it.*

When you don't have an opinion, you can use:

Je ne suis ni pour ni contre.	*I'm neither for nor against it.*
Je n'ai pas d'avis.	*I don't have an opinion.*
Je ne sais pas.	*I don't know.*

La fontaine célestin à Vichy

Activité 10.5.3

Track 10:24

Listen to Track 10:24, where you are asked to give your opinion. Speak following the prompts.

Donnez votre opinion en suivant les indications.

Alternative medicine

Alternative medicine is very popular in France. Homeopathy and acupuncture are the most popular, followed by herbal remedies, chiropractic treatments, osteopathy and thalassotherapy. Complementary or alternative medicine is most popular among younger and more educated people.

Some alternative treatments are not reimbursed by the *Sécurité sociale*, for example, osteopathy or chiropractic appointments. However, the usual 70% of the cost of other alternative treatments, such as acupuncture, homeopathy or GP-referred spa sessions is reimbursed. Whether the remainder of the cost is reimbursed by a *mutuelle* varies according to the type of insurance chosen by the patient.

The majority of people who choose alternative medicine do so for minor illnesses such as athlete's foot or flu, or for allergies and conditions such as eczema, although there are also those who rely on them to treat serious illnesses. In the twenty-first century there is a lot of interest in alternative remedies as part of a healthier lifestyle or disease prevention.

Activité 10.5.4

A

Look at these adverts for some herbal remedies. From the list given, work out the English equivalent of each of these plants.

Trouvez l'équivalent anglais de chaque plante.

Des plantes pour améliorer votre santé

Le ginseng pour lutter contre la fatigue

LA VALÉRIANE POUR COMBATTRE L'ANXIÉTÉ ET L'INSOMNIE

L'aloès pour traiter les infections de la peau

Le millepertuis pour soigner les dépressions légères

La menthe pour soulager les troubles digestifs

valerian • aloe vera • St John's wort • ginseng • mint

B

Read the adverts again and complete the following sentences in English to say which illnesses each plant treats.

Associez chaque plante à la maladie qu'elles soignent.

1 Ginseng is good for fighting __________.
2 Valerian helps to fight __________.
3 Aloe vera is used for __________.
4 St John's wort is used to treat __________.
5 Mint relieves __________.

C

You came across the following nouns, verbs and adjectives in step A. Using your dictionary, complete the table below with the missing nouns, verbs and adjectives as indicated. Where you do not need to provide an answer, this is indicated with a dash. The first line has been done for you.

Remplissez le tableau avec les mots manquants.

	Nom	**Adjectif**	**Verbe**
1	la fatigue	fatigué(e)	se fatiguer
2	l'anxiété		—
3	l'insomnie		—
4	l'infection		
5		—	traiter
6		—	soigner
7	la dépression		
8		—	soulager
9		digestif	
10		respiratoire	

Activité 10.5.5

A

Track 10:25

Listen to Track 10:25 and answer the questions.

Écoutez et répondez aux questions.

l'herboriste (m/f) *herbalist*
tiges (f.pl.) *stalks/stems*
racines (f.pl.) *roots*
le cerveau *brain*
effets secondaires (m.pl.) *side effects*

1 Pourquoi la cliente du dialogue 1 vient-elle chez l'herboriste ?
2 Que lui recommande l'herboriste ?
3 Comment doit-elle prendre le traitement ?
4 Quel est le problème de santé du client dans le dialogue 2 ?
5 Quelles sont les bienfaits de la plante que lui conseille l'herboriste ?
6 Comment doit-il prendre le traitement ?
7 Qu'est ce qui ne va pas chez la cliente du dialogue 3 ?
8 Qu'est-ce l'herboriste lui conseille ?
9 Quelles raisons donnent-elle pour ce traitement ?

B

Now it's your turn to be a herbalist. Read the following queries and answer them, using the *vous* form. Use the structures you have learned in this unit for how to give advice and the information about herbal remedies you have learned in this section, in particular that included in Track 10:20.

Maintenant à vous ! Répondez aux questions.

Exemple

Je suis très anxieuse la nuit et je ne dors pas. Pouvez-vous me conseiller un remède ?

Pour lutter contre l'anxiété, la valériane est très efficace. Prenez-en deux comprimés le soir avant d'aller au lit et couchez-vous tout de suite !

1 Je suis si stressée tout le temps ! Qu'est-ce que je dois faire ?
2 Je souffre de migraine très régulièrement, qu'est-ce que je peux prendre ?
3 Ma fille a de l'eczéma sur les jambes, qu'est-ce que vous me conseillez ?
4 Mon mari est déprimé, et son traitement par antidépresseurs, ça ne marche pas du tout, il ne se sent pas bien. Vous pouvez me recommander un remède ?

Des herbes médicinales

Writing skills

When you do some writing, as you have just done for *Activité 10.5.5*, it may seem difficult to check your work because what you have written may differ considerably from the suggested answer given in the *corrigé*. Writing your own material is nonetheless a very useful skill to develop. Rather like speaking, it is an opportunity for you to develop the ability to be creative and to produce spontaneous French, with the added advantage that once you have written your piece you can then check through it and correct details such as verb endings and agreements. When doing a writing activity:

- Concentrate on using structures that you have been practising in the exercises you have just been doing.
- Check what you have written against the exercises you have already done.
- Remember to make the necessary adjustments for masculine/feminine, where appropriate, or pronouns.
- Think about verb endings (for example, *je pense que* ***ça marche*** / *je pense que* ***les médecines marchent***).
- Keep it simple but try to say as much as you can, using as many structures and as much relevant vocabulary as you can remember.

Activité 10.5.6

Write a paragraph of about 200 words in French using the vocabulary and structures you have learned in this unit about alternative medicine.

- Give your general opinion about alternative medicine and why you think this.
- Give your opinion of two types of alternative medicine of your choice.
- Give two examples of successful or unsuccessful experiences of using alternative medicine (this can be true or made up).
- Add any other information you wish to give about alternative medicine.

Écrivez environ 200 mots.

L'intérieur d'une herboristerie

Unité 11

Unité 11 overview

Section	Language	Vocabulary	Skills	Cultural understanding
11.1 Comparing the past and the present	• Making comparisons using verbs with *plus*, *moins* and *autant* • Making comparisons using nouns • Making comparisons using adverbs • Pronouncing *plus*	• Past lifestyles • Inventions	• Start planning your revision	• *Mai 1968* • Regional languages in France • *Septante, huitante* and *nonante*
11.2 Talking about your family history		• Milestones in people's lives and family histories	• Understanding different accents	• The French colonial empire • French as a lingua franca • Algeria
11.3 Reading about and reporting news and other past events		• The press • Incidents and accidents	• Text structures and conventions	• Colloquial vocabulary • Newspapers and magazines published in France
11.4 Reading and writing stories about past events			• Understanding and writing short stories	

Section 11.1 Comparing the past and the present

In this section you will learn how to make comparisons between the present and the past and to talk about change. While finding out how French society evolved in the twentieth century, you will revise the use of the imperfect and practise combining it with the present tense. You will also revise themes and vocabulary from previous units.

Activité 11.1.1

A

What was life in France like in the 1940s, 50s, 60s and 70s? Read the statements overleaf and match them to the correct photos. Each photo has two matching statements.

Faites correspondre les descriptions et les photos.

(a) (b) (c) (d)

arrière-grand-mère (f.) *great-grandmother*

autrefois *in the past*

1 Dans les années 40, mon arrière-grand-mère n'avait pas l'électricité dans sa cuisine, mais elle avait un robinet d'eau froide, vrai luxe pour elle !

2 Dans les années 50, la France était encore très rurale, plus que certains pays voisins. Comme beaucoup de Français autrefois, mon arrière-grand-mère habitait un petit village à la campagne.

3 Au début des années 60, la mode était encore très classique. Ma mère et ma grand-mère portaient le même style de robes.

4 Dans les années 70, les couleurs vives étaient à la mode, pour les vêtements et pour la décoration. Chez moi il y avait un canapé orange et rose.

5 Quand j'étais petite, on n'avait pas l'internet. Pour les nouvelles, on lisait le journal et on utilisait de gros téléphones.

6 Pendant la guerre, et juste après, on ne mangeait que des choses simples préparées à la maison. La plupart des gens n'allaient jamais au restaurant.

7 Quand mes parents étaient jeunes, les divorces étaient rares et difficiles. Les familles avaient une structure traditionnelle ; il n'y avait pas souvent de familles recomposées.

8 Il y avait peu de voitures du temps de mon arrière-grand-mère, même en plein centre du village.

B

What tense is used in the statements above to describe what things were like in the past? Underline the verbs.

Dans les textes on utilise quel temps pour faire des descriptions au passé ? Soulignez les verbes.

Start planning your revision

As you begin this last unit of the module, you need to start planning your revision. Unit 11 has been designed in such a way that the activities revise a number of the points you have met while taking your learning a little further (as you will see in the next activity). This should provide a useful basis for you to organise your overall revision.

If you prepared vocabulary lists or flash cards during the year, check the relevant ones as you progress through this unit: you can reactivate words and structures you noted down earlier or add new ones. Use the Unit 11 activities to assess which areas of the module you are less confident about.

Activité 11.1.2

A

You are going to find out more about one of the periods pictured in the photos from the previous activity. Read the text and fill in the gaps by putting the verbs given into the correct tense.

Lisez le texte ci-dessous et complétez-le avec les verbes mis au temps qui convient.

Je suis née dans les années 70. Quand j'(être) __________ petite, je (vivre) __________ à Paris. À cette époque, Valéry Giscard d'Estaing (être) __________ Président de la République, c'(être) __________ les années des chocs pétroliers et de la crise économique, mais aussi des progrès sociaux après les événements de mai 1968. Mes parents, mes frères et moi (habiter) __________ dans un appartement. Dans les années 70, les couleurs vives (être) __________ à la mode ; chez moi, il y (avoir) __________ un canapé orange et rose. On (porter) __________ des vêtements colorés avec des formes et des matières nouvelles. Les femmes (mettre) __________ plus souvent un pantalon et (avoir) __________ plus souvent les cheveux courts qu'avant. À midi, beaucoup de gens (rentrer) __________ manger chez eux, c'(être) __________ rare de prendre un sandwich au bureau. On ne (trouver) __________ pas beaucoup de supérettes en ville autrefois, on (faire) __________ plutôt ses courses dans les petits commerces. Dans mon enfance, il n'y (avoir) __________ que trois chaînes de télévision et notre poste (être) __________ en noir et blanc. On (avoir) __________ un gros téléphone gris qu'on n'(utiliser) __________ pas beaucoup parce que téléphoner (coûter) __________ cher. En ce temps-là, on n'(avoir) __________ pas l'internet ; pour les nouvelles, on (regarder) __________ les informations à la télé à 20 h ou on (lire) __________ le journal. Pour les vacances, nous (partir) __________ à la campagne ou à la montagne avec mes grands-parents. Nous y (aller) __________ en voiture ou on (prendre) __________ le train, mais à l'époque le TGV n'(exister) __________ pas encore.

chocs pétroliers (m.pl.) *oil crises*

un poste (de télévision) *a TV set*

B

Read the completed text of step A, as given in the *corrigé*, and answer the questions in no more than about 40 words altogether.

Lisez le texte dans le corrigé et répondez aux questions ci-dessous en quelques mots (n'écrivez pas plus d'environ 40 mots).

1 Qui écrit ? Un homme ou une femme ? On le sait comment ?
2 Il ou elle parle de quoi ?
3 C'était quand ?
4 La personne se trouvait où ?

C

The text mentions several themes covered in previous units of the module. To do a bit of revision, fill in the table below with nouns and verbs from the text related to each theme. The first row has been completed for you.

Remplissez le tableau avec des noms et des verbes sur chaque thème.

Themes	**Nouns**	**Verbs**
Lieu/logement	un appartement – un canapé	vivre – habiter
Famille		
Politique/société		
Mode		
Communications/informations		
Vacances		
Transports		
Repas/nourriture		
Courses/magasins		

D

Note down the six phrases used in the text to refer to periods or dates in the past.

Notez les six expressions qui indiquent que le texte décrit une période du passé.

Exemple

dans les années 70

E

What were things like in the decade in which you grew up? Write five sentences to describe people, places or facts from your childhood. You can choose from the themes in the table in step C and reuse words or structures from the text in step A.

Ecrivez cinq phrases pour décrire des gens, des lieux ou des faits de votre enfance.

Mai 68

In the late 1960s, many countries in the Western world went through periods of unrest, such as the anti-Vietnam war movement in the United States and student protest movements in Germany. In France, a month of social and political unrest in May 1968 profoundly transformed French society. The events started with student protests at the University of Nanterre, just west of Paris, which quickly spread to the Sorbonne in central Paris. The extreme reaction of the police caused the situation to escalate into a general strike involving 7 million people across the country. There were violent confrontations with the police and barricades were set up in the streets of Paris, most famously in the Latin quarter. The riots and demonstrations led to the collapse of Charles de Gaulle's government at the end of the month, although he swiftly regained power by winning the early elections organised in June.

What was unique about the 1968 protests in France was that they sprang from a radical questioning of the traditional values of its society; the protesters' demands stemmed from the rejection of authority and of prevalent paternalistic attitudes. Among the resulting cultural and social changes were democratisation in the running of universities, the formation of new relationships between employers and workers' unions and the rise of the feminist movement in France.

Manifestation en mai 1968. Au premier rang sur la photo : des syndicalistes de la Confédération générale du travail (CGT)

syndicaliste (m.f.) trade unionist

Activité 11.1.3

A

In this activity, two lifestyles from two eras are compared. Read the text and fill in the table below by listing all the contrasts between the two lives described in the text. Reuse words from the text. The start of the table has been done for you.

Lisez le texte et complétez le tableau en notant autant de contrastes que possible entre les deux personnes. Utilisez les mots du texte.

la Bresse *a rural region in the south of Burgundy, north of Lyon*
l'eau (f.) courante *running water*
sûrement *probably*
les champs *fields*
se déplacer *to travel (literally: to get around)*
se consacrer à *to devote oneself to*

> Mon arrière-grand-mère vivait dans un petit village dans la Bresse, alors que moi je vis à Paris, la plus grande ville de France. Elle habitait une petite maison modeste. Elle avait l'eau courante mais pas l'électricité, tandis que moi, dans mon appartement, je bénéficie de tout le confort moderne. Par contre, son rythme de vie était sûrement plus régulier ; moi, mon emploi du temps change souvent. Mon arrière-grand-mère n'avait pas de diplômes ; en ce temps-là, les filles étudiaient moins. Moi, en revanche, j'ai un diplôme d'ingénieur en informatique et un poste à responsabilités. Mais cela ne veut pas dire qu'elle travaillait moins ; au contraire, c'était plus dur, elle travaillait dans les champs et s'occupait de vaches et de poules. À cette époque-là, on se déplaçait moins pour travailler : moi je passe beaucoup de temps dans les transports pour aller au travail. Elle partait moins en vacances que moi, et elle se consacrait autant à sa famille. Moi je me repose plus le week-end et en vacances, et je voyage beaucoup plus, alors que mon arrière-grand-mère ne quittait presque jamais son village. Elle ne prenait jamais

l'avion et n'allait jamais à l'étranger. Mais elle appréciait plus la nature, et elle participait plus à la vie de son voisinage, de son village. À l'époque, on y parlait encore patois ; maintenant seules quelques personnes très âgées connaissent encore cette langue régionale. En général les gens de ma génération ne la parlent plus.

le voisinage *the neighbourhood*
le patois *local dialect, patois*

Mon arrière-grand-mère	**Moi**
un petit village	une grande ville

B

Read the text again and circle the phrases used to express an opposition or a contrast.

Relisez le texte et encadrez les expressions utilisées pour exprimer une opposition ou un contraste.

Exemple

alors que

C

Find the missing words used in the text to complete the sentences below. Translate these words into your own language. What are they used for?

Cherchez dans le texte les mots qui manquent pour compléter les phrases ci-dessous. Traduisez-les. On les utilise pour quoi ?

Elle partait __________ en vacances que moi.

Elle se consacrait __________ à sa famille.

Je voyage beaucoup __________ .

D

Read the text again and complete the statements below using either *plus* or *moins* based on the information given in the text.

Relisez le texte et complétez les affirmations avec « plus » ou « moins » selon les informations données dans le texte.

1 Mon arrière-grand-mère travaillait __________ que moi.
2 Elle se déplaçait __________ que moi.
3 Elle se reposait __________ que moi.
4 Elle voyageait __________ que moi.
5 Elle appréciait __________ la nature que moi.
6 Elle participait __________ à la vie de son voisinage que moi.

Making comparisons using verbs with *plus, moins* and *autant*

You saw in Unit 9 that *plus*, *moins* and *aussi* can be used with adjectives to make comparisons:

Le pain bio est **plus** cher.	*Organic bread is **more** expensive.*
C'est **aussi** bon.	*It's **as** good.*

Plus and *moins* (*que/qu'*) are also used with verbs to make comparisons:

Elle partait **moins** en vacances **que** moi.	*She used to go on holiday less than me.*
Elle appréciait **plus** la nature.	*She used to appreciate nature more.*

But to express that two things are equal, using a verb, you need to use *autant (que/qu')*:

Elle se consacrait **autant** à sa famille (**que** moi).	*She used to dedicate as much time to her family (**as** I do).*
Ma grand-mère travaillait **autant que** mon grand-père.	*My grandmother used to work as much as my grandfather.*
J'aime **autant** la Bresse **que** la Bretagne.	*I like Bresse as much as Britanny.*

Regional languages in France

In the text of *Activité 11.1.3* you read that the writer's great-grandmother used to speak *patois*. This term refers to a regional dialect used in a small area or locality. French only became the official language in France in the sixteenth century, and at that time was not spoken by the majority of the population. Instead, dozens of regional languages and dialects were used across the country. Their decline started after the French Revolution (of 1789), when French was imposed as the language of the new Republic and as a tool for uniformisation and centralisation. This decline was accelerated when attendance of free primary school became compulsory at the end of the nineteenth century, since speaking regional languages and dialects was forbidden at school.

Although French remains the only official language in France, the importance of regional languages as part of France's cultural heritage has been acknowledged since the late twentieth century, as well as the importance of other languages spoken in French territories. Around the year 2000, a quarter of the French population had grown up being spoken to in a language other than French by their parents. It has been shown that there are 75 regional or minority languages spoken by French citizens living in French territories; these include some creoles, some Celtic languages (e.g. *breton*), Germanic languages (e.g. *alsacien*), Romance languages (e.g. *catalan*) and non-territorial languages like Berber, Romani or Yiddish; they also include the French sign language, LSF (*langue des signes française*).

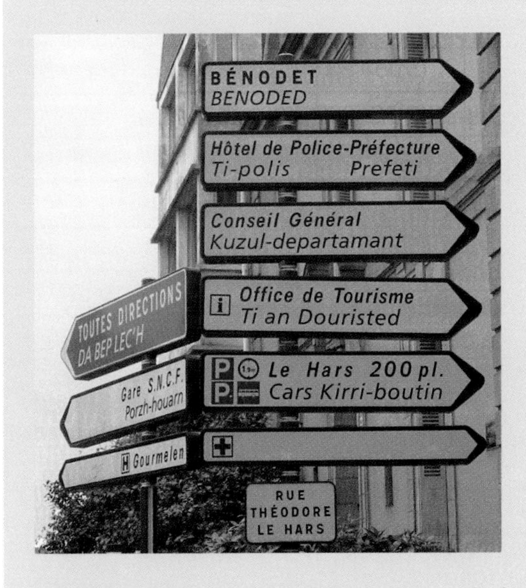

Panneaux bilingues français–breton à Quimper

Activité 11.1.4

What aspects of your life have changed since you began studying French? Compare your current life to what it was like before. Write five sentences using *plus*, *moins* and *autant* with verbs.

Faites cinq phrases avec « plus », « moins » et « autant » + verbe.

Exemple

Je dors plus la nuit mais je me repose moins la journée.

Activité 11.1.5

Track 11.1

A

Listen to Track 11:1, which contains interviews with two people called Agnès and Philippe talking about recent changes in their towns. Name the two towns and name one change about each that is mentioned.

Écoutez les interviews avec Agnès et Philippe. Ils parlent de changements récents dans deux villes. Nommez les deux villes et un changement mentionné pour chaque ville.

grâce à *thanks to*
un éco-quartier *environmentally friendly housing development*
un prix *a prize*
les technologies (f.pl.) de pointe *cutting-edge technology*
zone (f.) piétonne *pedestrian area*

B

Track 11:1

Listen again and complete the table by marking which points are mentioned about which towns. Some points may refer to both towns.

Réécoutez l'extrait. Les thèmes suivants sont évoqués pour quelle(s) ville(s) ?

	Grenoble	**La Rochelle**
des bâtiments écologiques		
des bâtiments historiques		
la circulation		
la zone piétonne		
le climat		
le tramway		
le vélo / les cyclistes		
les technologies de pointe		
l'université		
une population internationale		

Making comparisons using nouns

As you heard in Track 11:1, *plus de*, *moins de* and *autant de* are used with nouns to make comparisons:

Il y a **plus de** pistes cyclables..	*There are more cycle lanes.*
Il n'y avait pas **autant de** cadres internationaux autrefois.	*There weren't as many international executives before.*

These expressions may be followed by *que/qu'* (meaning 'than'):

Il y a **moins de** pollution **qu'**avant.	*There is less pollution than in the past.*

De plus en plus means 'more and more' and *de moins en moins* means 'less and less'. These can be followed by *de* + noun:

Il y a **de moins en moins d'**inconvénients.	*There are fewer and fewer drawbacks.*

or used on their own with verbs:

Je l'**aime de plus en plus** !	*I like it more and more!*

or followed by **adjectives**:

Les villes sont **de plus en plus** écologiques.	*Cities are greener and greener.*

Don't forget to include *de* at the start of these phrases: ***de** plus en plus*, ***de** moins en moins.*

Note the liaison, which sounds like /z/, in the pronunciation of these expressions:

De plus‿en plus / de moins‿en moins.

Grenoble

La Rochelle

Activité 11.1.6

Has your own town or area changed much, like Grenoble and La Rochelle have? Write five sentences using '*plus/moins* + noun' and '*de plus en plus / de moins en moins*'.

Faites cinq phrases avec « plus/moins + nom » et « de plus en plus / de moins en moins ».

Activité 11.1.7

A

In this activity you will find out more about some important social developments that have taken place in France since the end of the nineteenth century. Read the sentences below and fill in the first column of the table with the correct date of each event. Don't use your dictionary.

Lisez les phrases et mettez les bonnes date dans la première colonne du tableau. N'utilisez pas de dictionnaire.

Avant 1881, on n'allait pas à l'école primaire gratuitement en France.

Avant 1936, on n'avait pas droit à des vacances rémunérées en France.

Avant 1945, on ne votait pas en France si on était une femme.

Avant 1950, on n'avait pas de salaire garanti en France.

Avant 1967, on n'avait pas le droit de prendre la pillule en France.

Avant 1974, on devenait majeur à 21 ans en France.

Avant 1999, on ne pouvait pas s'unir si on était en couple avec une personne du même sexe.

Avant 2013, on ne pouvait pas se marier avec une personne du même sexe en France.

Date	**Event**
	Institution de l'instruction gratuite, publique et obligatoire
	Institution du SMIG (salaire minimum interprofessionel garanti)
	Institution du PACS (pacte civil de solidarité)
	La majorité légale passe à 18 ans
	Le droit de vote devient vraiment universel
	Légalisation de la contraception
	Les premiers congés payés
	Vote du mariage pour tous.

B

Read the list of events again, think about the content and answer the questions, in English.

Relisez la liste des événements, réfléchissez à son contenu et répondez aux questions en anglais.

Did any facts surprise you? Was anything different from what you might have expected? Is anything different from what you know about your own country?

Activité 11.1.8

A

Track 11:2

This activity is to revise pronouncing dates. Listen to Track 11:2 and repeat each date.

Écoutez et répétez.

1881 1950 1999 1974 1945 1967 1936

B

Track 11:3

Some dates are pronounced differently by speakers of French from Belgium and Switzerland compared to speakers from France. Listen to Track 11:3, which contains three dates pronounced by a speaker from Belgium and one from Switzerland, and try to guess what the dates are.

Écoutez et notez les dates.

Septante, huitante* and *nonante

The terms *soixante-dix*, *quatre-vingts* and *quatre-vingt-dix* are remnants in the French language of an old counting system based on twenties. In Belgium and Switzerland *soixante-dix* and *quatre-vingt-dix* are not used; instead there are terms derived from the decimal counting system: *septante* and *nonante*. In some parts of Switzerland, *huitante* is used instead of *quatre-vingts*; it is not used in Belgium. Another Swiss term for the same number, *octante*, has almost disappeared nowadays.

C

Track 11:4

Listen to Track 11:4 and fill in each gap in the sentences below with the correct date. Then listen again and repeat the sentences. This is also an opportunity to practise pronouncing verbs in the imperfect tense.

Maintenant écoutez et complétez les phrases. Ensuite réécoutez et répétez.

Avant __________ , la calculatrice n'existait pas.

Avant __________ , on ne buvait pas de champagne.

Avant __________ , on ne pouvait pas faire de photos.

Avant __________ , l'alphabet Braille n'existait pas.

Avant __________ , on ne pratiquait pas la pasteurisation.

Avant __________ , il n'y avait pas de poubelles à Paris.

Avant __________ , on n'avait pas inventé le cinéma.

Avant __________ , les cartes à puce n'existaient pas.

Avant __________ , on ne prenait pas le TGV.

Avant __________ , on ne payait pas en euros.

Activité 11.1.9

A

Track 11:5

faire les trois-huit *to work around the clock in eight-hour shifts*

Listen to Track 11:5, in which a French woman talks about her impressions of the past, and answer the questions.

Écoutez et répondez aux questions.

1 Qu'est-ce que elle pense du passé ? *(Answer this question very briefly* ***in English****.)*

2 Quand elle parle du passé, elle parle de quelle génération ? *(Answer this question and question 3 very briefly,* ***in French****.)*

   (a) la génération de ses parents

   (b) la génération de ses grands-parents

   (c) la génération de ses arrières-grands-parents

3 (a) Elle parle de trois thèmes principaux. Lesquels ?
(b) Qu'est-ce qui était différent dans le passé selon elle ? Donnez un exemple qu'elle cite pour chaque thème.

B

Track 11:5

Listen again and find the French words for the following.

Réécoutez l'extrait et trouvez l'équivalent des mots suivants en français.

1 the good old days
2 manual work
3 office work
4 a washing machine
5 a dishwasher
6 a vacuum cleaner
7 It wasn't all rosy.

C

Track 11:5

Each theme is introduced by a word which makes a logical connection with the previous part of the presentation. Listen again and write down the three connectors which are used at the start of each theme.

Écoutez et notez les trois connecteurs logiques qui introduisent chaque partie.

D

Track 11:5

Listen again and complete the following sentences.

Réécoutez l'extrait et complétez les phrases suivantes.

1 Autrefois on travaillait __________ et on se reposait __________ .
2 Les gens avaient __________ des emplois manuels.
3 On communique aussi __________ .
4 On guérissait __________ .
5 On peut voir un médecin ou aller à l'hôpital et se faire soigner __________ .
6 Du temps de mes grands-parents, ça ne se faisait pas __________ .

Making comparisons using adverbs

Adverbs, like adjectives, can be used in comparisons using *plus, moins* or *aussi* with *que/qu'*.

On travaillait certainement **plus** assidûment.	*People certainly used to work more assiduously.*
On se reposait **moins** souvent.	People used to rest less.

De plus en plus and *de moins en moins* can also be used before adverbs.

On voyage **de plus en plus** rapidement.	*We travel more and more quickly.*

Activité 11.1.10

Write six sentences about things that have changed in your own life, using comparisons and adverbs. You can use the vocabulary suggested below.

Écrivez six phrases sur des choses qui ont changé dans votre vie en utilisant des comparatifs et des adverbes.

Exemple

En ce moment je fume moins souvent que l'année dernière.

Maintenant Aujourd'hui De nos jours En ce moment Actuellement	plus moins aussi	souvent rapidement fréquemment régulièrement lentement facilement bien vite difficilement rarement	que qu'	avant dans le passé autrefois quand j'étais enfant

Activité 11.1.11

In this activity, you are going to look at the various meanings of the word *plus*, and the different ways the word is pronounced.

Track 11:6

A

As you practise pronouncing *plus* in different contexts, you will see why the correct pronunciation of *plus* can be important. Look at the two sentences below, listen to their pronunciation on Track 11:6, and answer the questions.

Regardez les deux phrases, écoutez leur prononciation dans l'extrait et répondez aux questions.

(a) On n'a plus de temps.

(b) On a plus de temps.

1 Translate the two sentences.

2 In writing, what indicates the difference between the two sentences (that one sentence is negative and one is not)? And orally, what indicates the difference?

Pronouncing *plus*

Plus is either pronounced as [ply] (which becomes [plyz] in a liaison) or [plys]. To avoid misunderstandings, if you are unsure how to pronounce *plus* in a particular sentence, the safest option is to pronounce it [plys] if you mean 'more' and [ply] if you are using the negation *ne ... plus*. In some cases it will not be accurate but you will be understood and it won't cause confusions in the meaning!

If you would like to know the detailed pronunciation rules, they are set out in the following table, but you are not expected to learn them at this stage.

Structure		**Example**	**Pronunciation**
plus + *adjective* ...	... beginning with a consonant	La Rochelle est beaucoup **plus** grande.	[ply]
	... beginning with a vowel	Grenoble est une ville **plus‿**écologique.	[plyz]
plus + *adverb* ...	... beginning with a consonant	On communique **plus** rapidement.	[ply]
	... beginning with a vowel	Elle s'habille plus‿élégamment.	[plyz]
plus de + *noun*		Il y a **plus de** grandes surfaces.	[plys]
***verb* + plus**		Elle appréciait **plus** la nature.	[plys]
ne ... plus (*negation*)		Nous **n**'y habitons **plus**.	[ply]

B

Track 11:7

To practise listening to the differences in pronunciation, listen to Track 11:7, in which you will hear several sentences containing *plus*. For each sentence, select the appropriate box to indicate if *plus* is pronounced /ply/ (like *plu*), /plys/ (like *plusse*) or /plyz/ (like *pluze*).

Écoutez l'extrait et cochez la prononciation de « plus » que vous entendez.

		/ply/	/plys/	/plyz/
1	Elle appréciait plus la nature.	❑	❑	❑
2	On communique plus rapidement.	❑	❑	❑
3	Grenoble est une ville plus animée.	❑	❑	❑
4	On n'a plus de temps.	❑	❑	❑
5	Il y a plus de grandes surfaces.	❑	❑	❑
6	On possède plus de voitures qu'avant.	❑	❑	❑
7	Ils n'habitent plus en ville.	❑	❑	❑
8	La Rochelle est beaucoup plus polluée.	❑	❑	❑
9	Je voyage plus que mon arrière-grand-mère.	❑	❑	❑
10	Elle s'habille plus élégamment.	❑	❑	❑

Activité 11.1.12

In this activity you will practise recognising and producing the pronunciation of the word *plus*.

Track 11:8

A

Listen to Track 11:8 and for each pair below select whether the sentence you hear is (a) or (b).

Écoutez l'extrait et cochez les phrases que vous entendez : a ou b ?

1	(a)	On a plus de grandes surfaces dans ma ville.	❑
	(b)	On n'a plus de grandes surfaces dans ma ville.	❑
2	(a)	On a plus de temps pour se détendre.	❑
	(b)	On n'a plus de temps pour se détendre.	❑
3	(a)	On utilise plus de téléphones portables.	❑
	(b)	On n'utilise plus de téléphones portables.	❑
4	(a)	On appréciait plus la nature.	❑
	(b)	On n'appréciait plus la nature.	❑
5	(a)	On aime plus les vacances à l'étranger.	❑
	(b)	On n'aime plus les vacances à l'étranger.	❑

Track 11:9

B

Now listen to Track 11:9 and repeat the sentences.

Maintenant écoutez l'extrait et répétez les phrases.

Activité 11.1.13

This final activity of the section provides an opportunity for you to practise your writing skills and to recap everything you have learned in the section.

Look at the two images below. They represent the same scene in Paris, fifty years apart, in 1950 and in 2000. Write about 100 words to express contrasts and comparisons between the two eras and the two lifestyles.

Regardez les deux images et écrivez environ 100 mots pour exprimer des contrastes entre les deux époques et les deux styles de vie.

Use the vocabulary and structures that you have practised in this section:

- *plus, moins* and *autant/aussi* with adjectives, verbs, nouns or adverbs
- some phrases to express opposition and contrast.

Include several elements, covering some of the following themes mentioned in the section:

- Transport
- People's appearances and clothes
- Technology and communication
- Work
- Food/shops.

You could start like this: *En 1950 il n'y avait pas beaucoup de voitures, mais en 2000...*

LES ANNÉES 1950
21 Dupont Menuisier père et fils
Chapellier
mercerie Louise
BOUCHERIE
Epicerie
EPICERIE
Café Royal
Café Royal
Café
MÉTROPOLITAIN
TAXI

LES ANNÉES 2000
PRESSE
banque
Location
24/24
immo
amiprix
SUPERMARCHÉS
un ami pour la vie
PROMO
PROMO
bar
royal
POLICE
POLICE
trions
TAXI
METRO
METRO

Section 11.2 Talking about your family history

In this section you will practise talking and writing about your family background or history. You will hear the story of several people's families from different parts of the French-speaking world. This will give you an opportunity to further practise the use of past tenses, combining the imperfect and the *passé composé*. You will also read about some aspects of France's colonial past.

Photo de mariage, France, 1910

Activité 11.2.1

A

Track 11:10

hameau (m.) hamlet
Jura *small mountain range north of the Alps*
jumeau (m.), jumelle (f.) *twin*
enfance (f.) *childhood*
viguétze (f.) (Swiss French) *party*

Listen to Track 11:10, in which Daniel talks about his family, and answer the questions.

Écoutez l'extrait et répondez aux questions.

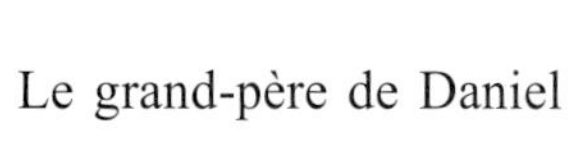

Le grand-père de Daniel

Le Jura suisse

1 Which country is Daniel's family from originally?
   (a) France
   (b) Switzerland
   (c) Belgium
   (d) England
2 Where did Daniel grow up?
   (a) France and Switzerland
   (b) France and Belgium
   (c) Switzerland and England
   (d) Switzerland and Belgium
3 Where does Daniel live now?
   (a) France
   (b) Switzerland
   (c) Belgium
   (d) England
4 What tense is used to list the important events in Daniel's life and the lives of his family?

B

Track 11:10

Listen again and complete the table with the relevant information.

Réécoutez l'extrait et complétez le tableau.

	Date	**Pays**
Naissance du grand-père		
Naissance de Daniel		
Enfance de Daniel		
Adolescence de Daniel		
Mariage et déménagement de Daniel		

C

Track 11:11

Now you are going to practise talking about the milestones in Daniel's life. Listen to Track 11:11 and speak in the pauses following the prompts.

Écoutez l'extrait et parlez dans les blancs.

D

Make some notes about your own life in the table overleaf. This is preparation for talking about your own life in the next step.

Prenez des notes dans le tableau.

Année de naissance ?	
Lieu de naissance? (pays/région/ville)	
Lieu de votre jeunesse ? (pays/région/ville)	
Déménagement ?	
Mariage ?	
Autres événements ou informations ?	

E

Now record an answer to the questions below, using your notes from the previous step. Add any other information you like about important events in your life.

Maintenant enregistrez votre réponse aux questions ci-dessous, en utilisant vos notes de l'étape précédente. Ajoutez d'autres informations sur les événements importants de votre vie si vous le voulez.

- Vous êtes né(e) en quelle année ? Dans quel pays ? Dans quel ville ?
- Vous avez passé votre jeunesse où ?
- Vous êtes marié(e) ?
- Vous vivez où maintenant ?

Activité 11.2.2

In this activity you will revise using both the *passé composé* and the imperfect in a story about the past.

Track 11:13

A

Listen to Track 11:13, in which Toan tells us about his family, and answer the questions, in French. Read the questions through before listening, and listen as many times as you need to.

le seul *the only one*

Écoutez l'extrait et répondez aux questions.

1 Toan vient de quel pays ?
2 Pendant son enfance, il vivait où ?
3 Ses parents faisaient quoi ? Et maintenant ?
4 Toan et son frère et ses sœurs se sont installés où ?
5 Maintenant, Toan fait quel métier ?
6 Il retrouve sa famille quand ?

Toan, et des membres de sa famille

B

Now read the transcript below and fill in the gaps by putting the verbs in brackets into the correct tense: present, *passé composé*, or imperfect.

Lisez la transcription et conjuguez les verbes indiqués au présent, au passé composé ou à l'imparfait.

> Je m'appelle Toan, et je (venir) _________ du Viêtnam. Mes grands-parents (être) _________ en vie à l'époque coloniale, quand le Viêtnam (être) _________ français. Mon grand-père (parler) _________ donc un peu français. Aujourd'hui nous (être) _________ une grande famille – mon père, ma mère et mes trois sœurs et frères. Quand j' (être) _________ petit, on (vivre) _________ tous à la campagne. Mes parents (être) _________ tous les deux agriculteurs. Le travail dans les champs (être) _________ très dur. Ils (être) _________ à la retraite maintenant.
>
> Mes deux sœurs, mon grand frère et moi nous (quitter) _________ le village et nous (s'installer) _________ dans une grande ville pour y chercher du travail et une meilleure vie. Mon grand frère (devenir) _________ donc coiffeur et mes deux sœurs commerçantes. Moi, j'(faire) _________ des études universitaires ; je suis le seul dans la famille. Et je (travailler) _________ maintenant comme enseignant de français. La fête de fin d'année est souvent la seule occasion où la famille (se réunir) _________. On se retrouve autour d'un repas et on passe de bons moments ensemble à la campagne.

C

Now match each tense to its correct use.

Faites correspondre chaque temps à l'emploi qui convient.

1 présent	(a) To talk about the events and actions in a story about the past.
2 passé composé	(b) To add background information and descriptions in a story about the past.
3 imparfait (*imperfect tense*)	(c) To talk about now or about general truths.

D

To learn or revise some vocabulary, complete this crossword puzzle. All the words needed are found in Toan's account.

Faites ces mots croisés.

Horizontalement	**Verticalement**
1 countryside	2 farmer
3 meal	7 opportunity
4 fields	8 teacher
5 female shop keeper	9 work
6 hairdresser	11 studies
10 Toan's country	13 family
12 life	
14 together	
15 party	

The French colonial empire

There were two main phases in the history of the French colonial empire. The first period of expansion took place in the sixteenth and seventeenth centuries during the era of great navigations and 'discoveries', when territories in North America, the Caribbean, Africa and India were colonised by France. This was linked to the trade in spices and other goods, and the slave trade that arose from colonial tropical plantations. Most of these territories were sold or lost by France at the end of the First French Empire (*le premier Empire*), of Napoleon I.

The second phase started in the nineteenth century under the Second Empire, headed by Napoleon III. Territories were invaded and conquered in Africa, North Africa, South-East Asia and Oceania.

Decolonisation started after the Second World War, and in many cases was a violent process, especially in Vietnam and Algeria.

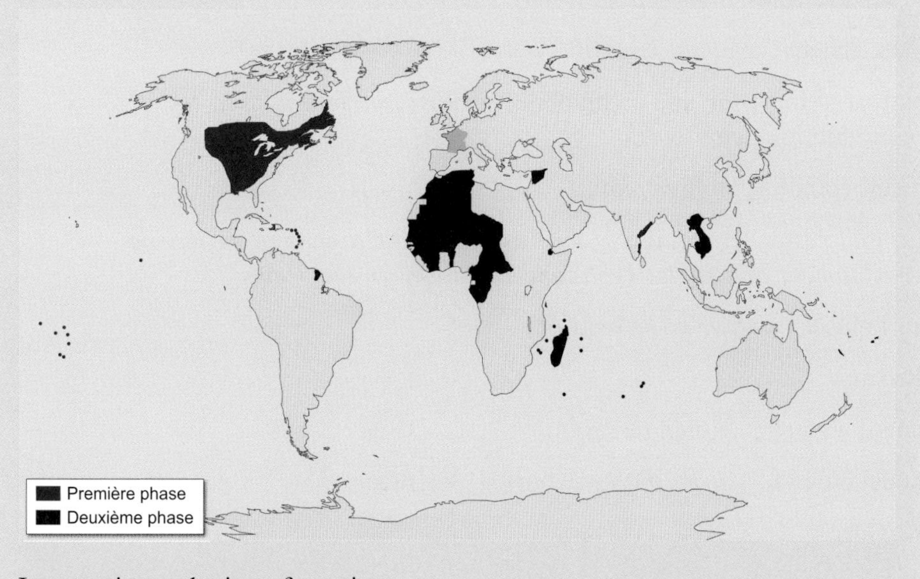

Les empires coloniaux français

Activité 11.2.3

In this activity you will find out about the family histories of some more French-speaking people.

A

Before listening to three people's family stories, look at the supporting vocabulary given below for Suzanne, Roxana and Xavière's accounts. See if you can predict something about each account from the vocabulary given and from the three images, one of which relates to each person's family history.

Regardez le vocabulaire et les trois photos et essayez de prédire quelques élements des histoires de Suzanne, Roxana et Xavière.

Suzanne

se sont connus *met*

la Seconde Guerre mondiale *the Second World War*

le village natal *the village where she was born*

s'est acheté *bought himself*

auto (f.) *(short for* une automobile; *in France,* auto *is used less frequently than* voiture*)* *car*

à son compte *self-employed*

La Révolution Tranquille *a period of political change, economic development and social evolution in Quebec in the 1960s*

au bout de *after, at the end of*

Roxana

une dictature *a dictatorship*

nous avons fui *(from the verb* fuir*)* *we fled*

Xavière

à cause de *because of*

l'une... l'autre... *one ... the other ...*

le Castillan *Castilian (i.e. Spanish)*

lointain(e) *distant*

Oran, Algérie

Vieille ville, Bucarest

Église de Vaudreuil, Québec

B

Track 11:14

Listen to Track 11:14, and match each name to the correct family.

Écoutez l'extrait 11:14 dans lequel trois femmes parlent de leur famille. Faites correspondre les noms aux familles.

1 Suzanne — (a) a Jewish family from North Africa
2 Roxana — (b) a Romanian family established in France
3 Xavière — (c) a family in Quebec

C

In which account are the following countries/provinces mentioned? There may be more than one answer for each.

Ces pays sont mentionnés dans quelle histoire ?

	Suzanne	**Roxana**	**Xavière**
France	❑	❑	❑
Algérie	❑	❑	❑
Roumanie	❑	❑	❑
Québec	❑	❑	❑
Australie	❑	❑	❑
Maroc	❑	❑	❑
États-Unis	❑	❑	❑

Track 11:15

Activité 11.2.4

Among the various people you have heard speaking French during the module are British, Swiss, Belgian, French Canadian and North African people. Listen to Track 11:15, in which you will hear five people from different parts of the world speaking French, and see if you can match each transcription (1–5) to the appropriate accent (a–e). (This activity is for general interest; you're not expected to be an expert at recognising accents!)

Écoutez l'extrait et faites correspondre les parties de l'extrait au bon accent.

1 La station est ouverte toute l'année et le domaine skiable est ouvert du 18 décembre au 17 avril.

2 Moi, je n'ai jamais fumé. Je n'ai jamais aimé cela, et je trouve que c'est très mauvais pour la santé.

3 Les médicaments et les frais hospitaliers sont gratuits avec la carte d'assurance maladie.

4 Vous devez normalement payer les médicaments prescrits par le docteur. Les médicaments sur ordonnance ont un prix fixe.

5 Pour pouvoir bénéficier des soins de santé et indemnités, il faut obligatoirement avoir une mutuelle. Une partie de votre salaire est utilisée pour payer les cotisations.

(a) accent britannique
(b) accent suisse
(c) accent belge
(d) accent québecois
(e) accent maghrébin

Understanding different accents

Although you have only practised the pronunciation of one variety of French, spoken in most parts of mainland France, you have learned that there are a variety of different accents in different regions and countries where French is spoken. In Unit 7 you listened to some examples, and in the module you have also heard some people who are not fluent speakers of French, such as recent migrants or tourists, and you will probably have interacted with fellow students. If you are not used to a particular accent you may find it difficult to understand, even if the language used is quite simple, but there are tips that can be helpful. Some of these can also be useful for understanding fast speech.

- The first thing to remember is not to panic when you struggle to understand somebody.
- It is always acceptable to ask, in French, if the speaker can repeat something or speak more slowly for you.

- It is important to persevere: the more you try to listen carefully, the more you are likely to understand.
- To pre-empt dealing with such difficulties, you can take every opportunity to listen to a variety of people speaking French, for instance by using online resources. Practice and pre-preparation are the best way to get used to different accents. If you are interested in this, or if you need to become accustomed to a different French accent, you could try finding an online radio broadcast from that area of the world. Even if you don't understand everything that you listen to, it will train your ear to pick up words and to recognise the accent.

Activité 11.2.5

In this activity and the next two, you will listen to the three stories of *Activité 11.2.3* again in more detail.

Suzanne et ses parents

A

Track 11:16

Listen to Track 11:16 and answer the questions below.

Écoutez l'extrait et répondez aux questions.

1 What were Suzanne's parents' names?
2 What were their occupations?
3 Why did her dad spend time in Australia?
4 Does Suzanne have any siblings?

Track 11:16

B

Listen again or read the transcript and note down the four phrases used to introduce time references in the story.

Réécoutez ou lisez la transcription et notez les quatre expressions utilisées pour introduire des références temporelles dans l'histoire.

Activité 11.2.6

Track 11:17

A

Listen to Track 11:17 and take brief notes in English to say what happened in each decade of Roxana's life.

Écoutez l'extrait et notez brièvement en anglais ce qui s'est passé à chaque décennie.

Université de Bucarest

La Sorbonne, Paris

1940s:

1960s:

1970s:

1980s:

B

Why did Roxana's family move to France? Select the correct reason.

Pourquoi est-ce que la famille de Roxana est partie en France ? Cochez la bonne raison.

1	Pour des raisons économiques : Roxana cherchait du travail.	❑
2	Pour des raisons de santé : Roxana avait besoin d'un traitement en France.	❑
3	Pour des raisons politiques : la famille fuyait un régime totalitaire.	❑
4	Pour des raisons culturelles : Roxana voulait apprendre le français.	❑

C

List the verbs in the past tenses used by Roxana.

Notez les verbes au passé utilisés par Roxana.

Verbs in the imperfect	Verbs in the *passé composé*

French as a lingua franca

For several centuries, French was used as a means of communication between people with different first languages. French became the language of diplomacy because of the economic and political importance of France in Europe from the sixteenth to the nineteenth century, combined with the extent of its colonial empire. As a result, it has remained one of the official languages of the United Nations and also of international postal services (which is why air mail stickers still include '*par avion*').

In the eighteenth and nineteenth centuries many European and Mediterranean elites used French as a common language. Romania is an example of a country where this had a lasting influence. For almost a century, from the middle of the nineteenth century, French was a compulsory subject in Romanian schools and there were strong cultural links between France and Romania. When the country was under Soviet occupation, French became a language of resistance in a country whose own language was also primarily of Latin origin. Cultural links to France played an important part in the development of Romania's identity, as is evidenced today by the membership of Romania in the *Organisation internationale de la Francophonie*. Although French is not an official language in Romania, nor indeed one of its minority languages, it is still learned and spoken by about 90% of the population.

Activité 11.2.7

A

Track 11:18

Now you will explore the story of Xavière's family in more detail. Listen to Track 11:18 and tick all the places mentioned in the recording.

Écoutez l'extrait et cochez tous les lieux qui sont mentionnés.

L'Afrique du nord	❑	Casablanca	❑
La ville d'Oran	❑	Marrakesh	❑
La ville d'Alger	❑	Tétouan	❑
L'Algérie	❑	Le Maroc espagnol	❑
Ce port situé au bord de la Méditerranée	❑	Essaouira	❑
La Kabylie	❑	L'Espagne	❑
Le Maroc	❑	Paris	❑

L'arrière-grand-père de Xavière reçoit la Légion d'honneur

B

Listen again and mark where each person was born.

Ces gens sont nés où ?

	En Algérie	**Au Maroc**	**En Espagne**	**En France**
Les parents de Xavière	❑	❑	❑	❑
Les frères et sœurs de Xavière	❑	❑	❑	❑
Xavière	❑	❑	❑	❑
Les grands-mères de Xavière	❑	❑	❑	❑
Les ancêtres de Xavière	❑	❑	❑	❑

C

Which of these maps shows the correct journey of Xavière's family members through the ages?

Quelle carte montre le voyage de la famille de Xavière à travers les époques ?

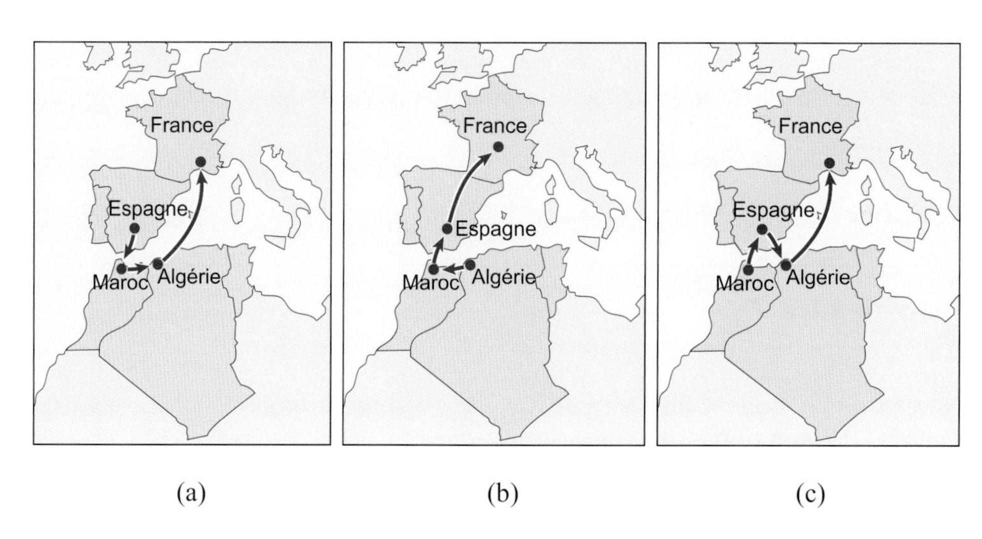

Algeria

The original inhabitants of the area that is now Algeria were Berbers. In the seventh century, North Africa was invaded and conquered by Arabs. In the fifteenth century, Jews were evicted from several parts of Spain and many settled in Algeria. In the sixteenth century, Algeria became part of the Turkish Ottoman Empire, while some northern towns, such as Oran, were invaded by Spain. In 1830, Algeria was conquered by France and was given the administrative status of a *département*, although there were inequalities in the way different categories of the population were regarded. Within 30 years, 50,000 French people had settled in Algeria. By 1960 there were about a million inhabitants not of Berber or Arab descent in Algeria, known as *les pieds-noirs*. This figure also included 140,000 Algerian Jews who had been granted French nationality in 1870.

La Grande Poste, Alger

Algeria's aspiration for independence resulted in a violent conflict with France which lasted over a decade. Although the struggle was only referred to as *les événements* in France at the time, it is now known as *la guerre d'Algérie*. Algeria became independent in 1962, and around 800,000 *pieds-noirs* had to move to mainland France. After independence the country struggled to find political and social stability.

Activité 11.2.8

In this activity, you will revise the use of a pronoun you have learned during the module. Complete the second sentence of each pair below by comparing it with the first sentence and filling in the gap with the correct pronoun. The same pronoun is used in all the gaps.

Complétez les phrases avec un pronom.

1 Nous vivions en Roumanie sous une dictature. En Roumanie la vie était difficile.
  Nous vivions en Roumanie sous une dictature. La vie __________ était difficile.
2 Je suis née dans une famille originaire de la ville d'Oran. Mes parents sont nés à Oran.
  Mes parents __________ sont nés.
3 Je me suis installé en Angleterre en 1991. J'habite toujours en Angleterre.
  J'__________ habite toujours.
4 Nous nous sommes installés dans une grande ville. Nous cherchions un travail dans une grande ville.
  Nous __________ cherchions du travail.

Activité 11.2.9

To practise using *y* in the *passé composé*, change the second sentence of each pair below to avoid a repetition by including *y*. Make sure you have identified the phrase to be replaced first; in the example, the phrase to be replaced has been underlined for you.

Changez la deuxième phrase pour éviter une répétition et inclure « y ».

Exemple

Mes parents habitaient à Avignon. Je suis née à Avignon.

→ **J'y suis née.**

1 J'aime beaucoup l'Algérie. Je suis arrivé en Algérie il y a cinq ans.
2 Il fait des études à l'Université de Bordeaux. Il a commencé une licence de langues à l'Université de Bordeaux.
3 Nous connaissons Bucarest. Nous sommes partis en voyage à Bucarest l'année dernière.
4 Elles étaient au Viêtnam l'été dernier. Elles ont passé trois semaines au Viêtnam.

Activité 11.2.10

A

Now it's your turn to write a story of your own family, or of a famous or fictional family if you prefer. First prepare some notes on what information you will include. You can use the mind map below or you can organise the information in a different way.

Maintenant à vous d'écrire l'histoire de votre famille, ou d'une famille célèbre ou fictive. D'abord préparez des notes sur le contenu. Vous pouvez utiliser le schéma ci-dessous ou organiser vos informations différemment si vous le préférez.

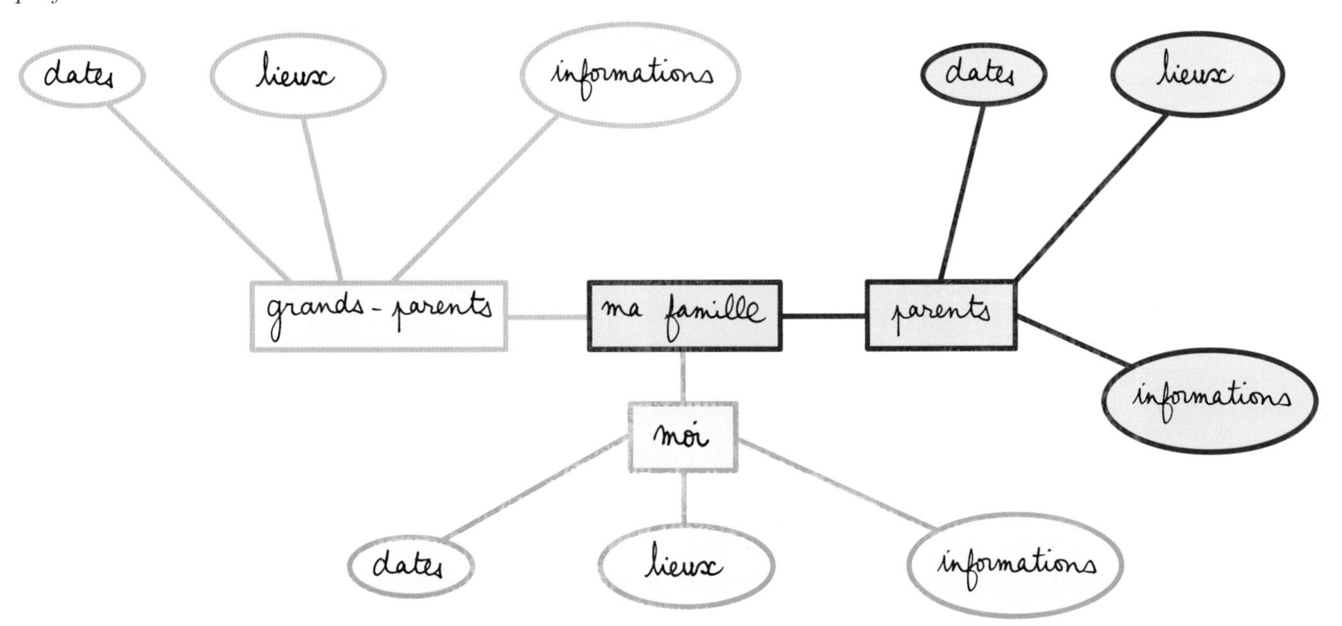

B

Now prepare a paragraph to tell your family's story. Include the information gathered in the previous step and the points listed below. Write 100 to 200 words.

Maintenant préparez un paragraphe pour raconter l'histoire de votre famille. Incluez les informations notées à l'étape précédente, et les points ci-dessous.

- Use the present tense, the *passé composé* and the imperfect, as appropriate.
- Use at least one occurrence of *y* with the *passé composé*.
- Use some phrases to introduce time references.
- Reuse as many expressions from the texts and recordings in this section as possible.

You could begin by talking about your grandparents, for example: *Mes grands-parents paternels étaient…*

Section 11.3 Reading about and reporting news and other past events

In this section you will begin by thinking about how information and communication technologies have evolved in the past decades and you will then explore the content and style of short newspaper articles. You can then do further revision of the imperfect and *passé composé*, look at how texts are structured and practise writing about an incident.

Activité 11.3.1

In this activity you will listen to accounts of how access to information and news has changed with the evolution of technology in France.

Track 11:19

A

Listen to Track 11:19 and match each of the three accounts you hear (1–3) to its main theme (a–c).

Écoutez l'extrait et faites correspondre chaque récit à son thème principal.

un quotidien national *a national daily newspaper*

une liseuse *an ebook reader*

Un téléphone des années 70

Un minitel

Des journaux nationaux et régionaux

(a) Lire les nouvelles, les journaux.
(b) Communiquer par téléphone.
(c) Chercher des renseignements, des informations.

B

Track 11:19

Listen again and tick all the items mentioned in each account. Some are mentioned more than once.

Réécoutez l'extrait et cochez tous les thèmes qui sont mentionnés dans chaque récit. Certains sont mentionnés plusieurs fois.

	1	**2**	**3**
l'annuaire	❑	❑	❑
l'email	❑	❑	❑
l'internet	❑	❑	❑
la liseuse	❑	❑	❑
l'ordinateur	❑	❑	❑
la tablette tactile	❑	❑	❑
le journal en ligne	❑	❑	❑
le journal papier	❑	❑	❑
le minitel	❑	❑	❑
le téléphone	❑	❑	❑
le téléphone portable	❑	❑	❑
les textos	❑	❑	❑

C

Complete the timelines below with the correct information, based on the items from the list in step B. The first one has been done for you.

Complétez les lignes des temps avec les éléments de la liste de l'étape B qui conviennent. Le premier a été noté pour vous.

	Autrefois	Ensuite	Aujourd'hui
Communiquer	***pas de téléphone***		
Chercher des renseignements			
Lire les nouvelles			

D

Now write six sentences to summarise each account (two sentences each). Only use the 'before' and 'now' stages of each timeline.

Maintenant écrivez six phrases pour résumer chaque récit. N'utilisez que deux étapes à chaque fois: « avant » et « maintenant ».

Exemple

1

(a) Autrefois, les gens n'avaient pas le téléphone.

(b) Aujourd'hui...

Activité 11.3.2

A

You are now going to look at vocabulary related to newspapers and the printed press. Which of the words in the list are not related to that domain? Cross out the odd ones. Look up any words you don't know in a dictionary.

Dans la liste ci-dessous, quels mots ne sont pas du domaine de la presse et des journaux ? Barrez les intrus. Cherchez dans le dictionnaire les mots que vous ne connaissez pas.

un article • la presse • un(e) journaliste • un micro • un écran • une interview • un titre • un sous-titre • les gros titres • une émission • un journal • les nouvelles • une dépêche • un magazine • les informations • une chaîne • un(e) reporter • zapper

B

Journalists use many metaphors in their professional jargon. Try to guess the correct explanation for each of the phrases below.

Devinez la bonne explication pour les expressions ci-dessous.

1 la une

(a) la première page d'un journal, où se trouvent les informations les plus importantes

(b) la première station de radio en France

2 un canard (= *a duck*)

(a) un mauvais journaliste

(b) un journal

3 les chiens écrasés (= *run-over dogs*)
   (a) les informations secrètes
   (b) les nouvelles moins importantes, souvent sordides
4 une feuille de chou (= *a cabbage leaf*)
   (a) un journal peu intéressant, de mauvaise qualité
   (b) un journal de petit format

Colloquial vocabulary

In French, as in most languages, there are words or structures that are of a particular register: they are suited to a particular style, a particular situation or a particular audience. For example, you learned in Unit 1 that *Salut* is an informal equivalent of *Bonjour*. Registers range from formal to vulgar. The phrases that you explored in the previous activity belong to the **colloquial** register (*le registre familier*): they are not rude or impolite but they would only be used in informal contexts, such as when talking to friends or close colleagues, for example.

When looking up a word in a bilingual dictionary, check if there are any indications about its register so that you avoid using it in the wrong context. Look out for abbreviations like *colloq* (colloquial), *frm* (formal) or *sl* (slang). Here are some examples of colloquial expressions you have come across in the module, with their standard equivalents given in brackets:

un bouquin (= un livre)
un boulot (= un travail)
un copain / une copine (= un ami / une amie)
avoir la trouille (= avoir peur)
rigoler (= rire)
crevé (= fatigué)

Activité 11.3.3

In this activity you will be reading some brief news items in French. This will help you to cope with real texts in French by looking at headlines and concentrating on what you do know instead of what you don't understand. You might find it useful to refresh your memory on the skills for approaching difficult texts, in Section 7.1 of *Livre 2*.

A

est prévue *is planned*
ont été interpellées *were arrested*

The following snippets of articles below are all from French regional newspapers. Match the headlines to the correct news items, without using a dictionary.

Faites correspondre les titres aux bonnes dépêches, sans utiliser de dictionnaire.

1 Opération antidrogue

2 Braquage: un blessé

3 Résultats des rugbymen

4 Reprise de la circulation des trains entre Rennes et Saint-Brieuc

5 Nouveau rassemblement contre l'aéroport samedi

(a) À l'appel de tous les opposants au projet de l'aéroport de Notre-Dame-des-Landes, une manifestation « pour l'arrêt immédiat du projet » est prévue samedi, à Nantes.

(b) En championnat de fédérale 2, Rodez s'est imposé devant Cahors 43 à 10 et Decazeville s'est incliné à Tulle 34 à 30.

(c) Soupçonnées de trafic de cannabis, plus de 20 personnes ont été interpellées hier, à Colmar.

(d) Lundi vers 17 h, un homme a braqué un bureau de tabac. Il a été blessé par les policiers puis arrêté.

(e) Depuis vendredi 22 h 30, les équipes de SNCF Infra réalisaient les travaux de déplacement des voies à l'Hermitage-Mordelles. Depuis 16 h ce dimanche, les travaux sont terminés. Les TGV et TER peuvent à nouveau circuler.

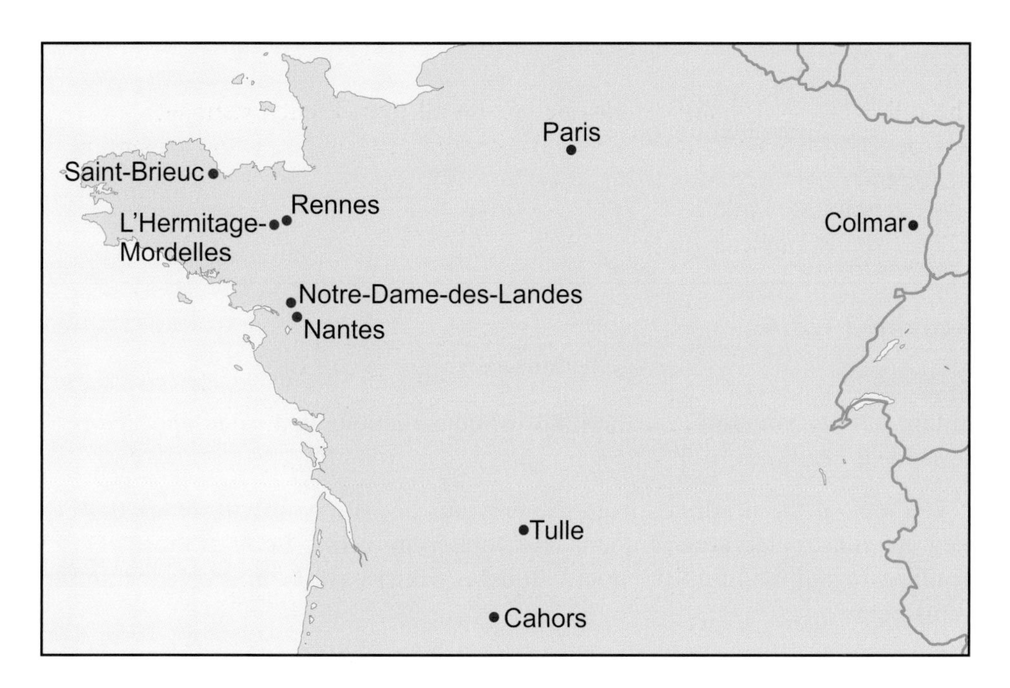

Cette carte indique les lieux mentionnées dans les articles

B

Which articles match which of the following topics?

Faites correspondre les articles aux bons thèmes.

1 sports results
2 a drugs raid
3 a demonstration
4 transport news
5 a hold-up

C

Find the French equivalent for the following phrases in the texts.

Trouvez les expressions françaises équivalentes dans les textes.

1 (text a)
   the opponents
   a demonstration
2 (text b)
   won
   lost
3 (text c)
   suspected
   arrested

4 (text d)
    attacked/held up
    was injured/wounded

5 (text e)
    building work
    run (trains can run)

Activité 11.3.4

A

In this activity you work on the kinds of constructions that often appear in newspaper headlines.

If you look at the headlines from the previous activity, you will notice that they are constructed around nouns and contain no verbs. Look at those headlines again, and find the nouns in them which have been derived from the verbs below.

Cherchez dans les titres les noms qui correspondent aux verbes suivants.

1 braquer
2 reprendre

B

Read the following headlines and work out the verbs which the underlined nouns derive from. Use a dictionary if necessary.

Cherchez les verbes qui correspondent aux noms suivants. Utilisez un dictionnaire si besoin.

Exemple

Circulation des trains coupée à cause d'un camion en feu

→ circuler

1 Livraison des plus grosses éoliennes de Bretagne
2 Réveil dans la neige dans les stations du Mercantour
3 Appel à une minute de silence devant l'hôtel de ville
4 Rassemblement des salariés de Visteon pour une manifestation

Newspapers and magazines published in France

The written press in France can be broadly divided into three sectors: the national daily press, the local daily press, and weeklies and magazines.

Some ten national daily newspapers are published in France, all of which are broadsheets, not tabloids. Their circulation has declined sharply and is lower than equivalent papers in neighbouring European countries. The most famous and widely respected title is *Le Monde*. Some papers are politically aligned: *Le Figaro* is the most famous conservative paper, and *Libération* a left-wing newspaper. *L'Équipe* is a sports daily.

The local press covers national as well as regional news. It is in better shape than the national titles, with about 50 local dailies nationwide. Readership has declined but not as sharply as that of the national press. Articles in the local press are often simpler to read than those from the national press: if you would like to have a go at reading news in French, a good starting point would be local titles such as *La Nouvelle République*, *Ouest-France*, *L'Est Républicain* and *La Provence*. In the decade from 2000 to 2010, free daily papers began to be circulated in larger cities, for example *Métro*, *20 minutes* and *Direct Matin* in Paris.

The abundance of magazines published in France is one aspect that characterises the French press. There are magazines covering numerous themes and domains, from weekly news titles (e.g. *L'Express, Le Nouvel Observateur*, *Paris Match*) to specialist weeklies about food, fashion, architecture, sports, DIY, motoring, etc. There are also numerous titles for children of different age groups. Over 90% of the population read at least one magazine a month.

Activité 11.3.5

A

Look at this newspaper article and label the different parts of it with the words given in the box below.

Regardez l'article et utilisez les mots ci-dessous pour désigner ses différentes parties.

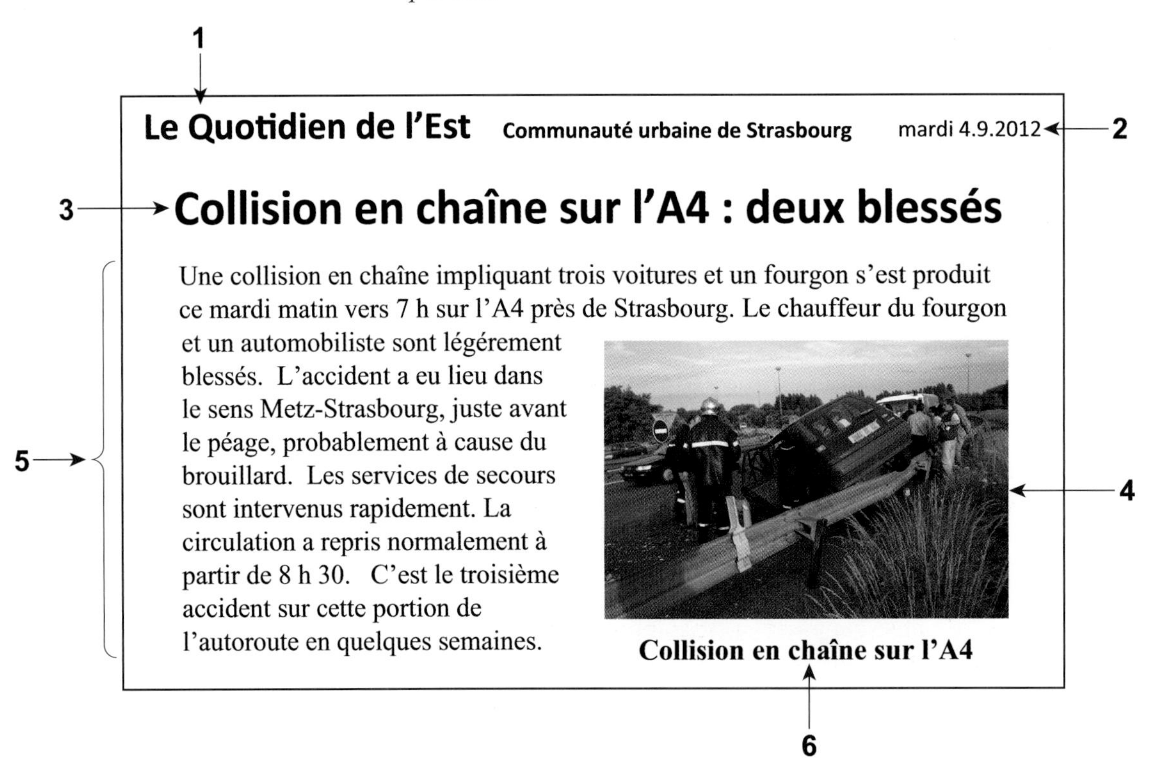

1

Le Quotidien de l'Est   Communauté urbaine de Strasbourg   mardi 4.9.2012 ← 2

3 → **Collision en chaîne sur l'A4 : deux blessés**

5 → Une collision en chaîne impliquant trois voitures et un fourgon s'est produit ce mardi matin vers 7 h sur l'A4 près de Strasbourg. Le chauffeur du fourgon et un automobiliste sont légérement blessés. L'accident a eu lieu dans le sens Metz-Strasbourg, juste avant le péage, probablement à cause du brouillard. Les services de secours sont intervenus rapidement. La circulation a repris normalement à partir de 8 h 30. C'est le troisième accident sur cette portion de l'autoroute en quelques semaines.

← 4

Collision en chaîne sur l'A4

6

impliquant *involving*

un fourgon *a van*

dans le sens Metz-Strasbourg *in the direction from Metz to Strasbourg / on the Metz to Strasbourg road*

le péage *the toll*

le corps de l'article • la date • le journal • la légende • la photo • le titre

B

Now read the article, trying not to use a dictionary, and answer the questions. Reuse words from the text to answer.

Maintenant lisez l'article (essayez de ne pas utiliser de dictionnaire) et répondez aux questions. Recopiez des mots du texte pour répondre.

1 Il s'est passé quoi ?
2 Quand ?
3 Où ?
4 Quelles sont les conséquences de l'événement ?

C

What is the main tense used in the article to list the events?

Quel est le temps utilisé dans l'article pour parler des événements ?

D

In what sequence are the following items presented in the article?

Dans quel ordre apparaissent ces éléments dans l'article ?

1 le lieu
2 la conséquence / le commentaire
3 la date
4 l'événement / l'information

Activité 11.3.6

The headline and the paragraphs of the next article have been jumbled up. Reorder them based on the sequence suggested in step D of the previous activity.

Le titre et les paragraphes de l'article sont mélangés. Remettez-les dans l'ordre en suivant la séquence proposée dans l'étape D de l'activité précédente.

1 Karen s'est classée 3e du slalom géant la semaine dernière à l'Alpe d'Huez. Mathieu s'est imposé dans le slalom du championnat de France qui avait lieu à Auron le week-end dernier.

s'est classée *came, was ranked*

2 Grâce à ces victoires les deux jeunes se sont qualifiés pour le championnat européen. La région de Nice est fière de ses deux nouveaux champions !

se sont qualifiés *qualified*

3 Deux skieurs de l'Inter Club de Nice, Mathieu Bailet (cadet) et Karen Smajda-Clément (benjamine) ont remporté le titre de champion de France de ski.

4 Deux Niçois champions de France de ski.

Text structures and conventions

As you know from reading in your own language, each type of text has a conventional structure. You have seen in the previous activity, for example, what the typical structure of a newspaper article might be. When you practise your writing or speaking skills, or when you prepare an assignment, take into account the fact that different types of texts have different formats: a newspaper article needs a headline, a letter needs a formulaic opening ('Dear ...') and ending ('Yours ...'), a phone call in French starts with '*Âllo ?*', etc. Make sure that you use the correct conventions for the type of text you are required to produce.

If you are asked to write more than a few sentences, it is a good idea to start your text or presentation with a short introduction, and to finish with a few concluding words.

Finally, if you are given a list of items to include, which happens frequently in this module, always double-check that you have included them all before submitting your work.

Activité 11.3.7

A

In this activity you are going to practise writing an account of an incident for a short news item in a local paper. This cartoon strip depicts what happened one evening in the village of Plessala in Britanny. Look at it carefully and then note down a few words to answer the four simple questions below.

Regardez la bande dessinée et notez quelques mots pour répondre aux quatre questions ci-dessous.

1 Quand ?
2 Où ?
3 Qui ?
4 Quoi ?

B

Now work on describing the scene. As this is part of the background of the story, you will need to use the imperfect tense. Complete the sentences based on the information given in the cartoon.

Complétez les phrases à partir des informations données dans la bande dessinée.

Weather: Il faisait __________ / il y avait __________ .

Day/date: On était __________ .

Time: Il était __________ .

Place: Ça se passait __________ .

C

Next, you are going to practise describing people. This is also part of the background so it will be done in the imperfect tense. Write three sentences to describe what the characters were wearing. You can either write one sentence for each character or three sentences about one of them.

Écrivez une petite description de ce que portaient les personnages. Faites trois phrases.

D

Next you need to list the actions that occurred during the event. Saying what happened is the main point of the news item, rather than part of the background, so you will need to use the *passé composé* when you relate what people did. Using the verbs in the box in the right sequence, write sentences to list what the two robbers and the petrol station employee did.

Avec les verbes de l'encadré, mis dans le bon ordre, faites des phrases pour dire ce que les deux voleurs et l'employée de la station service ont fait.

appeler au secours • arriver à la station service • attendre la police • entrer dans la boutique en criant • demander tout l'argent de la caisse • descendre de la voiture • faire démarrer la voiture • mettre les billets dans un sac en plastique • partir en trombe • sortir en courant

E

It's time to put the article together. Write it up using all the sentences you have written so far. Add a few connective words from the box provided to link events logically. Write a headline for your article as well.

Maintenant écrivez tout l'article. Utilisez toutes les phrases que vous avez écrites avant. Ajoutez quelques connecteurs de l'encadré pour que les événements s'enchaînent logiquement. Écrivez aussi un titre pour l'article.

mais • puis • alors • ensuite • après • et • donc

Section 11.4 Reading and writing stories about past events

In this section you will continue to look at texts written in the past tenses, starting by reading a short excerpt from a novel in French. You will also practise your writing skills further by writing a story.

Activité 11.4.1

This activity involves reading the beginning of a novel in French and exploring how it was written and why.

A

This first step will help you to understand some of the words you probably don't know. Read through the text once, without using a dictionary, to find the French words/expressions for the phrases in the list below. The words are in the correct order of appearance in the text.

Lisez le texte une fois, sans dictionnaire, et trouvez la traduction de ces mots en français dans le texte.

> Il devait être plus de deux heures du matin quand on a sonné à la porte, cette nuit-là. Deux coups de sonnette très longs, comme s'il y avait urgence. Tout de suite, j'ai pensé à maman qui vivait à l'autre bout de la ville.
>
> Cette nuit-là, je dormais chez mon père. C'était sa semaine. Une organisation qui durait depuis quatre ans, depuis leur séparation, et qui me convenait bien.
>
> Le dring de la sonnette en plein sommeil avait quelque chose de sinistre. Il ressemblait au cri d'un rapace. Comme si les deux coups stridents n'annonçaient pas simplement une visite, mais aussi des mauvaises nouvelles.
>
> Dans la chambre à côté, j'ai entendu mon père grogner et se lever. Lui non plus n'aime pas trop être réveillé en pleine nuit. Je me suis assis dans mon lit. La pensée qu'il était peut-être arrivé quelque chose à maman me hantait. J'étais comme pétrifié. Dehors, la pluie frappait le toit avec régularité.

Papa est passé devant ma chambre en pyjama, les cheveux en pétard, et s'est rendu compte que j'étais réveillé.

– Je vais voir ce que c'est ! il a dit d'une voix endormie.

J'ai écouté mon père descendre les escaliers de notre maison et je l'ai imaginé jeter un œil à travers la petite vitre découpée dans la porte. Il a ouvert au visiteur nocturne. J'ai entendu le grincement caractéristique de la porte.

(Extract from Robberecht, T. (2007) Le portrait de Léonora, Paris, Syros)

1 immediately
2 at the other end
3 which suited me
4 in mid-sleep
5 the cry of a bird of prey
6 to grunt
7 in the middle of the night
8 with untidy hair
9 (he) realised
10 in a sleepy voice
11 to have a look
12 glass pane
13 creaking

B

Now read the text again to get a first impression of the content. What type of story do you think it is?

Relisez le texte une fois pour vous faire une première impression. À votre avis, il s'agit de quel type d'histoire ?

1 a romance
2 a mystery story
3 an action novel
4 a historical novel

C

Which of these phrases taken from the text could be used as a title for the extract?

Quelle expression pourrait être un titre pour cet extrait ?

1 la séparation
2 le cri
3 la chambre à côté
4 le visiteur nocturne

D

Read the text a third time, concentrating on the main events and the characters, and answer the questions in English.

Relisez le texte en vous concentrant sur les événements principaux et sur les personnages, et répondez aux questions.

1 **Who?**
   (a) Who is telling the story? How much can you find out about him or her in the text?
   (b) Who else is present?
   (c) Who else is mentioned?
2 **When?**
   When does the scene take place?
3 **Where?**
   (a) Where does the scene take place?
   (b) Where does the mother live?
4 **What?**
   (a) What event is mentioned at the very start of the story?
   (b) What happens at the very end of the extract?
5 **Why?**
   (a) Why does the mother live somewhere else?
   (b) Why is the main character worried?

Activité 11.4.2

A

In this activity you look at how the author of the text has used particular words and devices to make the story more interesting. First you look at the elements of the text which create an atmosphere of mystery: the time and the weather. Answer the two questions in French.

Répondez aux deux questions.

1 L'incident est arrivé à quel moment, à quelle heure ?

2 Il faisait quel temps ?

B

Part of a mystery story is to create a feeling of fear. From the list of words below, pick the four that were chosen by the author to express or elicit a feeling of fear. Look up the words in a dictionary if necessary.

Cherchez les quatre mots de la liste qui évoquent un sentiment de peur. Cherchez les mots dans le dictionnaire si nécessaire.

organisation • séparation • sinistre • rapace • coups • visite • pensée • hantait • pétrifié

C

Another device used by the author is the use of several words that refer to noises and the sense of hearing. This adds another dimension to the story, and increases the feeling of fear and mystery because we rely on the character's interpretation of the sounds. Can you find at least three words in the text that refer to sounds or hearing?

Cherchez dans le texte au moins trois mots qui font référence à des sons, à ce qu'on entend.

D

The story is enhanced by the nature of the description because it goes beyond mere facts, relying on the main character's feelings and letting us into his thoughts and imagination. List or underline the three phrases from the text which relate to thinking or imagining.

Notez les trois expressions du texte qui font référence aux pensées ou à l'imagination.

E

Look at the expressions highlighted in bold in the phrases below. What are they all used for? Choose the correct option (1–3).

Regardez les expressions en gras. Elles sont utilisées pourquoi ? Choisissez la bonne réponse.

comme s'il y avait urgence

avait **quelque chose de** sinistre

il **ressemblait** au cri du rapace

comme si les deux coups…

1 pour faire des comparaisons
2 pour donner des faits objectifs
3 pour exprimer des oppositions

Activité 11.4.3

In this activity you will consider further how the text of the story is constructed.

A

You are now going to look at the different elements which build the story and the tenses used for each. The text of the extract is reprinted below. Read it again and relate the three elements shown after the text to the three coloured highlights used in the text.

Cochez la bonne couleur pour chaque catégorie.

Il devait être plus de deux heures du matin quand on a sonné à la porte, cette nuit-là. Deux coups de sonnette très longs, comme s'il y avait urgence. Tout de suite, j'ai pensé à maman qui vivait à l'autre bout de la ville.
Cette nuit-là, je dormais chez mon père. C'était sa semaine. Une organisation qui durait depuis quatre ans, depuis leur séparation, et qui me convenait bien.
Le dring de la sonnette en plein sommeil avait quelque chose de sinistre. Il ressemblait au cri d'un rapace. Comme si les deux coups stridents n'annonçaient pas simplement une visite, mais aussi des mauvaises nouvelles.
Dans la chambre à côté, j'ai entendu mon père grogner et se lever. Lui non plus n'aime pas trop être réveillé en pleine nuit. Je me suis assis dans mon lit. La pensée qu'il était peut-être arrivé quelque chose à maman me hantait. J'étais comme pétrifié. Dehors, la pluie frappait le toit avec régularité.
Papa est passé devant ma chambre en pyjama, les cheveux en pétard, et s'est rendu compte que j'étais réveillé.
— Je vais voir ce que c'est ! il a dit d'une voix endormie.
J'ai écouté mon père descendre les escaliers de notre maison et je l'ai imaginé jeter un œil à travers la petite vitre découpée dans la porte. Il a ouvert au visiteur nocturne. J'ai entendu le grincement caractéristique de la porte.

	Pink	Green	Yellow
1 the setting	❑	❑	❑
2 the character's feelings and thoughts	❑	❑	❑
3 the actions and events that make up the plot	❑	❑	❑

B

What tense is used in the sentences that make up each element of the story?

Quel temps est utilisé dans les phrases qui forment chaque élément de l'histoire ?

1 the setting
2 the character's feelings and thoughts
3 the actions and events that make up the plot

Activité 11.4.4

Now reorder the sentences below to create a simplified version of the story you read in the previous activities. Keep the elements in the same sequence as they appear in the original.

Remettez les phrases dans l'ordre pour obtenir une version simplifiée du texte que vous avez lu.

1 Il était plus de deux heures du matin.
2 Il pleuvait fort dehors.
3 J'ai entendu mon père se lever.
4 J'ai pensé que c'était ma mère qui habitait à l'autre bout de la ville.
5 J'avais peur, je pensais qu'il était arrivé quelque chose à ma mère.
6 Je dormais chez mon père. C'était sa semaine. Mes parents étaient divorcés.
7 Le bruit de la sonnette était sinistre.

8 Mon père s'est levé, il est passé devant ma chambre, m'a parlé. Il a descendu les escaliers, il a ouvert la porte.

9 Tout d'un coup, j'ai entendu la sonnette.

Activité 11.4.5

In this activity you are going to write about how you met somebody important in your life. The story can be true or invented.

A

First think about the basic information about the story. Make some brief notes in French in the table below.

Prenez des notes dans le tableau.

Qui ?	
Quand ?	
Où ?	
Quoi ?	

B

Now prepare more detailed notes, in French, on the following points.

Préparez des notes en français sur les points suivants.

Who was the person you met? Think about the background information you will mention, e.g. what was their relationship to you? what was their occupation? where did they live or work?

Where did the encounter happen? Think about the setting where you met, the background scene. Why were you, and the other person, there? What were you doing?

What happened? List the sequence of events that you will mention in the story.

And now? Do you still see each other? What is your present relationship?

C

Now write your story. Include all the points in step B. Think carefully about which past tense to use for each element in your story about the past. Use the language you have learned in the course of the module. (Obviously you are not expected to write a literary text as complex as the one you read at the beginning of this section!) Write about 250 words.

Maintenant rédigez votre histoire. Écrivez environ 250 mots.

Bibliothèque publique, centre Georges Pompidou

D

Finally, compare the text that you produced with the example given in the *corrigé* for step C. Answer the questions below.

Enfin comparez votre texte au corrigé de l'étape C. Répondez aux questions.

1 Have you included elements for each of the four questions indicated (*qui, quand, où, quoi*)?

2 The sentences below are all the sentences from the *corrigé* in the *passé composé*: they relate the actions and events that make up the story. Even looking at them on their own, you can understand the skeleton of the story.

   J'ai rencontré Antoine en juillet 2010.

   Un jour je suis allée à la bibliothèque pour me distraire.

   J'ai demandé de l'aide au bibliothécaire.

   J'ai reconnu Antoine.

   Nous avons discuté et j'ai choisi un livre grâce à ses conseils.

   Plus tard, je suis allée au cinéma avec mon beau-père et j'ai revu Antoine.

   Immédiatement on a commencé à discuter.

   Après le film on a décidé de rester en contact. Finalement on a passé beaucoup de temps ensemble pendant l'été.

   On est resté les meilleurs amis du monde.

   Now list the sentences in the *passé composé* from your own text and check that this gives you the outline of your story. If not, you may need to change the tense of some verbs.

3 Check that you have also included sentences in the imperfect tense to describe the setting of your story and give background information. Below are some examples from the *corrigé*.

C'était pendant des vacances chez ma mère vers Strasbourg.

Antoine travaillait à la bibliothèque municipale, il faisait un stage.

Moi j'étais étudiante à Paris, je préparais ma licence de physique à l'université.

En juillet 2010, c'était les vacances, je passais l'été chez ma mère et mon beau-père.

Je ne voyais plus mes amis de l'université, je m'ennuyais.

C'était le fils d'un voisin chez ma mère.

Il avait vingt ans, comme moi.

Il était petit, il avait les cheveux bruns courts, il portait un jean et un tee-shirt blanc.

4 The brief also asked you to write about now. Did you use the present tense as in this example from the *corrigé*?

Aujourd'hui je suis mariée, j'ai des enfants, et j'habite à Lille. Lui il travaille à Toulouse, à la bibliothèque universitaire. On ne se voit pas souvent, mais on garde le contact en ligne et on se retrouve au moins quelques jours tous les étés.

Corrigés

Unité 9

Activité 9.1.1

A

You may already know:

- une boulangerie (*baker's*)
- un supermarché (*supermarket*)
- une pharmacie (*chemist's*)
- une boucherie (*butcher's*)
- un fleuriste (*florist's*)
- un bureau de tabac (*tobacconist's/newsagent's*).

Le bureau de tabac can be recognised by its red sign, known as *la carotte*. It sells tobacco products, newspapers and magazines, some stationery items, stamps, phone cards and official documents (such as licences) and acts as an official agent for lottery tickets. The person who runs a *bureau de tabac* is called a *buraliste* (newsagent/tobacconist).

B

1 (e); 2 (h); 3 (a); 4 (g); 5 (f); 6 (b); 7 (c); 8 (d)

Une charcuterie-traiteur sells ready-made dishes to take away or to deliver, as well as charcuterie, cold meats and delicatessen items.

A 'grocer's' in French can be *un marchand de légumes*, *un primeur* or *une épicerie*.

C

1 (b); 2 (e); 3 (f); 4 (a); 5 (c); 6 (d)

Un traiteur chinois is a Chinese take-away.

Une épicerie fine is a shop that sells delicatessen items and locally or regionally sourced products *(les produits régionaux et gastronomiques).*

Activité 9.1.2

A

Au bureau de tabac, on achète...	**Dans une épicerie, il y a...**	**À la pharmacie, on vend...**	**À la boucherie, on peut acheter...**
des magazines des journaux des timbres des cigarettes	des produits surgelés des fruits et légumes des produits laitiers du vin des conserves de la charcuterie	des produits de beauté et d'hygiène des médicaments	des plats cuisinés de la viande de la charcuterie des conserves

B

The items in the list not normally sold in a supermarket in France are: *des médicaments* (medicines), *des cigarettes* (cigarettes) and *des timbres* (stamps).

Activité 9.1.3

A

1 True.

2 True.

3 False. (« *D'habitude, les boulangeries restent ouvertes jusqu'à 12 h 30–13 h* »)

4 False. (« *La plupart des centre-commerciaux, des grands magasins et des grandes surfaces font de plus en plus souvent la "journée continue "* »)

5 False. (« *seules les pharmacies (de garde* ») *assurent une permanence dans les villes* »

6 True.

B

1 en général
2 habituellement/d'habitude
3 toutefois
4 en particulier
5 traditionnellement
6 normalement

C

Describe a habit	Introduce a contrast	From generality to detail
habituellement/ d'habitude	toutefois	en général
traditionnellement		en particulier
normalement		

D

1 beaucoup de magasins
2 certains magasins
3 la plupart des magasins
4 quelques magasins
5 plusieurs magasins
6 aucun magasin

E

aucun magasin

quelques/certains magasins

plusieurs magasins

la plupart des magasins/beaucoup de magasins

Activité 9.1.4

A

Here is the completed text.

> En France, les magasins **sont ouverts / ouvrent** du lundi au samedi et sont fermés le **dimanche**. **En général, ils ferment / sont fermés** entre midi et deux heures. **Toutefois**, les habitudes changent et de plus en plus de petits magasins **ne ferment pas** pendant deux heures et les grandes surfaces font **la journée continue**. Habituellement, les boulangeries **ne ferment pas** à midi pile. Plusieurs supermarchés restent ouverts **jusqu'à** 20 heures. Quelques magasins **ouvrent / sont ouverts** le dimanche **matin** et **ferment / sont fermés** le lundi matin. Les pharmacies de garde **sont ouvertes / ouvrent** la nuit, mais aucun supermarché n'est ouvert **24h/24**.

B

Notes on shopping hours are provided in the instructions (*Exemple* of step B).

C

Here is a model answer based on the notes given in the instructions of step B.

> En Suisse, la plupart des magasins sont ouverts comme en France. Habituellement, les supermarchés ferment pendant deux heures à la pause de midi mais quelques supérettes et supermarchés restent ouverts dans les grandes villes comme Genève ou Zurich. En général, les supérettes et les supermarchés ferment à 18 h le samedi et n'ouvrent pas le dimanche. Les laiteries (les magasins où on achète le lait en Suisse) sont normalement ouvertes pendant deux heures le soir, de 17 h à 19 h. Tous les magasins sont fermés le dimanche.

Activité 9.1.5

A

1 (a); 2 (c); 3 (b); 4 (b) and (c)

B

1 Because it's better.
2 Because it's healthier.
3 Because they are a lot fresher than in shops.
4 Because there is a larger choice.
5 Because it's closer.
6 Because the meat is less expensive and as good.

C

more: *plus*

less: *moins*

as: *aussi*

D

1	plus cher	5	plus près
2	plus sain	6	moins cher / moins coûteux
3	plus frais	7	plus pratique
4	plus varié	8	aussi bon

E

The translation is:« *J'achète toujours ma baguette à la boulangerie, elle est meilleure* ».

The adjective *meilleur* is used here is the feminine form, because *baguette* is feminine.

Activité 9.1.6

1 La baguette de la boulangerie est **moins** chère **que** la baguette du magasin bio, mais elle est **plus** chère **qu**'au supermarché.

2 Les plats cuisinés du traiteur chinois sont **plus** gras **que** les plats du supermarché.

3 Les vins étrangers sont **aussi** bons **que** les vins français.

4 Le shampooing est **moins** coûteux à la parapharmacie **qu'**à la pharmacie.

Activité 9.1.7

A

1 (b); 2 (d); 3 (c); 4 (a)

B

Here are some possible answers.

Le Côte de Beaune est **aussi bon** que le Pouilly Fumé et il est **moins coûteux**, mais il est **plus léger**.

Le Côte de Beaune est **aussi bon** que le Sauterne et il est **beaucoup moins cher** mais il est **beaucoup plus sec**.

Le Rosé de Provence est **moins cher** que le Pouilly Fumé et il est **moins bon**, mais il est **plus doux**.

Le Pouilly Fumé est **meilleur** que le Rosé de Provence et il est **plus vieux**, mais il est **plus sec**.

Le Château Chinon est **moins bon** que le Pouilly Fumé mais il est **aussi cher** et **aussi corsé**.

Le Rosé de Provence est **bien moins cher** que le Sauterne, il est **plus jeune**, il est **moins bon** et **moins doux**.

Activité 9.1.8

A

1 (c); 2 (d); 3 (a); 4 (b)

B

	Quels produits?	**Où?**
Le premier monsieur	presque tous mes produits alimentaires	au supermarché
La demoiselle	presque tout	à la supérette (du coin)
Le deuxième monsieur	les produits du terroir notre viande des produits saisonniers notre pain fait maison	dans les petits commerces chez le boucher à l'épicerie à la boulangerie
La dame	mes produits alimentaires mes produits d'entretien mes fruits et légumes	au supermarché au supermarché au marché

C

1 He shops at the supermarket because it's more convenient and there is free parking.

2 Once a week.

3 She is a student. She doesn't have a car.

4 She can find almost everything and it's closer than the supermarket.

5 Local produce, good quality meat cuts, seasonal produce and homemade bread.

6 Because they are fresher.

D

1 le supermarché ; le magasin
2 un magasin
3 les petits commerces
4 le boucher
5 l'épicerie
6 la boulangerie
7 au marché

Activité 9.1.9

Listen to Track 9:3 again to check your answers. Pay particular attention to the use of comparatives (*plus/moins*) and the pronoun *où*.

Activité 9.2.1

1 (i); 2 (g); 3 (l); 4 (e); 5 (k); 6 (b); 7 (a); 8 (f); 9 (c); 10 (d); 11 (j); 12 (h)

Activité 9.2.2

A

Dialogue 1 Image (b)

Dialogue 2 Image (c)

Dialogue 3 Image (a)

Dialogue 4 Image (d)

B

1 A plug adaptor and a kettle.
2 He needs an adaptor for his mobile phone charger.
3 A tracksuit bottom and a pair of sports shoes.
4 14 years.
5 Fluorescent yellow.
6 39.
7 A red dress.
8 40.
9 Black and green.
10 A dress with straps.
11 A sofa.
12 A sofa-bed, with checks, and a sofa which is nicer but more bulky.
13 A shop assistant is coming to ask if they need some help.

C

1 The expressions used by sales assistants to approach customers are:
Je peux vous aider ?
Bonjour, je peux vous renseigner ?
On s'occupe de vous ?
2 The expressions used by customers to sales assistants are:
Oui, je cherche…
S'il vous plaît, est-ce que vous avez cette robe en rouge ?

D

1 ce
2 cet, cette
3 ces
4 cette
5 ces

Activité 9.2.3

1 cette
2 ces
3 cet
4 ces
5 ce

Activité 9.2.4

1 laquelle
2 lequel
3 laquelle
4 lequel

Activité 9.2.5

1 celui-ci
2 celui-ci
3 celles-là; celles-ci

4 celle-ci
5 celui-ci; celui-là

Activité 9.2.6

1 Ce canapé est en cuir. **Celui-ci** est en tissu, **celui-là** est en laine. Vous préférez **lequel** ?
2 Vous avez choisi vos chaussures ? **Lesquelles** vous voulez essayer ? **Celles-ci** ou **celles-là** ?
3 Ces deux bouilloires sont très pratiques. **Celle-ci** est de voyage, et **celle-là** est sans fil. **Laquelle** vous voulez acheter ?
4 Voici les costumes de la dernière collection. **Ceux-ci** sont classiques et **ceux-là** sont plus modernes. **Lesquels** vous préférez ?

Activité 9.2.7

A

The items mentioned in the dialogue are:

un agenda
des enveloppes
une carte de vœux
un stylo plume.

B

Here are the vocabulary items from the drawing, with English translations.

un agenda = *a diary*

des enveloppes à fenêtre = *window envelopes*

une carte de vœux = *a greetings card*

un stylo plume = *a fountain pen*

du papier cadeau = *wrapping paper*

des ciseaux = *a pair of scissors, some scissors*
(une paire de ciseaux = *a pair of scissors)*

une gomme = *rubber, eraser*

une boîte de peinture = *paint tubes, a painting set*

un roller = *a rollerball (pen)*

un stylo bille = *a ballpoint pen, a biro®*

un crayon de couleur = *a crayon*

un crayon à papier = *pencil*

un classeur = *folder, ring binder*

du papier à lettre = *writing paper*

un cahier = *exercise book*

C

1 False. It takes place in a stationery shop.
2 True.
3 False. He is buying a fountain pen.
4 True.
5 False. It's a gift for the start of a new school year.
6 False. It's 48 euros 90.

D

Here is a possible answer:

> Le client se trouve dans une papeterie. Il achète un agenda, des enveloppes, une carte de vœux et un stylo plume. Il choisit un stylo plume pour son neveu. C'est un cadeau, c'est pour la rentrée des classes. Il doit 48 euros 90.

Activité 9.2.8

Listen to Track 9:6 again to check your answers. Pay particular attention to the use of *ce/cette*, etc., *lequel/laquelle*, etc. and *celui-ci*, *celle-ci*, etc.

Activité 9.2.9

A

1 pour rigoler
2 suer
3 Elle est à la bonne taille?
4 le SMIC (le salaire minimum interprofessionnel de croissance)
5 les soldes

B

1 Cher is a boutique for luxury goods.
2 They are browsing, trying to guess the price of some items and expressing astonishment.

3 They can't believe what they see and wonder who buys these goods.
4 She wants to try a dress on.
5 She is trying to discourage her.
6 She is very friendly and helpful. She is smiling, perhaps because she thinks she might be on the point of selling the dress.
7 She wants to know if the dress is going to be in the sales.
8 There aren't any sales in that shop.

C

1 The expressions used by Joséphine and Chloé to express their astonishment are:
« Oh, mon Dieu ! / Mais il est en quoi le prix ? En roubles ? / Mais qui achète ça ? / Je rêve ! / Tu crois qu'elles sont en or ? »
2 The expressions used by the sales assistant to be helpful are:
« Je peux vous renseigner, Madame ? / Tout se passe bien, Madame ? / Elle est à la bonne taille ? »
3 The expressions used by Chloé to discourage Joséphine are:
« Non, malheureuse ! / Sors de là tout de suite ! / Cette robe coûte un SMIC ! »

Activité 9.2.10

A

Dialogue 1: Image (c)

Dialogue 2: Image (b)

Dialogue 3: Image (a)

Dialogue 4: Image (d)

B

1 1.400 euros
2 8,50 euros
3 125.000 euros
4 36 euros

C

Sentences (d), (e), (g), (j) and (k).

Activité 9.2.11

Listen to Track 9:8 as many times as necessary to reproduce the right intonation of each sentence.

Activité 9.2.12

Listen to Track 9:9 again to check your answers.

Activité 9.3.1

A

1	Help	*Aide*
2	My account	*Mon compte*
3	My basket	*Mon panier*
4	Search site	*Rechercher*
5	Gift vouchers	*Chèques-cadeaux*
6	Free delivery	*Livraison gratuite*
7	Best sellers	*Nos meilleures ventes*
8	Recently viewed items	*Vos derniers articles consultés*
9	Store finder	*Rechercher un magasin*
10	Subscribe	*Devenez adhérent/ s'inscrire*
11	Customer services	*Service clientèle*
12	Terms and conditions	*Conditions générales*

B

Here is an example of a customer's details:

Champs obligatoires means that you need to fill in the boxes marked with an asterisk.

You should have ticked the first box (to accept terms and conditions) but not the second box as you do not wish to receive mailings.

LCJS

Complétez votre inscription * Champs obligatoires

Pays de résidence * France — Choisissez votre pays de livraison

Civilité * ○ M. ◉ Mme ○ Mlle

Prénom * Gisèle

Nom * Tronche

Date de naissance * 18 Avril 1976

Profession * Cadre

Code postal * 34000

Ville de résidence * Montpellier

E-mail * g.tronche @googlemail.fr

Confirmez votre email * g.tronche @googlemail.fr

Mot de passe * ••••••••••••••

Confirmez votre mot de passe * ••••••••••••••

☑ J'accepte sans réserve les conditions générales de vente du site LCJS.fr

☐ Je souhaite recevoir par e-mail les offres et cadeaux

S'inscrire

C

1 Vrai.

2 Faux (« en stock » *shows for the two items*).

3 Vrai.

4 Vrai.

D

1 Step 1 – view my basket
Step 2 – enter customer reference number
Step 3 – check delivery
Step 4 – payment
Step 5 – confirm the order.

2 Two books: *La couleur des sentiments* and *Dans les forêts de Sibérie*.

3 Monday to Saturday 9.00 a.m. – 7.30 p.m.

4 Enter the e-voucher number in step 4 when paying.

5 39,62 euros.

6 *Validez et commandez.*

Activité 9.3.2

A

The answer is: 1.

B

1 commande

2 Nous vous remercions de votre confiance. Nous vous remercions de votre fidélité

3 récapitulatif de votre commande

4 vous identifier (s'identifier)

5 suivi de commande en ligne

6 droit de rétractation

7 annuler

8 vos coordonnées

9 adresse de facturation

10 imprimer

C

1 The customer has ordered a gift wrap and the billing address is different from the delivery address.

2 11 January.

3 You can consult your 'manage your account' page.

4 You can consult the 'help' on the website, send an email or phone.

5 Send an email before 8 January.

6 You are advised to print it for your records and not to reply to it.

D

1 Il vous suffit de vous identifier.
2 Consultez nos pages 'aide en ligne'.
3 Vous pouvez également contacter notre service clientèle.
4 Vous devez nous prévenir avant le 8 janvier.
5 Veuillez nous signaler tout changement éventuel le plus vite possible.
6 Nous vous conseillons d'imprimer cette page.
7 Merci de ne pas répondre à ce message.

Activité 9.3.3

A

1 merci de / veuillez
2 devez
3 pouvez
4 conseillons
5 il vous suffit de
6 consultez
7 veuillez / merci de

B

1 Il vous suffit de vous identifier.
2 Vous devez / Il faut remplir toutes les cases.
3 Merci de ne pas nous contacter par téléphone.
4 Vous devez / Il faut lire et accepter les conditions générales de vente.
5 Merci de / Veuillez nous informer de tout changement éventuel.
6 Nous vous conseillons de saisir votre numéro de bon de réduction.

Activité 9.3.4

Here is a sample answer:

> Pour passer une commande en ligne, il faut tout d'abord aller sur la page d'accueil et puis il faut vous identifier. Vous pouvez consulter les meilleures ventes et les offres exceptionnelles pour vous aider. Pour commander un article, vous devez tout d'abord choisir l'article et ajouter chaque article au panier, puis vous devez cliquer sur « validez la commande ». Ensuite vous devez saisir votre adresse de facturation et vous pouvez choisir une adresse de livraison différente si vous faites un cadeau. Pour le paiement, il vous suffit d'entrer vos coordonnées bancaires. Finalement, vous devez confirmer la commande. Nous vous conseillons d'imprimer le mail de confirmation pour conserver les références de votre commande. Merci de ne pas répondre au mail de confirmation. Veuillez consulter votre compte pour le suivi de votre commande en ligne.

Activité 9.4.1

1	coins	**des pièces (n.f)**
2	a note	**un billet**
3	a cheque	**un chèque**
4	a credit card	**une carte bancaire**, *sometimes referred to as* **une carte bleue**
5	a voucher	**un bon d'achat** (*or sometimes* **un chèque-cadeau**)
6	a loyalty card	**une carte de fidélité**
7	cash	**du liquide**
8	a coupon	**un bon de réduction**
9	a restaurant voucher	**un chèque-restaurant** (*sometimes* **un ticket-restaurant**)
10	a cash point	**un distributeur (de billets)**
11	change	**la monnaie**

Activité 9.4.2

A

1 (e); 2 (b); 3 (a); 4 (f); 5 (c); 6 (d)

B

	Cash	Cheque	Card
Dialogue 1	✓		
Dialogue 2			✓
Dialogue 3	✓		
Dialogue 4	✓		
Dialogue 5		✓	
Dialogue 6			✓

C

In Dialogue 2, the customer cannot pay by credit card because she is spending less than 15 euros.

Activité 9.4.3

	Asking the price	Indicating how to pay
Dialogue 1	Je vous dois combien ?	Voici un billet de 20 euros. Excusez-moi, je n'ai pas de monnaie.
Dialogue 2	Ça fait combien ?	Je peux régler par carte ?
	Asking the price	**Indicating how to pay**
Dialogue 4		Il faut insérer les pièces. L'appareil ne prend pas les billets.
Dialogue 5		Je peux vous faire un chèque ?
Dialogue 6		Je paie par carte.

Activité 9.4.4

1 (c); 2 (d); 3 (b); 4 (a)

Activité 9.4.5

Listen to Track 9:10 again to check your answers. Pay particular attention to the expressions used to ask for prices and methods of payment, as well as the intonation in the last sentence.

Activité 9.4.6

A

1 At a supermarket till.
2 178,45 euros.
3 A coupon.
4 She can't use it because it's out of date.
5 She wants to know if she has a loyalty card.
6 By credit card.
7 Her payment is refused because the code is invalid.
8 She has two other cards but she can't find them.

B

1 *l'* replaces *le bon de réduction*
2 *la* replaces *une carte de fidélité*
3 *les* replaces *deux autres cartes*

Activité 9.4.7

A

1 les
2 le
3 les
4 le
5 la
6 l'

B

1 Non, je ne **les** passe pas par catalogue. Je **les** passe sur internet.
2 Non, je ne **la** regarde pas tous les jours. Je **la** regarde tous les lundis.
3 Oui, je **les** aime beaucoup.
4 Non, je ne **le** porte pas souvent. Je **le** porte seulement pour les grandes occasions.
5 Non, je ne **le** prend pas à 8 heures. Je **le** prends à 7 heures.
6 Oui, je **l'**écoute toujours sur mon ordinateur.
7 Non, je ne **les** fais pas à la maison. Je **les** fais à la gym.
8 Oui, je **le** lis dans le métro tous les jours.
9 Non, je ne **les** achète pas au supermarché. Je **les** achète chez le fleuriste.
10 Non, je ne **l'**invite pas samedi prochain. Je **l'**invite dimanche prochain.

Activité 9.4.8

A

Listen to Track 9:12 again to check your answers. Pay particular attention to the use of pronouns.

B

Listen to Track 9:13 again for sample answers.

Activité 9.4.9

A

1 Frais de livraison
2 Le numéro de contrôle
3 Date d'expiration
4 au verso de votre carte bancaire
5 Veuillez saisir vos coordonnées bancaires
6 paiement sécurisé
7 moyen de paiement
8 en plusieurs fois

B

1 Les frais de livraison sont gratuits.
2 L'emballage cadeau coûte 2,70 euros.
3 On peut régler par carte, par téléphone, par paiement sécurisé ou en plusieurs fois.
4 Vous devez saisir vos coordonnées bancaires.
5 Le numéro de contrôle se trouve au verso de votre carte bancaire.
6 Oui, on peut cliquer sur « modifier ».

Activité 9.4.10

A

1 (c); 2 (a); 3 (e); 4 (f); 5 (g); 6 (b); 7 (d)

B

The answer is 2, to enquire about an order.

C

1 Vrai.
2 Faux (« je l'ai trouvé »).
3 Faux (« oui, vous l'avez confirmée, mais je n'ai toujours pas reçu mes billets »).
4 Vrai.
5 Vrai.
6 Faux (« nous n'avons pas vos coordonnées bancaires »).

D

1 Je **l'**ai trouvé. (**le numéro de commande**)
2 Vous **l'**avez confirmée. (**la commande**)
3 Je **les** ai données. (**les coordonnées bancaires**)

The past participles change according to the word they replace.

Activité 9.4.11

A

1 Je l'ai invitée pour dimanche prochain.
2 Nous les avons commandés sur internet.
3 Vous l'avez achetée en solde ?
4 Il les a obtenus gratuitement.
5 Elle l'a retrouvé à la poste.

B

1 Les vêtements (*because the past participle* commandés *refers to a masculine plural noun*).
2 Cette robe (*because the past participle* achetée *refers to a feminine singular noun*).
3 Les tickets de concert (*because the past participle* obtenus *refers to a masculine plural noun*).
4 Son chien (*because the past participle* retrouvé *refers to a masculine singular noun*).

C

1 bu
2 vue
3 prises
4 achetées
5 perdu
6 invités

Activité 9.4.12

A

1 l'
2 l'
3 l'
4 l'
5 l'
6 les
7 les
8 l'
9 les
10 l'
11 l'

B

Listen to Track 9:15 again to check your answers. Pay particular attention to the pronunciation of the past participles.

Activité 9.5.1

A

1 (c); 2 (a); 3 (b)

B

Email 1

1 China bowls and a coffee machine by mail order.

2 One of the bowls was broken and the coffee machine was damaged.

3 The customer is asking for a replacement of the goods.

Email 2

4 By internet.

5 A delivery within 15 days.

6 The goods have not been delivered to date.

7 Lodge a complaint and cancel the order.

Email 3

8 A pair of trousers and a jumper by phone.

9 The pair of trousers were the wrong style and the jumper was not the right size.

10 The customer returned the items and sent two emails to cancel the order.

11 He/she hasn't had any replies and the repayment hasn't yet come through.

12 Immediate refund of the amount paid by credit card.

C

The three sentences which express requests are:

1 Pourriez-vous remplacer ces articles dans les plus brefs délais, s'il vous plaît ?
Please could you replace these items as soon as possible?

2 Je voudrais faire une réclamation et annuler ma commande.
I would like to lodge a complaint and cancel my order.

3 Je vous demande de me rembourser immédiatement la somme versée par carte bancaire.
I request an immediate refund of the amount paid by credit card.

D

The three sentences which express dissatisfaction are:

1 Je suis très déçue .
I am very disappointed.

2 Je dois vous dire que je ne suis pas du tout satisfaite de votre service.
I must say that I am not at all satisfied with your service.

3 C'est vraiment inacceptable !
It's really unacceptable.

Activité 9.5.2

A

The customer is not at all happy. She has been waiting for a book which hasn't arrived. She wants to cancel her order and demands her money back.

B

1 End of May.

2 A DVD and a book.

3 She received the DVD but she is still waiting for the book.

4 It's out of stock.

5 She is asked to wait for another 2 to 3 days.

6 She wants to cancel the order.

7 No, it's the last time she'll order with them.

C

1 (a) Ça fait cinq minutes que je patiente.

2 (a) Ça fait trois semaines que j'attends mon livre.

3 (b) Ça fait dix ans que je suis cliente chez vous.

Activité 9.5.3

1 Ça fait trente ans qu'il est facteur.

2 Ça fait une dizaine de jours que j'attends le colis.

3 Ça fait un quart d'heure qu'on fait la queue à la caisse.

4 Ça fait dix minutes qu'il patiente et le poste est toujours occupé !
5 Ça fait une semaine que vous attendez votre remboursement ?

Activité 9.5.4

Listen to Track 9:17 again to check your answers. Make sure you have used the present tense in your answers.

Activité 9.5.5

Listen to Track 9:18 again to check your answers. Pay particular attention to vocabulary and expressions you have learned in this section.

Activité 9.5.6

A

1 Monsieur Lemoine is ringing *Billetterie-Réservations* about the delivery of tickets he ordered for a rugby match.
2 Because the match is on Saturday and he still hasn't received his tickets.
3 The manager says that the tickets have arrived. She will contact the colleagues in Brive and they'll send the tickets to Monsieur Lemoine immediately. Mr Lemoine should receive his tickets the day after tomorrow at the latest.

B

1 No, Mr Lemoine still hasn't received his tickets.
2 He sent an email and he rang twice.
3 The tickets were due to arrive this morning.
4 He spoke to the manager and asked her to solve his problem immediately but it is already too late and she can't do anything about it. So he wrote to the managing director, he sent a letter recorded delivery to request compensation.

C

1 Je lui téléphone tout de suite.
2 Je vais leur envoyer un courriel d'urgence.
3 Tu peux lui dire qu'il va les recevoir après-demain au plus tard.
4 Je leur ai envoyé un courriel.
5 Je leur ai téléphoné deux fois.
6 Je lui ai téléphoné.
7 Je lui ai demandé de résoudre mon problème immédiatement.
8 Je lui ai envoyé une lettre recommandée.

Activité 9.5.7

1 Oui, je lui écris de temps en temps.
2 Non, elle ne lui a pas téléphoné.
3 Oui, je lui ai parlé hier.
4 Oui, je leur envoie des courriels tous les jours.
5 Non, elle ne lui a pas montré son album.
6 Oui, je lui ai demandé mon remboursement par téléphone.
7 Oui, je leur ai répondu il y a deux jours.
8 Non, je ne lui ai pas dit bonjour.

Activité 9.5.8

1 (a) invite = *inviter* (no preposition)
(b) Likely pronouns = *le/la/les*
(c) Past tense (*a invité*)
(d) *Elle les a invités/invitées.*

2 (a) phone = *téléphoner à*
(b) Likely pronouns = *lui/leur*
(c) Present tense (*téléphonons*)
(d) *Nous lui téléphonons deux fois par jour.*

3 (a) speak to = *parler à*
(b) Likely pronouns = *lui/leur*
(c) Present tense (*parlent à*)
(d) *Henri et Sophie lui parlent tous les jours.*

4 (a) see = *voir* (no preposition)
(b) Likely pronouns = *le/la/les*
(c) Past tense (*ont vu*)
(d) *Ils l'ont vu la semaine dernière.*

5 (a) order = *commander* (no preposition)
(b) Likely pronouns = *le/la/les*
(c) Past tense (*ont commandé*)
(d) *Les livres, ils les ont commandés par téléphone.*

6 (a) buy = *acheter* (no preposition)
(b) Likely pronouns = *le/la/les*
(c) Past tense (*a acheté*)
(d) *Sa voiture, il l'a achetée il y a deux jours.*

7 (a) show = *montrer à*
(b) Likely pronouns = *lui/leur*
(c) Past tense (*a montré*)
(d) *Elle leur a montré sa robe dans le magasin.*

8 (a) say = *dire à*
(b) Likely pronouns = *lui/leur*
(c) Past tense negative (*n'a pas dit*)
(d) *Il ne lui a pas dit bonjour.*

9 (a) give = *donner à*
(b) Likely pronouns = *lui/leur*
(c) Past tense negative (*n'avons pas donné*)
(d) *Nous ne lui avons pas donné les fleurs.*

Activité 9.5.9

Here is a sample answer. Note the layout of the letter.

Monsieur/Madame Leblanc
78, rue des Pervenches
46100 Figeac

Société Lokia
Zone Industrielle du Pradeau
10-15 avenue du Puy
46000 Cahors

Figeac, le 5 mai 2012

Objet : Commande Référence 481000ZL

Monsieur,

J'ai passé une commande récemment par internet. J'ai commandé une bouilloire électrique et un téléphone sans fil. Je devais recevoir les articles dans un délai de 15 jours. Au bout de trois semaines, j'ai téléphoné aux services clientèle, je leur ai demandé de résoudre mon problème immédiatement, mais jusqu'ici je n'ai rien reçu. J'ai envoyé un courriel au responsable pour annuler ma commande. Je lui ai demandé un remboursement immédiat. Ça fait 10 jours que j'attends une réponse. C'est inadmissible. Je dois dire que je ne suis pas du tout satisfait/e de votre service. Je vous demande de répondre à cette lettre recommandée et j'exige le remboursement immédiat de la somme versée par carte bancaire.

Cordialement

Monsieur/Madame Leblanc

Activité 9.6.1

A

1 low prices = *prix bas*
2 deals = *bonnes affaires*
3 instant discount = *remise immédiate*

B

1 (c); 2 (e); 3 (b); 4 (a); 5 (d)

Activité 9.6.2

A

1 (b); 2 (a); 3 (b); 4 (a); 5 (c); 6 (b); 7 (c)

B

Here is a possible answer.

> J'ai acheté une tablette tactile récemment. C'est un modèle noir avec wifi et Bluetooth. Le magasin où je l'ai achetée ne fait pas de remise, mais si je trouve le même article meilleur marché dans un autre magasin, ils me remboursent la différence. Je bénéficie de plusieurs services gratuits compris dans le prix. Il y a la livraison gratuite, une garantie gratuite pendant un an, une assistance téléphonique si j'ai besoin d'aide, et la possibilité d'échange ou de remboursement de la tablette si je change d'avis dans les 10 jours. Le modèle que j'ai choisi n'était pas disponible alors le magasin l'a commandé et je vais le recevoir dans 48 heures. La livraison est gratuite.

Activité 9.6.3

A

1 On the phone.
2 A tablet from a shop.
3 He would like to swap it for a white one.
4 Tablet TT32 with wifi and Bluetooth.
5 You can return any item within ten days. Yes, he can do a swap. The tablet is in stock.
6 The shop assistant can order the replacement item and the customer can go and collect it from the shop.

B

1 il y a (*ago*)
2 dans (*in*)
3 dans (*in*)

Activité 9.6.4

A

1 il y a ; dans
2 il y a ; dans
3 il y a ; dans
4 il y a ; dans
5 il y a ; dans
6 il y a ; dans

B

Listen to Track 9:21 to check your answers. Pay particular attention to the verbs and their tenses used with *il y a* and *dans*.

Activité 9.6.5

A

1 Vrai.
2 Vrai.
3 Faux (« non, celui-ci, il a un zoom optique »).
4 Faux (« et ce noir, là, celui qui se trouve dans la vitrine »).
5 Vrai.
6 Vrai.
7 Vrai.
8 Vrai.
9 Vrai.
10 Faux (« si vous l'achetez sur internet, vous bénéficiez d'une réduction de 10% »).

B

1 (f); 2 (h); 3 (c); 4 (b); 5 (a); 6 (g); 7 (e); 8 (d)

Activité 9.6.6

A

1 celui que
2 celui qu'
3 celle qui
4 celles que
5 celles qui
6 ceux qui

B

Here are some sample answers.

Photo 1

Ce restaurant, c'est celui où je mange tous les jours.

Ce restaurant, c'est celui que je conseille à mes amis.

Ce restaurant, c'est celui qui offre une réduction aux étudiants.

Photo 2

Cette petite ville, c'est celle que j'ai visitée l'année dernière.

Cette petite ville, c'est celle où je suis né(e).

Cette petite ville, c'est celle qui accueille le festival des Beaux-Arts.

Photo 3

Ce village, c'est celui où j'aime venir me promener.

Ce village, c'est celui que je préfère.

Ce village, c'est celui qui a le musée Renoir.

Photo 4

Ces amis, ce sont ceux qui habitent en Dordogne.

Ces amis, ce sont ceux que j'ai rencontrés en Australie il y a trois ans.

Activité 9.6.7

Listen to Track 9:23 again to check your answers. Pay particular attention to the pronouns (*celui qui*, *lequel*, *celle-ci…*) and the tenses used with *il y a* and *dans*.

Activité 9.6.8

A

1 Haggling in Marrakech.
2 Comment bien négocier à Marrakech ?

The original thread was: *Technique pour négocier ses achats à Marrakech*.

B

1 Je ne sais pas.
2 Faux – « je voudrais savoir plusieurs choses. Je ne suis vraiment pas habitué ».
3 Vrai.
4 Vrai.
5 Faux – « je te conseille le centre artisanal près de la place Djama el Fna où les prix sont quasiment fixes ».
6 Vrai.
7 Faux – « c'est une coutume, voire une tradition ».
8 Vrai.

C

1 Tu divises le prix par 2 ou 3.
2 Tu offres un prix inférieur à celui que tu veux réellement obtenir.
3 Il ne faut pas refuser un petit verre de thé.
4 Il faut se fixer un prix maximum.
5 Il faut proposer un prix minimum au vendeur.
6 Je te conseille le centre artisanal.
7 Le principe de base c'est d'être courtois et avenant.
8 Il faut savoir le prix que tu veux dépenser.
9 Il ne faut jamais changer d'avis.
10 Reviens avec des images plein la tête.

D

1 Diviser le prix par (*to divide the price by*)
2 Les arnaques (*tricks*)
3 Baisser le prix (*to lower the price*)
4 Monter le prix (*to increase the price*)
5 Une règle élémentaire / un principe de base (*a basic rule*)
6 Dépasser un prix (*to go over a price*)
7 Marchander (*to bargain*)
8 Affiché (*posted up, declared*)
9 Être abordé (*to be approached*)
10 Avenant (*pleasant*)
11 Le marchandage (*bargaining*)
12 Faire une bonne affaire (*to strike/get a bargain*)

Tips to remember:

- You often only need to look for one word to make sense of a long expression.
- Looking for one word leads to finding the meaning of related words (e.g. verb *marchander* and noun *le marchandage*).
- Sometimes the related words have an English equivalent which will help you to remember (*diviser* = to divide; *la division* = division).
- Always note the gender of nouns (*une arnaque*).

E

1 For *le cadre*, depending on which dictionary you use, you might have found:

(a) frame

(b) surroundings

(c) framework

(d) manager.

The correct answer is (b).

2 For *les bricoles*, you might have found:

(a) a little something

(b) trifle

(c) breast harness (for a horse).

The correct answer is (a)

3 For *un souvenir*, you might have found:

(a) memory

(b) souvenir

(c) remembrance.

The correct answer is (a).

If you came up with the right answers, how did you do so?

F

1 It does not go down well. (look up the past participle *vu*)

2 I am not used to it. (look up the verb *habituer*)

3 Everybody gets something out of it. (look up the noun *compte*)

4 It's priceless. (look up the noun *prix*)

Activité 9.6.9

Here is a possible answer:

> Merci pour tous vos conseils. J'ai adoré Marrakech et même le marchandage ! J'ai acheté un tapis de qualité supérieure dans un souk et j'ai fait une bonne affaire ! J'ai négocié pendant deux heures mais on est arrivés à un consensus. Enfin, on y a trouvé notre compte le vendeur et moi. D'abord, le marchand a proposé 800 dirhams et enfin j'ai acheté le tapis pour mon prix maximum de 500 dirhams. Je suis revenu du Maroc il y a deux semaines et puis je suis allé en Espagne et j'ai vu le même tapis à 45 euros, c'est un prix inférieur !!! Mais, mon tapis, c'est celui que je préfère, et je suis revenu du Maroc avec plein de couleurs, d'images et d'odeurs dans ma tête, et cela n'a pas de prix. Je repars au Maroc dans trois mois !

Unité 10

Activité 10.1.1

A

1 (e); 2 (g); 3 (h); 4 (d); 5 (a); 6 (l); 7 (j); 8 (f); 9 (k); 10 (b); 11 (c); 12 (i)

B

There is no *corrigé* for this step, as your answers will be personal.

Activité 10.1.2

A

1

(a) Pixel wants to know what to do to stay healthy while studying.

(b) She is advised to lead a healthy life, e.g. doing exercise, eating healthily and getting lots of sleep.

2 You should have identified the following expressions.

Garder la forme	*To stay healthy/to keep fit*
Garder la pêche	*To stay healthy/to keep fit (familiar)*
Éviter le stress	*To avoid stress*
Je suis toujours en forme	*I am always in good shape*
Je me sens bien dans ma peau	*I feel good in myself*
Être en bonne santé	*To be in good health*
J'ai toujours la pêche	*I am always full of beans*
Être en bonne condition physique	*To be healthy*
Se maintenir en forme	*To keep fit*
Je pète la forme !	*I am on top form! (informal language)*

B

1

Prénom	Pour être en bonne santé, il faut...
Agnès	• bien dormir • manger sainement • profiter de la vie au maximum

Philippe	• faire du sport • manger équilibré • dormir beaucoup
Pascaline	• bien manger • marcher une heure par jour
Jean-Claude	• bien dormir • avoir un bon métier • penser positivement
Leïla	• garder le sourire • manger sainement
Sandrine	• éviter le stress • se détendre suffisamment
Ahmed	• dormir beaucoup • faire de l'exercice régulièrement
Céline	• boire deux verres de vin tous les jours • sortir avec ses amis

C

1 Il faut **bien** dormir.
2 Il faut manger **sainement**.
3 Il faut dormir **beaucoup**.
4 Il faut **bien** manger.
5 Il faut penser **positivement**.
6 Il faut se détendre **suffisamment**.
7 Il faut faire de l'exercice **régulièrement**.

Activité 10.1.3

A

1 longuement
2 anciennement
3 constamment
4 durement
5 généreusement
6 prudemment
7 faiblement
8 franchement

B

1 (b); 2 (f); 3(h); 4 (g); 5 (a); 6 (e); 7 (c); 8 (d)

Activité 10.1.4

A

Qui vit sainement ?	Qui ne vit pas sainement ?
Frédérique	Arlette
Thierry	Régis
Fatoum	Grégoire
	Joseph
	Farad

B

1 He goes to bed early: *je me couche assez tôt.*
2 It destresses you and allows you to clear your head: *c'est un sport complet qui permet d'évacuer tout le stress et de se vider la tête complètement.*
3 It's too tiring: *c'est trop fatigant.*
4 Housework is the only 'sport' Grégoire mentions: *Le seul sport que je pratique par obligation, c'est le ménage !*
5 He drinks a lot of alcohol: *Je bois un demi-litre de vin par jour, plus les apéritifs et les pousse-cafés.*
6 He has a lot of responsibilities in his job and too much work, so he doesn't have time: *j'ai beaucoup de responsabilités et j'ai toujours trop de travail. Je n'ai pas le temps de faire de sport.*

C

Here are some sample answers for what you could have written.

Régis ne mange pas **très bien**. Il mange trop de viande.

Thierry vit **sainement**.

Grégoire fume **beaucoup** et il ne fait pas **suffisamment** de sport.

Fatoum pratique une activité physique **très fréquemment**.

Joseph boit **beaucoup**.

Farad travaille **énormément/beaucoup** et il ne se détend pas **assez**.

Activité 10.1.5

A

1 Faux : « je ne fume plus ».
2 Faux : « je fume depuis dix, quinze ans ».
3 Vrai.
4 Faux : « quand j'étais adolescente, j'ai fumé ».
5 Faux : « je n'ai jamais fumé ».
6 Vrai.

B

1 Nathan stopped smoking because he's now got children. Vanessa gave up because it's quite harmful to your health. Marine stopped because she became pregnant with her first daughter.
2 10 to 15 years.
3 About ten.
4 He doesn't like it at all. He thinks it's bad for your health and he'd like to see smoking banned from restaurant terraces because he hates eating in a smoky environment.
5 Buying patches or consulting a tobacco addiction specialist.

C

1 ne ... jamais.
2 ne ... plus.
3 ne ... rien.

Activité 10.1.6

1 Je ne bois jamais.
2 Je n'ai jamais fumé dans ma chambre.
3 Il ne joue plus au tennis.
4 Ils ne se sont rien dit.
5 Elles ne se voient plus.
6 Je ne veux rien.
7 Il ne parle à personne.
8 Nous n'avons consulté personne.

Activité 10.1.7

Listen to Track 10:3 to check your answers. Pay particular attention to the negative sentences.

Activité 10.1.8

A

1 (b); 2 (d); 3 (a); 4 (c)

B

Astuces means 'tricks' or 'tips'. (But your answers might include 'suggestions' or 'recommendations', both of which give a good idea about what the text is about.)

In this context, synonyms for *astuces* include *conseils* or *suggestions.*

C

1 le surpoids
2 l'hypertension (f.)
3 le diabète
4 le cœur
5 le tabagisme
6 l'abus (m.) d'alcool
7 le colorant
8 les conservateurs
9 le grignotage (*Note that the verb* grignoter *is more frequently used than the noun.)*
10 avoir le moral

D

1 To stay in good health. (Excess weight and obesity are generally the cause of high blood pressure, diabetes and heart problems.)
2 Exercise is good for the heart, muscle development, relaxation, and for getting air into your lungs.
3 The advice given is to live healthily: to eat at regular hours, drink 1.5 litres of water a day, get enough sleep, and avoid smoking and excess drinking.
4 If you're happy, your body generates endorphins which make you feel good.
5 Unhealthy snacks, smoking and excess drinking.

Activité 10.1.9

Here is a possible answer.

> Pour rester en bonne santé, je mange sainement : trois repas par jour à heures régulières. J'essaie de consommer des produits frais, ni trop salés, ni trop

gras. Je ne grignote jamais entre les repas, mais je mange beaucoup de fruits dans la journée. Je surveille mon poids constamment pour éviter les maladies cardiovasculaires. Je ne bois pas beaucoup d'alcool et je ne fume plus. Malheureusement, je ne fais pas suffisamment d'activités physiques. Je pratique la marche pour m'oxygéner le week-end, mais je ne fais rien en semaine. J'ai un bon métier mais je travaille tard le soir. Rarement, je vais faire un soin dans un institut de beauté. Cela me permet de retrouver mon énergie et d'avoir la pêche !

Activité 10.2.1

A

1 (a); 2 (c); 3 (b)

B

You should have ticked: 1, 3, 5, 7, 8, 10, 12.

Note that *Bof, ça va, sans plus* is a colloquial expression and should be used mainly in informal contexts with friends, for example.

C

1 J'ai mal à la tête.
2 J'ai chaud et froid.
3 La grippe.
4 J'ai attrapé un mauvais rhume.
5 Il est toujours … fatigué.
6 Il a des vertiges.
7 Il a mal au ventre.
8 Il souffre de rhumatismes.
9 Il est toujours stressé.

Activité 10.2.2

A

Listen to Track 10:5 again to check your answers and pay particular attention to the expressions relating to health.

B

Listen to Track 10:6 again to check your answers and pay particular attention to the expressions relating to health.

Activité 10.2.3

A

Fatigué and *crevée.* (Note that *crevé(e)* is colloquial language and should not be used in formal situations.)

B

There are three meanings for the word *crevé*: (1) punctured/burst; (2) exhausted, worn out; (3) dead.

C

1 I got a puncture/flat tyre on the motorway.
2 She is working too much, she is exhausted.
3 There is a dead sheep in the field.

Activité 10.2.4

A

(a) The meaning of *forme* here corresponds with definition 1: shape.
(b) The meaning of *forme* here corresponds with definition 4 *(Ling)*: form.
(c) The meaning of *forme* here corresponds with definition 6 *(gén, Sport)*: form/fitness.

B

(a) This vase is in the shape of a bottle.
(b) It's not the same verb form.
(c) I started Zumba a month ago and since then I'm in great shape.

Activité 10.2.5

1 toi
2 moi
3 lui

Activité 10.2.6

A

1 Et **toi**, tu as mal au ventre ?
2 **Eux**, ils ont faim.
3 **Elles**, elles n'ont pas la grippe.
4 **Lui**, il est souvent malade.

5 **Toi**, tu souffres de diabète ?
6 Et **vous**, vous surveillez votre poids ?

B

1 **Moi**, je suis en pleine forme. Paul, je vais venir avec **toi** au tennis.
2 Mon père, **lui**, il est très fatigué, il reste toujours chez **lui**.
3 Ah, oui, j'ai commandé un coca, oui, c'est pour **moi**.
4 Attendez ! Ne partez pas sans **eux**, ils arrivent dans deux minutes.
5 Martine ne fait pas assez d'activité physique, va marcher avec **elle**.

Activité 10.2.7

A

Listen to Track 10:7 again and practise as often as necessary until you can pronounce the sound [w].

B

Listen to Track 10:8 again and practise as often as necessary until you can pronounce the sound [ɥ].

Activité 10.2.8

A

Listen to Track 10:9 again as many times as necessary.

B

Listen to Track 10:10 and practise as many times as necessary until you can pronounce the sounds [ɥ] and [w] to your satisfaction.

C

Listen to Track 10:11 again to check your answers. Pay particular attention to the pronunciation of the sounds [ɥ] and [w].

Activité 10.2.9

A

1 la tête
2 les yeux *(Note that the singular is* l'œil.*)*
3 le nez
4 le bras
5 le ventre
6 le poignet
7 le genou
8 le pied
9 la cheville
10 la jambe
11 la main
12 l'épaule (f.)
13 le cou
14 la bouche
15 l'oreille (f.)

B

1 (d); 2 (f); 3 (e); 4 (a); 5 (c); 6 (b)

Activité 10.2.10

A

1 (e) or (d); 2 (d) or (e); 3 (a); 4 (g); 5 (b); 6 (c); 7 (f)

B

Name	Accident	Injury	Treatment
Jacques	serious motorbike accident	broken arm, leg and pelvis	2 months in hospital, physiotherapy
Guillaume	playing rugby	broken nose and dislocated shoulder	physio
Margaux	slipped in the snow	broken ankle	wore plaster cast for 6 weeks
Annie	playing with matches	burnt left hand	3 weeks in hospital and skin graft
Raoul	accident at work	cut finger	surgery, 6 months off work

C

1 False. His leg hurts from time to time and he has a limp.

2 False. He no longer rides a motorbike (*ne ... plus*).
3 True.
4 True.
5 True.
6 False. She has kept the cast (*le plâtre*) with all her friends' signatures on it as a nice souvenir.
7 True.

D

The five expressions used to ask somebody if they have recovered fully are:

Et maintenant, ... vous êtes tout à fait rétabli ?

Et maintenant, ça va ?

Et... vous êtes complètement remise aujourd'hui ?

Et... aujourd'hui, tout va bien ?

Et... vous êtes complètement remis maintenant ?

Activité 10.2.11

Here are some possible answers.

1 Il s'est cassé la jambe. / Il s'est fait mal à la jambe. / Il a la jambe cassée.
2 Il s'est cassé le nez. / Il a le nez cassé.
3 Elle s'est brûlé la main. / Elle s'est fait mal à la main.
4 Il s'est fracturé/cassé le doigt. / Il s'est fait mal au doigt. / Il a le doigt cassé/fracturé.
5 Elle s'est cassé le genou. / Elle s'est fait mal au genou. / Elle a le genou cassé.

Activité 10.2.12

A

1 (c); 2 (a); 3 (b), (c), (f); 4 (a); 5 (b)

B

1 Je me suis coincé le doigt.
2 Je me suis cogné la tête.
3 Je me suis foulé la cheville.
4 Elle a une jambe cassée.

Activité 10.2.13

A

1 J'ai le nez tordu.
2 Je suis tombé(e) dans les escaliers il y a deux ans.
3 Je me suis fait mal au dos.
4 J'ai eu mal au dos pendant six mois.
5 J'ai beaucoup grossi.
6 Mon dos me fait toujours mal de temps en temps.
7 Je suis tombé(e) d'une échelle.
8 Je me suis fracturé le bassin.
9 J'ai eu un plâtre.
10 J'ai fait de la rééducation pendant six mois.

B

Listen to Track 10:13 to check your answers.

You will have heard *'j'ai eu un accident de travail'* ('I had a work-related accident') used in the dialogue, but *j'ai eu un accident au travail* ('I had an accident at work') is also correct.

C

Here is a sample answer.

J'ai eu un accident de travail. Je suis tombé(e) d'une échelle il y a deux mois. J'ai eu un bras cassé et je me suis déboîté une épaule. Je suis resté(e) à l'hôpital pendant deux semaines. Maintenant, je vais mieux mais j'ai mal à l'épaule de temps en temps. Je ne fais plus de sport et j'ai beaucoup grossi.

Activité 10.3.1

A

1 True.
2 False. You can see a specialist if you want to. (*Vous pouvez aussi bien choisir un médecin généraliste ou un spécialiste...*)
3 True.
4 False. (*Vous pouvez aussi bien choisir un médecin... sans contrainte géographique particulière.*)

B

1 vous prescrit des médicaments
2 vous ausculte
3 écoute votre cœur
4 une ordonnance
5 une analyse de sang (*Note that this refers both to the blood test and its results, though you will also hear* prise de sang *for blood test.)*
6 prend votre tension artérielle

C

1 Over-the-counter medicines.
2 Prescription medicines.
3 Any medicine that has not been prescribed by a doctor.
4 You need to go to casualty.
5 You should call the fire brigade. Note that in France it is firefighters (*les pompiers*) who are trained in emergency first aid.

D

1 un téléphone fixe
2 médicaments contre le rhume
3 des pilules contraceptives (*also called* la pilule)
4 un téléphone portable
5 sirops pour la toux

Activité 10.3.2

A

You should have underlined: *serez, choisirez, deviendra, irez, voir.*

B

The infinitives are:

serez : être
choisirez : choisir
deviendra : devenir
irez : aller
voir is already in the infinitive.

Activité 10.3.3

	être	**avoir**	**aller**	**faire**	**prendre**
je/j’	serai	aurai	irai	ferai	prendrai
tu	seras	auras	iras	feras	prendras
il/elle/on	sera	aura	ira	fera	prendra
nous	serons	aurons	irons	ferons	prendrons
vous	serez	aurez	irez	ferez	prendrez
ils/elles	seront	auront	iront	feront	prendront

	venir	**pouvoir**	**devoir**	**vouloir**	**voir**
je	viendrai	pourrai	devrai	voudrai	verrai
tu	viendras	pourras	devras	voudras	verras
il/elle/on	viendra	pourra	devra	voudra	verra
nous	viendrons	pourrons	devrons	voudrons	verrons
vous	viendrez	pourrez	devrez	voudrez	verrez
ils/elles	viendront	pourront	devront	voudront	verront

Activité 10.3.4

1 parlerai
2 prendront
3 remplirons
4 achèteras
5 appellerez
6 irai
7 te sentiras
8 devrez
9 seront
10 fera ; sera
11 viendront
12 aurons

Activité 10.3.5

A

1 accouchera
2 aura droit

3 sera

4 payera *or* paiera *(the latter is more frequently used)*

5 devra

B

1 J'accoucherai en France.

2 Je devrai demander une carte européenne d'assurance maladie.

3 Avec ma carte européenne d'assurance maladie j'aurai droit aux soins médicaux.

4 Je serai traitée comme si j'étais assurée en France.

5 Je paierai les frais d'accouchement et je devrai demander le remboursement.

C

Listen to Track 10:14 again to check your answers.

Activité 10.3.6

A

Here are some sample notes to compare with your own.

Comment s'appelle le système de santé dans votre pays ?

NHS

Comment ça marche ?

Gratuit : paiements → salaire

Est-ce que l'équivalent de la carte vitale existe dans votre pays ?

Non

Devez-vous payer les consultations chez le médecin traitant, ou chez les spécialistes comme les dentistes, les ophtalmologistes et les gynécologues, etc. ?

médecin traitant : non

spécialistes : non

dentistes : oui, normalement on paie

Est-ce que le système des mutuelles existe ?

Non

Faut-il payer les médicaments chez le pharmacien et les frais à l'hôpital ?

Médicaments : oui (mais certaines personnes ne paient pas). Prix fixe pour méds. sur ordonnance

Frais à l'hôpital : non

B

Here are some sample answers to compare with your own.

– **Comment s'appelle le système de santé dans votre pays ?**

– En Angleterre, le système de santé s'appelle le *National Health Service* (*NHS*).

– **Comment ça marche ?**

– C'est un système de santé public gratuit. Une partie de votre salaire est utilisée pour payer le système.

– **Est-ce que l'équivalent de la carte vitale existe dans votre pays ?**

– Non.

– **Devez-vous payer les consultations chez le médecin traitant, ou chez les spécialistes comme les dentistes, etc. ?**

– Non, toutes les consultations chez le médecin traitant sont gratuites, mais vous devez payer si vous allez au dentiste normalement. Beaucoup de dentistes sont privés.

– **Est-ce que le système des mutuelles existe ?**

– Non, mais vous pouvez avoir une assurance privée qui remboursera les soins médicaux privés.

– **Faut-il payer les médicaments chez le pharmacien et les frais à l'hôpital ?**

– Oui, vous devez normalement payer les médicaments prescrits par le docteur (mais certaines personnes ne doivent pas payer). Les médicaments sur ordonnance ont un prix fixe. À l'hôpital, les soins sont gratuits.

Activité 10.4.1

A

1 (h); 2 (d); 3 (f); 4 (b); 5 (e); 6 (g); 7 (c); 8 (a)

B

1 (c); 2 (a); 3 (b)

C

	Dialogue 1	Dialogue 2	Dialogue 3
J'ai une rougeur.			✓
J'ai chaud, j'ai froid.	✓		
J'ai mal au cœur.			✓
J'ai très mal à la gorge.		✓	
J'ai des vertiges.			✓
J'ai un peu mal à la tête.			✓
J'ai des douleurs.	✓		
Je ne mange pas beaucoup.		✓	
Je suis très fatigué(e).	✓		
J'ai un peu de fièvre.		✓	
Je suis épuisé(e).		✓	

D

1 (a) and (c); 2 (b); 3 (a); 4 (c); 5 (c); 6 (b)

E

Prenez du paracétamol : **prendre**

Buvez beaucoup : **boire**

reposez-vous : **se reposer**

Prenez-le : **prendre**

ne le **prenez** pas : **prendre**

revenez : **revenir**

Prenez deux comprimés : **prendre**

Prenez-les : **prendre**

arrêtez : **arrêter**

Ne vous **fatiguez** pas : **se fatiguer**

finissez : **finir**

Prends-les : **prendre**

ne les **prends** pas : **prendre**

Ne **mange** pas : **manger**

ne **bois** pas : **boire**

Ne t'**inquiète** pas : **s'inquiéter**

Repose-toi : **se reposer**

va voir le médecin : **aller**

Activité 10.4.2

Here are some suggestions.

1 Prends du paracétamol.
2 Mangez équilibré et faites de l'exercice !
3 Prends des anti-inflammatoires.
4 Buvez beaucoup et prenez du paracétamol.
5 Couche-toi, bois beaucoup et arrête de fumer !
6 Va chez le dentiste.
7 Reposez-vous un moment. Ne vous couchez pas trop tard.
8 Téléphonez au médecin !

Activité 10.4.3

1 Ne les prends pas à jeun.
2 Buvez-le lentement.
3 Ne les donne pas à ta fille.
4 Ne le prenez pas plus de trois fois par jour.
5 Ne les oublie pas à midi.
6 Prends-les avant d'aller au lit.
7 Ne les mange pas, tu es allergique.
8 Appelle-le le plus tôt possible.

Activité 10.4.4

Listen to Track 10:18 again to check your answers. Pay particular attention to the use and position of the imperative and pronouns.

Activité 10.4.5

A

1 (b); 2 (e); 3 (f); 4 (a); 5 (g); 6 (d); 7 (c)

B

The three people are asked what they have in their medicine cabinet: '*Qu'est-ce que vous avez dans votre armoire à pharmacie ?*'.

C

1 **Pierre** : Alors, moi, j'ai de l'aspirine, des **gélules** d'ibuprofen, j'ai du bicarbonate de soude et des **pastilles** pour le mal de gorge.
2 **Pierre** : Ça se vend en **comprimés effervescents**. Il faut diluer un ou deux **comprimés** dans un verre d'eau.
3 **Julien** : J'ai des **sachets** de paracétamol.

D

comprimés effervescents : *effervescent tablets*

pastilles : *pastilles/lozenges*

gélules : *capsules*

sachets : *sachets of powdered paracetamol/ aspirin, etc.*

comprimés : *tablets*

E

Pierre	Julien	Marie
aspirine, ibuprofen, bicarbonate de soude, pastilles pour le mal de gorge	paracétamol, somnifères, pommade à l'arnica	médicaments homéopathiques, crème au propolis, magnésium

Activité 10.4.6

En is used in sentences 1–4 to avoid repetition of the following words:

1 des médicaments homéopathiques
2 de la crème au propolis
3 du magnésium
4 de l'aspirine

Activité 10.4.7

1 Oui, j'en ai quatre.
2 Oui, elle en fait trois fois par semaine.
3 Oui, elle en mange tous les soirs.
4 Oui, il y en a deux boîtes.
5 Oui, j'en prends tous les mois.
6 Oui, il en parle tout le temps.

Activité 10.4.8

A

1 (c); 2 (a); 3 (b)

B

Dialogue 1

Amélie ne dort pas parce qu'**elle pense toujours au travail**.

Elle est **fatiguée**.

Elle a besoin de **décompresser**.

Dialogue 2

Thierry n'est pas **en forme**.

Il a souvent des **migraines**.

Dialogue 3

Thomas a toujours des **brûlures d'estomac**.

Il est souvent **en déplacement d'affaires**.

Il mange **régulièrement au restaurant**.

C

1 (b) or (d); 2 (h); 3 (e); 4 (a); 5 (g); 6 (d) or (b); 7 (c); 8 (f)

D

Rassurez-vous

Tu verras, ça ira mieux

Ne vous inquiétez pas

Ce n'est pas grave

Ça devrait passer

Activité 10.4.9

A

Here are some sample sentences.

1 Tu devrais/vous devriez faire du sport.
Tu devrais/vous devriez faire un régime.
Tu devrais/vous devriez manger plus équilibré.
2 Tu devrais/vous devriez prendre de la camomille.
Tu devrais/vous devriez boire une tisane.
Tu devrais/vous devriez te coucher.
3 Tu devrais/vous devriez prendre un rendez-vous chez le dentiste.
Tu devrais/vous devriez faire des bains de bouche.
4 Tu devrais/vous devriez arrêter de faire du sport.
Tu devrais/vous devriez utiliser de la pommade à l'arnica.

B

1 Fais/faites du sport. Fais/faites un régime. Il faudrait manger/Mange/Mangez plus équilibré.
2 Je te/vous recommande la camomille. Bois-en/buvez-en une tisane et couche-toi/couchez-vous.
3 Prends/prenez un rendez-vous chez le dentiste. Fais/faites des bains de bouche.
4 Arrête/arrêtez de faire du sport. Je te/vous conseille d'utiliser de la pommade à l'arnica.

C

Listen to Track 10:22 for some sample answers.

Activité 10.4.10

Here are some sample answers, but you may have used alternative expressions of reassurance.

1 Ce n'est pas grave. Envoie des fleurs.
2 Rassure-toi ! Il y a beaucoup de circulation.
3 Ça ne fait rien, tu les prendras ce soir.
4 Ne t'inquiète pas ! Tu pourras la regarder en ligne sur l'ordinateur.
5 Rassure-toi ! Mon ami peut le réparer.
6 Ce n'est pas grave. Voici un sparadrap.
7 Ne t'en fais pas. Il y a un paquet dans le placard.
8 Ne t'inquiète pas ! Fais une omelette.

Activité 10.5.1

A

les médecines douces

B

1 (c); 2 (e); 3 (a); 4 (b); 5 (d); 6 (g); 7 (f)

C

1 self-knowledge
2 needles
3 is based on (from the verb *reposer sur*)
4 heavily diluted
5 gentle manipulations
6 treats (from the verb *soigner*)

Activité 10.5.2

A

1 (c) it works really well; 2 (f) it's a load of rubbish/a joke; 3 (e) it didn't work at all; 4 (a) I am totally cured; 5 (d) it's unacceptable; 6 (g) it's controversial; 7 (b) it's all in the mind

B

	Nicolas	Isabelle	Alice	Martin	Philippe
homéopathie	✓	✓			
acupuncture		✓	✓		
réflexologie	✓				
ostéopathie				✓	
cures	✓				

C

1
(a) Nicolas: for
(b) Isabelle: against

(c) Alice: against
(d) Martin: for
(e) Philippe: neither for nor against

2 (a) Isabelle; (b) Martin; (c) Philippe; (d) Alice; (e) Nicolas

D

Je suis tout à fait contre.

Je trouve que…

Je ne suis pas d'accord avec vous.

Je suis contre.

Je suis plutôt pour.

Je pense que…

Je suis tout à fait d'accord avec vous.

Je ne sais pas.

Je suis ni pour, ni contre.

Je n'ai pas d'exemples.

Je n'ai rien qui prouve le contraire.

Je sais que…

À mon avis…

Activité 10.5.3

Listen to Track 10:24 again to check your answers.

Activité 10.5.4

A

le ginseng *ginseng*
la valériane *valerian*
l'aloès *aloe vera*
le millepertuis *St John's wort*

B

1 tiredness
2 anxiety and insomnia
3 skin infections
4 mild depression
5 digestion problems

C

	Nom	Adjectif	Verbe
1	la fatigue	fatigué(e)	se fatiguer
2	l'anxiété	anxieux/se	—
3	l'insomnie	insomniaque	—
4	l'infection	infectieux/se	infecter
5	le traitement	—	traiter
6	le soin	—	soigner
7	la dépression	dépressif/ déprimé(e)	déprimer
8	le soulagement	—	soulager
9	la digestion	digestif	digérer
10	la respiration	respiratoire	respirer

Activité 10.5.5

A

1 La cliente a des insomnies. Son médecin lui a prescrit des somnifères mais elle ne se sent pas bien le matin.
2 Elle lui recommande la valériane.
3 Elle doit la prendre en tisane, une tasse le soir avant de se coucher.
4 Il est toujours fatigué, il manque d'énergie.
5 Le ginseng augmente la performance intellectuelle et la résistance au stress.
6 Il doit le prendre en poudre. Il doit diluer une cuillère dans le thé ou le café tous les matins.
7 Elle est un peu déprimée.
8 L'herboriste lui conseille de prendre du millepertuis.
9 La substance du millepertuis a le même effet sur le cerveau que les antidépresseurs mais avec moins d'effets secondaires.

B

Here are some sample answers.

1 Le magnésium est très efficace pour lutter contre le stress. Faites-en une cure une fois par mois. Prenez-en un comprimé tous les matins pendant 7 jours.

2 Pour combattre les migraines, je vous recommande la camomille. Il faudrait en prendre une tisane trois fois par jour.

3 L'aloès, ça marche vraiment bien pour l'eczéma. Achetez une pommade à l'aloès et ça ira mieux.

4 Les antidépresseurs ne sont pas toujours très efficaces et ils peuvent avoir des effets secondaires. Vous pourriez essayer des gélules de millepertuis, c'est plus naturel et ça marche.

Activité 10.5.6

Here is a sample answer.

> Les médecines douces sont de plus en plus populaires aujourd'hui, mais je pense qu'elles ne sont pas très efficaces pour soigner les maladies graves. Cependant, je sais que certaines peuvent être efficaces pour les problèmes musculaires, par exemple.
>
> Je n'ai jamais essayé l'homéopathie, tout simplement parce que quand je suis malade, je vais chez le docteur, il me prescrit des médicaments et c'est assez efficace. La phytothérapie ou la réflexologie, je n'y crois pas. Pour moi, c'est du pipeau. Je ne vais jamais chez un herboriste. Par contre, je suis assez pour l'ostéopathie et les cures thermales. Je souffrais beaucoup de douleurs dans le cou et les épaules, et les séances chez l'ostéopathe ont été vraiment efficaces. Je ne souffre plus du tout maintenant. Mon fils a fait des cures thermales pendant 4 ans pour combattre l'asthme, et il est complètement guéri aujourd'hui. Donc, je pense que certaines médecines douces marchent vraiment bien.
>
> Je trouve que les médecines douces sont très contestées parce qu'on ne peut pas vraiment prouver que ça marche. À mon avis, c'est tout dans la tête: si on y croit, ça marche, et si on n'y croit pas, ça ne marche pas !

Unité 11

Activité 11.1.1

A

1 (d); 2 (b); 3 (c); 4 (a); 5 (a); 6 (d); 7 (c); 8 (b)

B

The imperfect is used in descriptions in the past. Here are the texts with the verbs in the imperfect highlighted in bold.

1 Dans les années 40, mon arrière-grand-mère n'**avait** pas l'électricité dans sa cuisine, mais elle **avait** un robinet d'eau froide, vrai luxe pour elle !

2 Dans les années 50, la France **était** encore très rurale, plus que certains pays voisins. Comme beaucoup de Français autrefois, mon arrière-grand-mère **habitait** un petit village à la campagne.

3 Au début des années 60, la mode **était** encore très classique. Ma mère et ma grand-mère **portaient** le même style de robes.

4 Dans les années 70, les couleurs vives **étaient** à la mode, pour les vêtements et pour la décoration. Chez moi il y **avait** un canapé orange et rose.

5 Quand j'**étais** petite, on n'avait pas l'internet. Pour les nouvelles, on **lisait** le journal et on **utilisait** de gros téléphones.

6 Pendant la guerre, et juste après, on ne **mangeait** que des choses simples préparées à la maison. La plupart des gens n'**allaient** jamais au restaurant.

7 Quand mes parents **étaient** jeunes, les divorces **étaient** rares et difficiles. Les familles **avaient** une structure traditionnelle ; il n'y **avait** pas souvent de familles recomposées.

8 Il y **avait** peu de voitures du temps de mon arrière-grand-mère, même en plein centre du village.

Activité 11.1.2

A

Here is the text with the verbs in the imperfect highlighted in bold.

> Je suis née dans les années 70. Quand j'**étais** petite, je **vivais** à Paris. À cette époque, Valéry Giscard d'Estaing **était** Président de la République, c'**était** les années des chocs pétroliers et de la crise économique, mais aussi des progrès sociaux après les événements de mai 1968. Mes parents, mes frères et moi **habitions** dans un appartement. Dans les années 70, les couleurs vives **étaient** à la mode ; chez moi, il y **avait** un canapé orange et rose. On **portait** des vêtements colorés avec des formes et des matières nouvelles. Les femmes **mettaient** plus souvent un pantalon et **avaient** plus souvent les cheveux courts qu'avant. À midi, beaucoup de gens **rentraient** manger chez eux, c'**était** rare de prendre un sandwich au bureau. On ne **trouvait** pas beaucoup de supérettes en ville autrefois, on **faisait** plutôt ses courses dans les petits commerces. Dans mon enfance, il n'y **avait** que trois chaînes de télévision et notre poste **était** en noir et blanc. On **avait** un gros téléphone gris qu'on n'**utilisait** pas beaucoup parce que téléphoner **coûtait** cher. En ce temps-là, on n'avait pas l'internet ; pour les nouvelles, on **regardait** les informations à la télé à 20 h ou on **lisait** le journal. Pour les vacances, nous **partions** à la campagne ou à la montagne avec mes grands-parents. Nous y **allions** en voiture ou on **prenait** le train, mais à l'époque le TGV n'**existait** pas encore.

B

1 Une femme. *(The agreement of the past participle* née *in the first sentence and that of the adjective* petite *in the second sentence indicates this.)*

2 Elle parle de son enfance.

3 C'était dans les années 70.

4 Elle se trouvait à Paris.

C

Here are some possible answers.

	Noms	**Verbes**
Lieu/logement	un appartement – un canapé	vivre – habiter
Famille	un parent – un frère – un grand-parent	
Politique/société	(le) Président de la République – une crise économique – un progrès social (des progrès sociaux)	
Mode	un vêtement – une forme – une matière – les cheveux (m.) courts	porter – mettre – avoir (les cheveux courts)
Communications/ informations	une chaîne de télévision – un poste – un téléphone – l'internet (m.) – les nouvelles (f.) – les informations (f.) – la télé – un journal	téléphoner – regarder (la télévision) – lire (le journal)
Vacances	(à) la campagne – (à) la montagne	partir – aller
Transports	une voiture – un train – un TGV	prendre
Repas/nourriture	un sandwich	manger – prendre (un sandwich / un repas)
Courses/ magasins	une supérette – un petit commerce – les courses (f.)	faire ses/les courses

D

The expressions in the text that refer to periods or points in the past are:

> dans les années 70 ; à cette époque ; autrefois ; dans mon enfance ; en ce temps-là ; à l'époque.

E

Here is a possible answer. Note the different ways of dating descriptions.

> Dans mon enfance, on ne partait pas en vacances à l'étranger.
>
> Quand j'étais petit(e), les filles ne portaient pas de pantalons.
>
> Quand j'avais 10 ans, je n'avais pas beaucoup de jouets mais je lisais beaucoup.
>
> Dans les années 40, pendant la Seconde Guerre mondiale, on ne mangeait pas beaucoup de viande.
>
> Dans les années 1980 on ne travaillait pas avec des ordinateurs.

Activité 11.1.3

A

Mon arrière-grand-mère	Moi
un petit village	une grande ville
une petite maison modeste	un appartement
pas d'électricité	tout le confort moderne
un rythme de vie plus régulier	un emploi du temps (qui) change souvent
pas de diplômes	un diplôme d'ingénieur en informatique
le travail dans les champs	un poste à responsabilités
se déplaçait moins	beaucoup de temps dans les transports
partait moins en vacances	je me repose plus le week-end et en vacances
ne quittait presque jamais son village, ne prenait jamais l'avion, n'allait jamais à l'étranger	je voyage beaucoup plus
parlait patois	je ne parle pas cette langue régionale

B

alors que ; mais ; tandis que ; par contre ; en revanche ; mais ; au contraire ; alors que ; mais

C

Elle partait **moins** en vacances que moi.

Elle se consacrait **autant** à sa famille.

Je voyage beaucoup **plus**.

moins = *less*; autant = *as much*; plus = *more*

These words are used to make comparisons.

D

1 plus
2 moins
3 moins
4 moins
5 plus
6 plus

Activité 11.1.4

A

Here are some possible answers.

> Je dors **plus** la nuit mais je me repose **moins** la journée.
>
> Je voyage **moins** mais je vais **plus** en France.
>
> Je m'occupe de mes enfants **autant qu'**avant.
>
> Je sors **moins** le soir et je travaille **plus** après le dîner.
>
> Je lis **autant** mais pas des romans : je lis mes livres de français.

Activité 11.1.5

A

The two towns described are Grenoble and La Rochelle.

Grenoble : moins de circulation, plus de transports en commun, plus de pistes cyclables, plus de bâtiments écologiques, moins de pollution, plus de cadres internationaux.

La Rochelle : plus grande, plus de jeunes, une université, moins de voitures, plus de piétons, plus de vélos / de cyclistes.

B

	Grenoble	La Rochelle
Des bâtiments écologiques	✓	
Des bâtiments historiques		✓
La circulation	✓	✓
La zone piétonne		✓
Le climat		✓
Le tramway	✓	
Le vélo / les cyclistes	✓	✓
Les technologies de pointe	✓	
L'université	✓	✓
Une population internationale	✓	

Activité 11.1.6

Here is a possible answer.

> Dans ma ville, à Oxford, il y a toujours **plus d'**étudiants, et aussi **de plus en plus de** touristes.
>
> Dans le centre, il y a **moins de** voitures et **plus de** zones piétonnes.
>
> Il y a **autant de** cyclistes qu'avant : le vélo est toujours populaire.
>
> Il y a **moins de** parkings en ville, on doit prendre le bus.
>
> On ne peut pas circuler très vite, il y a **de plus en plus d'**embouteillages.

Activité 11.1.7

A

Date	Event
1881	Institution de l'instruction gratuite, publique et obligatoire
1950	Institution du SMIG (salaire minimum interprofessionel garanti)
1999	Institution du PACS (pacte civil de solidarité)
1974	La majorité légale passe à 18 ans
1945	Le droit de vote devient vraiment universel
1967	Légalisation de la contraception
1936	Les premiers congés payés
2013	Mariage pour tous

B

Here is a possible answer.

> A few facts surprised me. The introduction of a national minimum wage happened earlier than I would have thought, and women's suffrage later than I expected. In my country, England, a guaranteed national minimum wage was introduced later (in 1999), but all women gained the right to vote earlier (in 1928). Other events happened at about the same time, for example compulsory education and the legal majority age of 18.

Activité 11.1.8

A

Listen to Track 11:2 again to check your pronunciation. You can also read the transcript if you would like to check how each date is formed.

B

The three dates included in the recording are:

1881 mille huit cent huitante-et-un

1999 mille neuf cent nonante-neuf

1974 mille neuf cent septante-quatre

C

Here are the sentences with the correct dates in them. Listen to Track 11:4 again to check your pronunciation of dates and of verbs in the imperfect.

Avant 1642, la calculatrice n'existait pas.

Avant 1688, on ne buvait pas de champagne.

Avant 1816, on ne pouvait pas faire de photos.

Avant 1829, l'alphabet Braille n'existait pas.

Avant 1865, on ne pratiquait pas la pasteurisation.

Avant 1884, il n'y avait pas de poubelles à Paris.

Avant 1894, on n'avait pas inventé le cinéma.

Avant 1974, les cartes à puce n'existaient pas.

Avant 1980, on ne prenait pas le TGV.

Avant 2002, on ne payait pas en euros.

Did you guess that all the sentences describe some famous French inventions?

The calculator was invented by Pascal, champagne by the French monk Dom Pérignon, photography by Louis Daguerre, and the Braille alphabet by Louis Braille.

Louis Pasteur gave his name to pasteurisation.

Eugène Poubelle introduced the first bins in the streets of Paris.

The Lumière brothers, Auguste and Louis, are credited with inventing film-making.

Roland Moreno patented the first chip cards which were soon used in France.

The French high-speed train (TGV [= Train à Grande Vitesse]) carried its first passengers in 1980 between Paris and Lyons.

The euro was first used, in France and other countries, on 1 January 2002.

Activité 11.1.9

A

1 She doesn't think that the past was better than the present.

2 (b)

3 (a) Le travail, la technologie et la santé.

(b) Here are some possible answers. Check the speaker's arguments and examples in the transcript.

Travail : on travaillait plus dur, les congés payés n'existaient pas.

Technologie : on n'avait pas de machines pour nous aider.

Santé : quand on tombait malade, on guérissait moins rapidement.

B

1 le bon vieux temps
2 des emplois manuels / un emploi manuel
3 un emploi de bureau / des emplois de bureau
4 une machine à laver (le linge)
5 un lave-vaisselle
6 un aspirateur
7 Tout n'était pas rose.

C

tout d'abord ; ensuite ; enfin

D

1 plus assidûment ; moins souvent
2 plus fréquemment
3 plus rapidement
4 moins rapidement
5 plus vite
6 aussi facilement

Activité 11.1.10

Here are some possible answers.

Maintenant j'arrive plus rapidement au bureau grâce au nouveau tramway.

De nos jours mes enfants mangent mieux que quand ils étaient petits. *(Note that* bien *becomes* mieux *in a comparison.)*

Aujourd'hui je regarde plus rarement la télévision qu'avant, parce que je suis étudiant(e).

Maintenant je comprends plus facilement le français qu'au début du cours.

Actuellement je sors aussi fréquemment qu'avant, j'ai besoin de me détendre !

Activité 11.1.11

A

1 (a) We no longer have any time.
(b) We have more time.

2 In writing, the difference is indicated by the *n'* part of the negation (*ne ... plus*) in the first sentence. In speaking there is no difference between *on a* and *on n'a* because *on‿a* must be pronounced with a liaison. The only difference between the two sentences is therefore the pronunciation of *plus* : [ply]/ in the first sentence, and [plys] in the second one. It is one of the cases where correct pronunciation is crucial to the meaning of a sentence.

B

		[ply]	[plys]	[plyz]
1	Elle appréciait plus la nature.		✓	
2	On communique plus rapidement.	✓		
3	Grenoble est une ville plus animée.			✓
4	On n'a plus de temps.	✓		
5	Il y a plus de grandes surfaces.		✓	
6	On possède plus de voitures qu'avant.		✓	
7	Ils n'habitent plus en ville.	✓		
8	La Rochelle est beaucoup plus polluée.	✓		
9	Je voyage plus que mon arrière-grand-mère.		✓	
10	Elle s'habille plus élégamment.			✓

Activité 11.1.12

A

1 (b); 2 (b); 3 (a); 4 (a); 5 (b)

B

Listen to Track 11:9 again to check your pronunciation.

Activité 11.1.13

Here is a possible answer.

Sur l'image on voit qu'en 1950 il n'y avait pas beaucoup de voitures, alors qu'en 2000 il y a plus de circulation. Autrefois les dames portaient des chapeaux, mais pas en 2000. En 2000 il y a des antennes satellites sur les toits ; en revanche elles n'existaient pas en 1950. Il y a autant de bâtiments sur les deux images, mais certains sont plus modernes aujourd'hui qu'en 1950. En 2000 on ne voit qu'une supérette tandis qu'en 1950 il y avait plusieurs petits commerces pour acheter sa nourriture, par exemple une boucherie et une épicerie. Il y avait aussi des gens qui vendaient des choses dans la rue.

Activité 11.2.1

A

1 (b)
2 (d)
3 (d)
4 The *passé composé*.

B

	Date	Pays
Naissance du grand-père	1912	Suisse
Naissance de Daniel	1966	Suisse
Enfance de Daniel		Suisse
Adolescence de Daniel		Belgique
Mariage et déménagement de Daniel	1991	Angleterre

C

Listen to Track 11:11 to check your answers.

D

Here is a possible answer.

Année de naissance ?	1971
Lieu de naissance ? (pays / région / ville)	Lyon, France
Lieu de votre jeunesse ? (pays / région / ville)	Paris
Déménagement ?	Oui, Allemagne
Mariage ?	Oui
Autres événements ou informations ?	Deux frères

E

Listen to Track 11:12 for a sample answer, and compare it with your own recording. Check if you used the correct verb forms and listen carefully to see if you pronounced them correctly.

Activité 11.2.2

A

1 Il vient du Viêtnam.
2 Il vivait à la campagne, au Viêtnam.
3 Ils étaient agriculteurs, maintenant ils sont à la retraite.
4 Ils se sont installés dans une grande ville.
5 Il est enseignant de français.
6 Pour la fête de fin d'année.

B

Here is the completed transcript with the verbs highlighted in bold.

> Je m'appelle Toan, et je **viens** du Viêtnam. Mes grands-parents **étaient** en vie à l'époque coloniale, quand le Viêtnam **était** français. Mon grand-père **parlait** donc un peu français. Aujourd'hui nous **sommes** une grande famille – mon père, ma mère et mes trois sœurs et frères. Quand j'**étais** petit, on **vivait** tous à la campagne. Mes parents **étaient** tous les deux agriculteurs. Le travail dans les champs **était** très dur. Ils **sont** à la retraite maintenant.
>
> Mes deux sœurs, mon grand frère et moi, nous **avons quitté** le village et nous **nous sommes installés** dans une grande ville pour y chercher du travail et une meilleure vie. Mon grand frère **est devenu** donc coiffeur et mes deux sœurs commerçantes. Moi, j'**ai fait** des études universitaires; je suis le seul dans la famille. Et je **travaille** maintenant comme enseignant de français. La fête de fin d'année est souvent la seule occasion où la famille **se réunit**. On se retrouve autour d'un repas et on passe de bons moments ensemble à la campagne.

C

1 (c); 2 (a); 3 (b)

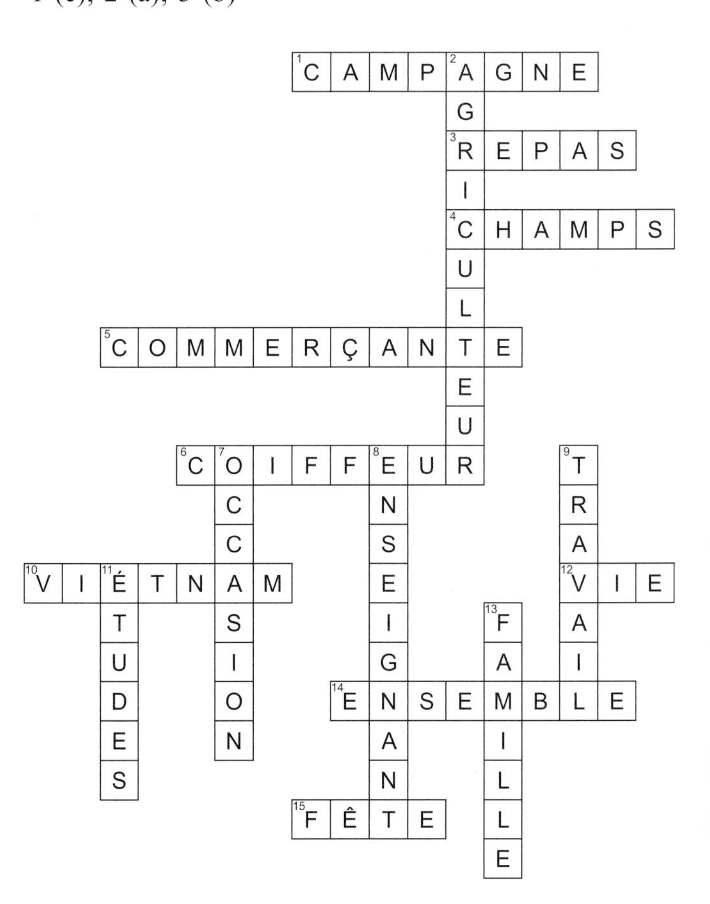

D

(Note: the spellings Viêtnam and Viétnam are both valid.)

Activité 11.2.3

A

There is no *corrigé* for this step of the activity. Read on to check if your predictions were close.

B

1 (c); 2 (b); 3 (a)

C

	Suzanne	Roxana	Xavière
France		✓	✓
Algérie			✓
Roumanie		✓	
Québec	✓		
Australie	✓		
Maroc			✓
États-Unis		✓	

Activité 11.2.4

1 (b); 2 (e); 3 (d); 4 (a); 5 (c)

Activité 11.2.5

A

1 Jacques and Thérèse.

2 Policeman, then taxi driver, and schoolteacher.

3 He took part in the Second World War.

4 She has one brother.

B

The four phrases are:

ensuite; après quelques années; au bout de 5 ans; un peu plus tard.

Activité 11.2.6

A

Here is the information about each decade mentioned.

1940s: Roxana's birth. Childhood.

1960s: Marriage.

1970s: Daughters born.

1980s: Arrival in France.

You may have noticed the verb *était persecutée*, meaning 'was persecuted'. This is a passive verb construction you have not come across yet in the module; it functions the same way as in English so the meaning is fairly easy to understand or guess.

B

The correct answer is 3.

C

Verbs in the imperfect	Verbs in the *passé composé*
mon père était ma mère était nous vivions la vie y était la population était nous parlions	je me suis mariée j'ai grandi j'ai eu nous avons décidé mon frère et ma sœur ont préféré nous avons fui nous sommes arrivés

Activité 11.2.7

A

L'Afrique du nord ✓	Casablanca ✓
La ville d'Oran ✓	Marrakesh ×
La ville d'Alger ×	Tétouan ✓
L'Algérie ✓	Le Maroc espagnol ✓
Ce port situé au bord de la Méditerranée ✓	Essaouira ×
La Kabylie ×	L'Espagne ✓
Le Maroc ✓	Paris ×

B

	En Algérie	Au Maroc	En Espagne	En France
Les parents de Xavière	✓			
Les frères et sœurs de Xavière	✓			
Xavière				✓
Les grands-mères de Xavière		✓		
Les ancêtres de Xavière			✓	

C

The correct information is shown on map (a).

Activité 11.2.8

The pronoun *y* was used in all of these sentences. If you would like to revise how to use *y* please refer back to Unit 4. Note that *y* is always placed in front of the conjugated verb.

Activité 11.2.9

1 J'**y** suis arrivé il y a cinq ans.

2 Il **y** a commencé une licence de langues. *(Note that this use of* y *with a verb in the* passé composé *(i.e.* il **y** a commencé*) is completely separate from the expression* il y a *meaning 'there is/are' or* il y a *meaning 'ago'.)*

3 Nous **y** sommes partis en voyage l'année dernière.

4 Elles **y** ont passé trois semaines.

Activité 11.2.10

A

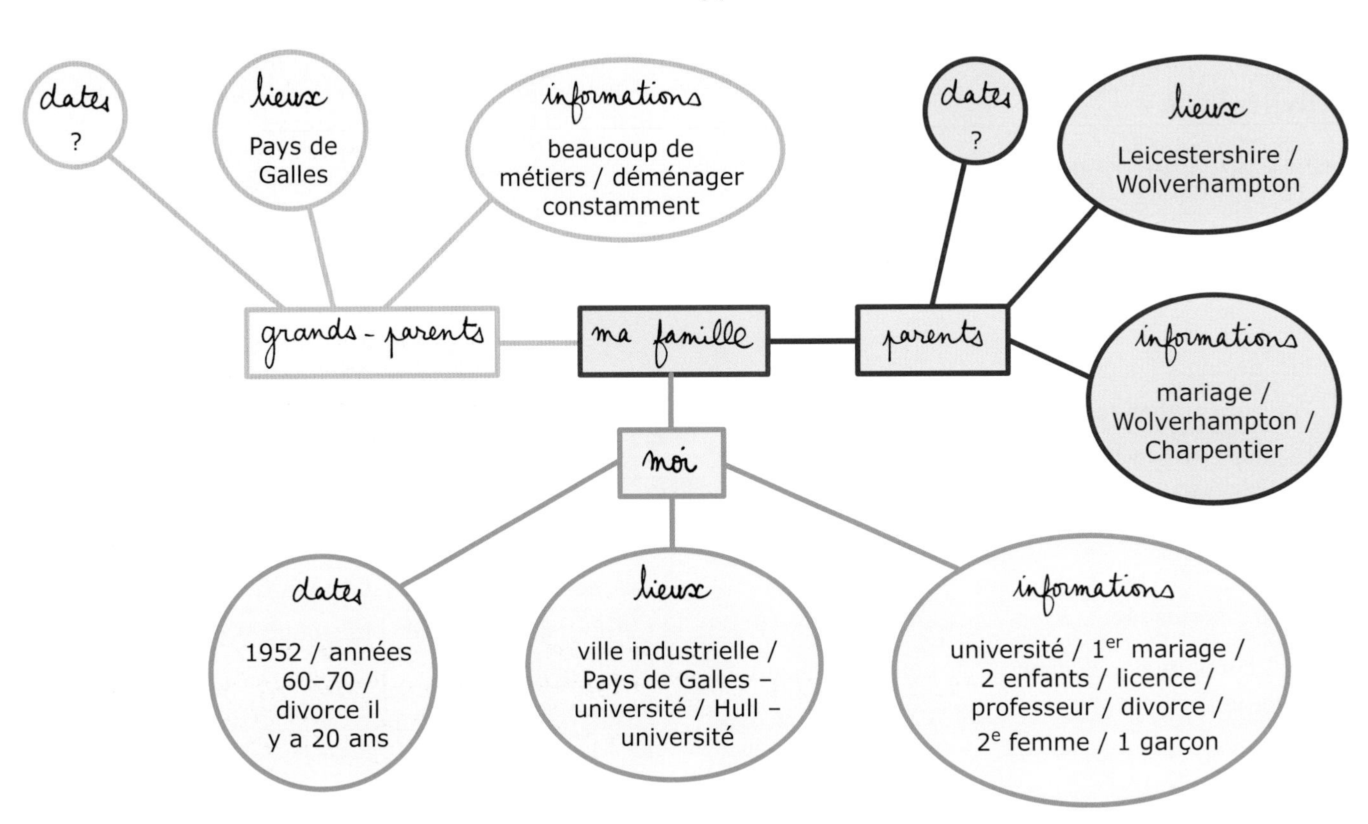

B

Here is a possible answer (based on the sample notes in step A).

> Mes grands-parents paternels étaient gallois. Mon grand-père changeait de métier fréquemment et ma famille a dû déménager constamment pendant des années. Mon père est né dans le Leicestershire, son frère dans le Yorkshire et ses deux sœurs près de Manchester. Mes parents se sont rencontrés à Wolverhampton et ils se sont mariés à la fin de la Deuxième Guerre mondiale. Mon père était charpentier. Ma sœur est née en 1945, et je suis né en 1952. Pendant mon enfance j'habitais dans une ville industrielle. J'ai grandi pendant la révolution des années 60. Dans le milieu des années 70, je suis allé à l'université au Pays de Galles où j'ai rencontré ma première femme. Nous avons eu deux enfants. J'étais le premier enfant de ma famille à étudier à l'université. J'ai obtenu une licence de mathématiques et je suis devenu professeur d'informatique dans une école secondaire. J'ai divorcé il y a vingt ans et je suis allé à l'université de Hull pour faire un mastère en communication. C'est là que j'ai rencontré ma deuxième femme : une Française exceptionnelle. Nous avons un petit garcon qui est adorable !

Activité 11.3.1

A

1 (b); 2 (c); 3 (a)

B

	1	2	3
l'annuaire		✓	
l'email	✓		
l'internet		✓	✓
la liseuse			✓
l'ordinateur		✓	
la tablette tactile		✓	
le journal en ligne			✓
le journal papier			✓
le minitel		✓	
le téléphone	✓	✓	
le téléphone portable	✓	✓	
les textos	✓		

C

	Autrefois	Ensuite	Aujourd'hui
Communiquer	*pas de téléphone*	*un gros téléphone gris*	*un téléphone portable*
Chercher des renseignements	*l'annuaire / la bibliothèque*	*le minitel*	*l'internet*
Lire les nouvelles	*le journal papier*	*le journal en ligne / sur la liseuse*	

D

Here are some possible answers.

1 (a) Autrefois les gens n'avaient pas le téléphone.
  (b) Aujourd'hui on a tous des téléphones portables.

2 (a) Avant en France il y avait le minitel.
  (b) Maintenant ça n'existe plus, il y a l'internet.

3 (a) Mon père achetait le journal tous les jours.
  (b) Moi, aujourd'hui, je lis le journal en ligne ou sur ma liseuse.

Activité 11.3.2

A

The odd ones out are: *un micro, un écran, une émission, une chaîne, zapper*. These words are all related to television rather than newspapers.

B

1 (a); 2 (b); 3 (b); 4 (a)

Activité 11.3.3

A

1 (c); 2 (d); 3 (b); 4 (e); 5 (a)

B

1 (b); 2 (c); 3 (a); 4 (e); 5 (d)

C

1 les opposants, une manifestation, est prévue
2 s'est imposé, s'est incliné *(literally: 'imposed itself', 'inclined itself/bowed').*
3 soupçonné(es), interpellé(es)
4 a braqué, (a été) arrêté
5 les travaux, circuler

Activité 11.3.4

A

1 le braquage
2 la reprise

B

1 livrer
2 réveiller
3 appeler
4 rassembler

Activité 11.3.5

A

(1) le journal ; (2) la date ; (3) le titre ; (4) la photo ; (5) l'article ; (6) la légende

B

1 un accident (de voiture) / une collision; deux personnes légèrement blessées.
2 Mardi, vers 7 h.
3 Sur l'A4, près de Strasbourg.
4 La circulation a été fortement ralentie.

C

The *passé composé.*

D

4, 3, 1, 2.

Activité 11.3.6

The correct order of the paragraphs is: 4, 3, 1, 2.

Here is the reordered article in full.

> **Deux Niçois champions de France de ski**
>
> Deux skieurs de l'Inter Club de Nice, Mathieu Bailet (cadet) et Karen Smajda-Clément (benjamine) ont remporté le titre de champion de France de ski.
>
> Karen s'est classée 3e du slalom géant la semaine dernière à l'Alpe d'Huez. Mathieu s'est imposé dans le slalom du championnat de France qui avait lieu à Auron le week-end dernier.
>
> Grâce à ces victoires les deux jeunes se sont qualifiés pour le championnat européen. La région de Nice est fière de ses deux nouveaux champions !

Activité 11.3.7

A

1 Le samedi 16 mars, à 19 h.
2 Station service. Plessala.
3 Deux voleurs, une employée.
4 Agression. 500 € volés.

B

Here is the information, taken from the cartoon.

> **Weather**: « Il faisait **froid**, il y avait **de la pluie** »
>
> **Day/date**: « On était **le samedi 16 mars** »
>
> **Time**: « Il était **7 h du soir / 19 h** »
>
> **Place**: « Ça se passait **dans une station service à Plessala** »

C

Here is a description of each character. (You only needed to produce three such sentences.)

> L'employée de la station service était âgée. Elle avait les cheveux blancs. Elle portait des lunettes. Elle avait un haut rouge.

Les voleurs portaient tous les deux un sweat à capuche et un pantalon.

Le premier voleur avait un pantalon noir, un sweat à capuche bleu et des tennis blanches. Le deuxième voleur était une femme, avec un jean, un sweat à capuche gris et des bottes noires. Elle était blonde.

D

Here are the actions that occurred in the incident.

Deux voleurs sont arrivés à la station service. Ils sont descendus de la voiture. Ils sont entrés dans la boutique en criant. Ils ont demandé tout l'argent de la caisse. L'employée a mis les billets dans un sac en plastique. Ils sont sortis en courant. L'employée a appelé au secours. Les voleurs ont fait démarrer la voiture. Ils sont partis en trombe. La dame a attendu la police.

E

Here is a possible answer.

Braquage à Plessala

Le samedi 16 mars, à 7 heures du soir, deux voleurs sont arrivés à la station service à Plessala. Il faisait froid, il y avait de la pluie. Ils portaient tous les deux un sweat à capuche. Ils sont descendus de la voiture et ils sont entrés dans la boutique en criant. Ils ont demandé tout l'argent de la caisse, donc l'employée a mis les billets dans un sac en plastique. Ensuite ils sont sortis en courant. Alors l'employée a appelé au secours. Les voleurs ont fait démarrer la voiture, puis ils sont partis en trombe. La dame a attendu la police.

Activité 11.4.1

A

1 immediately *tout de suite*

2 at the other end *à l'autre bout*

3 which suited me *qui me convenait (bien)*

4 in mid-sleep *en plein sommeil*

5 the cry of a bird of prey *le cri d'un rapace*

6 to grunt *grogner*

7 in the middle of the night *en pleine nuit*

8 with untidy hair *les cheveux en pétard*

9 (he) realised *(il) s'est rendu compte*

10 in a sleepy voice *d'une voix endormie*

11 to have a look *jeter un œil*

12 glass pane *la vitre*

13 creaking *le grincement*

B

The answer is 2. There are elements in the excerpt that point to the text being the start of a mystery: the main character describes an unexpected and as yet unexplained event, and seems to be frightened.

C

Phrase 4 would probably make the best title. The other three points are all mentioned or happen in the passage but the main emphasis is on the night visitor.

D

1 (a) The story is told by a boy (we can tell from the fact that past participles in some verbs are in the masculine form, e.g. *assis*, *réveillé*). He lives with his father.
  (b) The boy's father is also in the house.
  (c) The boy's mother is mentioned too, and a night visitor is mentioned at the end.

2 The scene takes place in the middle of the night, at two in the morning.

3 (a) At the father's house.
  (b) The mother lives at the other end of town.

4 (a) The door bell ringing in the night.
  (b) The father opens the door to a night visitor.

5 (a) Because the parents are separated.
  (b) Because he thinks the door bell might be to announce bad news and something might have happened to his mum.

Activité 11.4.2

A

1 Il est arrivé la nuit, à deux heures du matin.

2 Il pleuvait.

B

The four words are: *sinistre, rapace, hantait, pétrifié.*

C

Here are the words from the text which refer to sounds or hearing: *sonner, coups de sonnette, le dring, le cri, deux coups stridents, j'ai entendu, j'ai écouté.*

D

The three phrases which relate to thinking or imagining are:

j'ai pensé à maman…

La pensée qu'il était peut-être…

je l'ai imaginé jeter…

E

The answer is 1: the phrases are all used to make comparisons. It is a device used to make the account of events subjective, because an innocent event (a door bell ringing) is compared to scary and dramatic events. This is another way of presenting the story through the main character's imagination and so increasing the sense of fear and mystery.

Activité 11.4.3

A

1 yellow

2 pink

3 green

B

1 the imperfect

2 the imperfect

3 the *passé composé*

Note that there is a verb in a tense that you have not studied yet. In 'La pensée qu'il **était** peut-être **arrivé** quelque chose à maman me hantait', 'il était arrivé' means (something) 'had happened' and is in the pluperfect tense (called the *plus-que-parfait* in French). You will learn about this later in your French studies.

Activité 11.4.4

The correct order of the sentences is:

1 Il était plus de deux heures du matin.

9 Tout d'un coup, j'ai entendu la sonnette.

4 J'ai pensé que c'était ma mère qui habitait à l'autre bout de la ville.

6 Je dormais chez mon père. C'était sa semaine. Mes parents étaient divorcés.

7 Le bruit de la sonnette était sinistre.

3 J'ai entendu mon père se lever.

5 J'avais peur, je pensais qu'il était arrivé quelque chose à ma mère.

2 Il pleuvait fort dehors.

8 Mon père s'est levé, il est passé devant ma chambre, m'a parlé. Il a descendu les escaliers, il a ouvert la porte.

Activité 11.4.5

A

Here is an example of some possible notes for a story.

Qui ?	Antoine, mon meilleur ami.
Quand ?	Juillet 2010. Vacances.
Où ?	Chez ma mère, dans sa ville.
Quoi ?	Rencontre à la bibliothèque et au cinéma.

B

Here are some sample notes on each point.

Qui ? Antoine, mon meilleur ami. Le fils d'un voisin de ma mère, vers Strasbourg. Stage à la bibliothèque. Petit. Cheveux bruns courts. Jean et tee-shirt blanc.

Où ? Rencontre : à la bibliothèque. En vacances chez ma mère. Je cherchais un livre. Il travaillait. Le soir, au cinéma. Le même film.

Quoi ? Je suis allée à la bibliothèque. J'ai demandé de l'aide. J'ai reconnu Antoine. On a discuté. Au cinéma, j'ai revu Antoine. On a commencé à discuter. On a passé beaucoup de temps ensemble.

Et maintenant ? Aujourd'hui : moi à Lille, lui à Toulouse. On garde le contact. On se retrouve tous les étés.

C

Here is a possible answer.

> J'ai rencontré Antoine en juillet 2010. Aujourd'hui c'est mon meilleur ami. C'était pendant des vacances chez ma mère vers Strasbourg. Antoine travaillait à la bibliothèque municipale, il faisait un stage. Moi j'étais étudiante à Paris, je préparais ma licence de physique à l'université. En juillet 2010, c'était les vacances, je passais l'été chez ma mère et mon beau-père. Je ne voyais plus mes amis de l'université, je m'ennuyais. Un jour je suis allée à la bibliothèque pour me distraire. J'avais besoin de conseils pour trouver un livre alors j'ai demandé de l'aide au bibliothécaire. J'ai reconnu Antoine : c'était le fils d'un voisin chez ma mère. Il avait 20 ans, comme moi. Il était petit, il avait les cheveux bruns courts, il portait un jean et un tee-shirt blanc. Nous avons discuté et j'ai choisi un livre grâce à ses conseils. Plus tard, je suis allée au cinéma avec mon beau-père et j'ai revu Antoine. Il allait voir le même film. Immédiatement on a commencé à discuter. Après le film on a décidé de rester en contact. Finalement on a passé beaucoup de temps ensemble pendant l'été. Aujourd'hui je suis mariée, j'ai des enfants, et j'habite à Lille. Lui il travaille à Toulouse, à la bibliothèque universitaire. On ne se voit pas souvent, mais on garde le contact en ligne et on se retrouve au moins quelques jours tous les étés. On est resté les meilleurs amis du monde.

D

There is no *corrigé* for this step of the activity.

Transcriptions

Unité 9

Track 9:1

Interviewer Euh, s'il vous plaît, je fais une enquête sur les habitudes d'achat. Je peux vous poser quelques questions ?

Passante Euh, je n'ai pas beaucoup de temps, mais oui, allez-y.

Interviewer Où est-ce que vous achetez votre pain ?

Passante Eh bien... j'achète toujours ma baguette à la boulangerie, elle est meilleure que la baguette du supermarché. Euh, de temps en temps, j'achète du pain bio. C'est plus cher, mais c'est plus sain que le pain blanc.

Interviewer Et, où est-ce que vous achetez vos fruits et légumes ?

Passante Euh, mon mari, lui, il va régulièrement au marché pour acheter les fruits et légumes, ils sont bien plus frais que dans les magasins. Mais, moi, je préfère aller chez le marchand de légumes, c'est plus varié.

Interviewer Et, vous allez à la poste pour acheter vos timbres ?

Passante Euh, non. Je vais au bureau de tabac, c'est plus près.

Interviewer Et où est-ce que vous achetez vos produits de beauté ?

Passante Ah, les produits de beauté, c'est à la parapharmacie. Ils sont beaucoup moins coûteux qu'à la pharmacie ! Je n'aime pas les marques des supermarchés.

Interviewer Où est-ce que vous achetez votre viande ?

Passante Ça dépend... Euh, quelquefois, je vais à la boucherie, c'est plus pratique, mais... euh... ça coûte plus cher ! De temps en temps, je vais au supermarché, c'est moins cher et vous savez, c'est aussi bon.

Interviewer Ben, je vous remercie, madame.

Passante Mais je vous en prie.

Track 9:2

Micro-trottoir. Une étudiante en marketing fait une enquête devant un supermarché.

Interviewer Euh, bonjour monsieur, vous faites vos courses souvent ici ?

Le premier monsieur [euh] En général, je viens une fois par semaine. Ben, le supermarché, c'est le magasin... euh... où j'achète presque tous mes produits alimentaires. C'est plus pratique et le parking est gratuit.

Interviewer Euh, pardon, mademoiselle. Vous venez souvent ici ?

La demoiselle Euh, ben, non... euh... très très rarement... euh... moi, je suis étudiante. Je n'ai pas de voiture, alors je vais normalement à la supérette du coin. C'est un magasin où je trouve presque tout. C'est plus cher qu'au supermarché mais c'est beaucoup moins loin.

Interviewer Ah, euh, bonjour messieurs-dames, vous venez faire vos courses souvent ici ?

Le deuxième monsieur Alors, euh... non, jamais. Nous, nous faisons nos courses au marché et en particulier dans les petits commerces où nous achetons les produits du terroir. Nous prenons notre viande chez le boucher où on trouve des morceaux de meilleure qualité. Euh... de temps en temps, nous allons à l'épicerie où on vend des produits saisonniers, et bien sûr à la boulangerie où nous achetons notre pain fait maison.

Interviewer Mais... qu'est-ce que vous faites ici ?

Le deuxième monsieur Ah, on se promène dans la galerie marchande, on est venus pour aller à la parapharmacie.

Interviewer Euh... s'il vous plaît madame, vous venez souvent ici ?

La dame [*elle rit*] Euh, oui, tous les jours sauf le dimanche... je travaille ici.

Interviewer Et… donc… vous faites vos courses ici tous les jours ?

La dame Euh, ben… non, ça dépend. D'habitude j'achète mes produits alimentaires et mes produits d'entretien ici, mais… euh, je préfère acheter mes fruits et légumes au marché où les produits sont plus frais.

Track 9:3

Interviewer Bonjour, où est-ce que vous faites vos courses ?

(Say you normally shop at the supermarket where you buy nearly all of your food products.)

Vous D'habitude, je fais mes courses au supermarché où j'achète presque tous mes produits alimentaires.

(Say it's cheaper and car parking is free. Say you go there once a week.)

Vous C'est moins cher et le parking est gratuit. J'y vais une fois par semaine.

Interviewer Qu'est-ce que vous n'achetez pas au supermarché ?

(Say you buy your baguette at the boulangerie. *It's better, and it's more convenient.)*

Vous J'achète ma baguette à la boulangerie. Elle est meilleure et c'est plus pratique.

(And you also go to the bureau de tabac *everyday where you buy your newspapers.)*

Vous Je vais aussi tous les jours au bureau de tabac où j'achète mon journal.

Interviewer Et vos fruits et légumes ?

(Say: Generally you prefer to buy your fruit and veg at the market where they sell seasonal products; it's also fresher.)

Vous Je préfère en général acheter mes fruits et légumes au marché où on vend des produits saisonniers. C'est aussi plus frais.

Interviewer Et vos produits de beauté ?

(Say it depends. Say usually you go to the parapharmacie *where it's cheaper.)*

Vous Ça dépend. Normalement, je vais à la parapharmacie où c'est moins cher.

(Say: But from time to time you buy shampoo at the chemist's. It's better quality.)

Vous Mais de temps en temps j'achète du shampooing à la pharmacie. C'est de meilleure qualité.

Track 9:4

Dialogue 1

Le vendeur Je peux vous aider, monsieur ?

Le client Euh, oui, s'il vous plaît, je cherche un adaptateur pour chargeur de téléphone portable.

Le vendeur Euh, oui, c'est pour quel pays ? Vous êtes américain ?

Le client Euh, non, c'est pour une prise britannique.

Le vendeur Ah, d'accord, alors… voici un adaptateur pour prise britannique. Vous désirez autre chose ?

Le client Euh, oui, je voudrais une bouilloire électrique sans fil.

Le vendeur Alors, laquelle vous voulez ? J'ai ce modèle qui contient 2 litres ou celui-ci, plus petit, de voyage.

Le client Euh, je voudrais la grande, s'il vous plaît.

Le vendeur Alors, vous prenez cet adaptateur-là et cette bouilloire ?

Le client Oui, merci.

Dialogue 2

La vendeuse Bonjour, je peux vous renseigner ?

La cliente Euh, oui, je cherche un bas de jogging et des chaussures de sport pour ce jeune garçon.

La vendeuse Oui, vous cherchez un jogging en coton ou en nylon ?

Le garçon J'aime bien celui-ci.

La vendeuse Lequel ?

Le garçon Celui-ci, le noir.

La vendeuse Celui-ci, oui… il est en nylon, c'est bien comme matière, c'est plus résistant et c'est plus chaud aussi. C'est plus facile d'entretien, ça sèche vite, et le noir, vous avez raison, c'est moins salissant. [*à la mère*] Quelle est sa taille ?

La cliente Il fait du 14 ans.

La vendeuse Alors, attendez, je regarde, voilà. Allez essayer.

[un moment plus tard]

La vendeuse Alors, ça va ?

Le garçon Oui, ça va, il est bien ce jogging-là.

La vendeuse Et pour les chaussures ? Qu'est-ce que vous cherchez ?

La cliente J'ai vu ces chaussures bleues, celles-là, en vitrine.

Le garçon Mais maman, j'aime pas le bleu…

La vendeuse Et, celles-ci en noir, elles te plaisent ?

Le garçon Oui, mais je préfére ces jaune-fluo.

La cliente Quelle est ta pointure ?

Le garçon Je fais du 39.

Dialogue 3

La cliente S'il vous plaît, est-ce que vous avez cette robe en rouge ?

La vendeuse Vous faites quelle taille ?

La cliente Du 40.

La vendeuse Je suis désolée, en 40, je n'ai plus que la verte ou la noire.

La cliente Et celle-ci, vous l'avez en 40 ?

La vendeuse Laquelle ?

La cliente Celle-ci avec les bretelles.

La vendeuse Oui, attendez un instant…

Dialogue 4

Gabin Tiens, regarde, j'aime bien ces deux canapés. Tu préfères lequel ?

Julien Ben, celui-ci, c'est un canapé-lit, c'est plus pratique pour les invités, mais je n'aime pas trop les carreaux, et celui-là est plus classe, mais plus encombrant.

Gabin Le canapé-lit, peut-être, c'est plus utile, mais j'aime bien la forme de celui-là, il existe en blanc et en bleu.

Julien Je préfère le bleu, c'est moins salissant, et j'aime bien la forme des coussins aussi.

Gabin Alors, qu'est-ce qu'on fait ?

La vendeuse On s'occupe de vous, messieurs ?

Track 9:5

Dialogue – Dans une papeterie

Le vendeur C'est à qui ?

Hugo Oui, c'est à moi. J'ai cet agenda, ces enveloppes, cette carte de vœux et je voudrais un stylo.

Le vendeur Alors, vous avez le stylo bille, le roller ou le stylo plume. Lequel vous préférez ?

Hugo J'ai vu un stylo plume dans la vitrine.

Le vendeur Oui, dans laquelle ?

Hugo Celle-là à droite.

Le vendeur Oui, alors, j'ai deux modèles. Vous avez celui-ci, très fin, très léger, ou celui-là, moins fragile.

Hugo Oui, celui-là, c'est bien, c'est pour mon neveu, pour le lycée. Je vais prendre celui-là.

Le vendeur Je vous fais un paquet cadeau ?

Hugo Oui, s'il vous plaît… C'est pour offrir, c'est pour la rentrée scolaire.

Le vendeur Alors, un agenda, des enveloppes, une carte de vœux et un stylo plume. Ça fait 48 euros 90.

Track 9:6

La vendeuse Bonjour. Je peux vous aider ?

(Say yes, you are looking for a diary.)

Vous Oui, je cherche un agenda.

La vendeuse Oui, alors, j'ai plusieurs modèles à des prix différents. Par exemple, j'ai celui-ci, très pratique pour mettre dans le sac, et celui-là, un peu moins cher mais un peu plus grand.

	(Say you have seen a red diary in the window.)
Vous	J'ai vu un agenda rouge dans la vitrine.
La vendeuse	Lequel ?
	(Say: this one, on the left.)
Vous	Celui-ci, à gauche.
La vendeuse	Ah, celui-ci est en cuir, et ceux-là sont aussi en cuir, mais plus grands, pour le bureau. Ils sont plus chers.
	(Say you are going to have this one, in leather.)
Vous	Je vais prendre celui-ci, en cuir.
La vendeuse	Lequel ? Et en quelle couleur ?
	(Say you want this big model in red.)
Vous	Je veux ce grand modèle en rouge.
La vendeuse	Je vous fais un paquet cadeau ?
	(Say yes please, it's for a gift.)
Vous	Oui, s'il vous plaît… C'est pour offrir.

Track 9:7

1 – Pardon madame, elle coûte combien cette robe ?
– 1.400 euros.
– Oh, mon Dieu! Mais il est en quoi le prix, en roubles ?

2 – C'est combien le kilo de pêches ?
– 8 euros 50.
– 8 euros 50, mais c'est pas possible ! Vous plaisantez ?

3 – Regarde le prix de cette montre: 125.000 euros !
– Mais je rêve ! Mais qui achète ça ?
– Ils sont fous !

4 – Ah, que c'est agréable, un bon sandwich et un café avec une vue panoramique superbe.
– Oui, mais regarde l'addition, 36 euros !
– Quoi ? Tu rigoles ?

Track 9:8

1 Je n'y crois pas !
2 C'est incroyable !
3 Mais j'hallucine !
4 Je rêve !
5 C'est pas possible !
6 C'est pas vrai !
7 Vous rigolez ?
8 Vous plaisantez ?
9 Ah bon !
10 Ça alors !
11 Ils sont fous !
12 Tu rigoles ?
13 Tu plaisantes !
14 Tu te moques de moi ?
15 Vous vous moquez de moi !
16 C'est une plaisanterie !

Track 9:9

Le serveur	Voilà, un café, deux croissants, un chocolat et une brioche. Ça fait 38 euros.
	(Say: How much? Say: It's impossible! You're having a laugh!)
Vous	Combien ? C'est pas possible ! Vous vous moquez de moi !
Une amie	Regarde cette robe, elle est chouette. Ah, mais elle coûte 500 euros !
	(Say: It's incredible!)
Vous	C'est incroyable !
La cliente	C'est combien ce stylo ? 80 euros ? Mais c'est une plaisanterie ?
	(Say: Well, I can't believe it!)
Vous	Ça alors ! Je n'y crois pas !

Track 9:10

La vendeuse	Voilà. Un beau paquet cadeau !
	(Say thank you and ask how much you owe.)
Vous	Merci. Combien je vous dois ?
La vendeuse	Alors, ça fait 72 euros. Vous réglez comment ?
	(Ask if they accept cheques.)
Vous	Vous acceptez les chèques ?

La vendeuse	Oui. Vous avez une pièce d'identité ?
	(Say sorry, you have no identity card with you.)
Vous	Ah, désolé(e), je n'ai pas de pièce d'identité sur moi.
La vendeuse	Alors, je ne peux pas accepter de paiement par chèque.
	(Say: Well, I can't believe it!)
Vous	Ça alors, c'est incroyable !

Track 9:11

Dialogue – À la caisse d'un supermarché

La caissière	178 euros 45, s'il vous plaît madame.
La cliente	Combien vous m'avez dit ?
La caissière	Ça fait 178 euros 45. Vous réglez comment ?
La cliente	Par carte. Euh, attendez, j'ai un bon de réduction pour la lessive.
La caissière	Merci. [...] Ah, je suis désolée madame, je ne peux pas l'accepter, il est périmé.
La cliente	Ah, bon ? Tant pis !
La caissière	Vous avez une carte de fidélité ? Je peux la valider.
La cliente	Oui.
La caissière	Voilà, merci. Vous avez votre carte de crédit, s'il vous plaît ?
La cliente	Oui, je vous la donne... Ah, voilà.
La caissière	Alors... Patientez un moment... Voilà. Tapez votre code s'il vous plaît.
[...]	Toutes mes excuses, madame. Je ne peux pas la prendre, on me dit que le code est érroné. Vous avez une autre carte ?
La cliente	Oui, j'ai deux autres cartes, attendez... Euh... Je ne les trouve pas...

Track 9:12

1 Tu aimes le chocolat ?
(oui – beaucoup)
Oui, je l'aime beaucoup.

2 Tu achètes tes légumes au marché ?
(non – au supermarché)
Non, je les achète au supermarché.

3 Tu passes tes commandes par catalogue ?
(oui – toujours)
Oui, je les passe toujours par catalogue.

4 Tu lis le journal dans le métro ?
(non – à la maison)
Non, je le lis à la maison.

5 Tu regardes souvent la télévision ?
(non – jamais)
Non, je ne la regarde jamais.

6 Tu écoutes cette émission à la radio ?
(non – sur internet)
Non, je l'écoute sur internet.

Track 9:13

1 Vous aimez le chocolat ?
(a) Oui, je l'aime beaucoup.
(b) Non, je ne l'aime pas du tout.

2 Vous achetez vos légumes au marché ?
(a) Oui, je les achète souvent au marché.
(b) Non, je les achète au supermarché.

3 Vous passez vos commandes par téléphone ?
(a) Oui, je les passe par téléphone de temps en temps.
(b) Non, je les passe toujours par internet.

4 Vous lisez le journal dans le métro ?
(a) Oui, je le lis dans le métro tous les matins.
(b) Non, je ne le lis jamais dans le métro.

5 Vous regardez souvent la télévision ?
(a) Oui, je la regarde très souvent.
(b) Non, je ne la regarde pas très souvent.

6 Vous écoutez cette émission à la radio ?
(a) Oui, je l'écoute tous les jours.
(b) Non, je ne l'écoute jamais.

Track 9:14

L'employée	Service billetterie et réservations, bonjour.
Le client	Oui bonjour. Je téléphone au sujet d'une commande.

L'employée Oui, vous pouvez me donner le numéro de référence de la commande ?

Le client Euh, attendez… Euh, non, je ne le trouve pas.

L'employée Vous avez commandé par internet? Vous avez dû recevoir un message de confirmation.

Le client Ah oui, ici, je l'ai trouvé. J'ai réservé deux billets pour le match de rugby Brive-Leicester. La référence, c'est RBL009.

L'employée Alors, un instant s'il vous plaît… Oui, alors nous avons bien enregistré votre commande.

Le client Oui, et vous l'avez confirmée effectivement, mais je n'ai toujours pas reçu mes billets.

L'employée Attendez, je vérifie… Vous avez réglé comment ?

Le client Eh ben, j'ai payé quand j'ai passé ma commande, par carte bleue en paiement sécurisé.

L'employée Écoutez, je ne comprends pas. Nous n'avons pas vos coordonnées bancaires. Je vais les reprendre.

Le client Mais je les ai données au moment de la commande.

L'employée Je suis vraiment désolée, monsieur, nous ne les avons pas conservées. Je dois absolument avoir ces informations, sinon je ne peux pas autoriser l'expédition des billets.

Le client Bon, bon, d'accord…

Track 9:15

Votre amie Regarde ce stylo plume.

(Say it's beautiful. Ask: Have you bought it in a paper shop?)

Vous Il est beau. Tu l'a acheté dans une papeterie ?

Votre amie Oui, je l'ai acheté aux Galeries Lafayette. Et, j'ai cette écharpe aussi.

(Say it's magnificent. Ask: Have you bought it at the Galeries Lafayette too?)

Vous C'est magnifique. Tu l'as achetée aux Galeries Lafayette aussi ?

(Say no, you didn't buy it there. You bought it in a small leather shop.)

Vous Non, je ne l'ai pas achetée là-bas. Je l'ai achetée dans une petite maroquinerie.

Votre amie Ils sont beaux ces cadeaux. Ils sont pour toi ?

(Say: no, you bought them for your friends Maurice and Elisabeth.)

Vous Non, je les ai achetés pour mes amis Maurice et Elisabeth.

(Ask: Have you invited them to your party?)

Vous Tu les a invités à ta fête ?

Votre amie Non, toute la famille est partie en week-end. Tu sais, ils ont acheté une maison de campagne.

(Say: Ah, yes, have you visited it?)

Vous Ah, oui ! Tu l'as visitée ?

Votre amie Oui, elle est superbe. Regarde, j'ai des photos.

(Say: Ah, when did you take them?)

Vous Ah, tu les as prises quand ?

Votre amie Cet été. Tu vois la piscine, c'est Maurice qui l'a faite lui-même.

(Repeat: Maurice has made it himself! But it's incredible!)

Vous Maurice l'a faite lui-même ! Mais c'est incroyable !

Track 9:16

Répondeur Bonjour, vous êtes bien chez LCJS. Tous nos opérateurs sont en ligne. Veuillez patienter quelques instants. Nous allons donner suite à votre appel.

L'employé LCJS, bonjour.

La cliente Ah, enfin ! Ça fait cinq minutes que je patiente…

L'employé Je suis vraiment désolé madame, mais nous sommes très occupés, nous avons beaucoup d'appels. Je pourrais avoir votre numéro de cliente, s'il vous plaît ?

La cliente Euh, oui, c'est ACL 269. J'ai passé une commande par internet, euh, fin mai, mais mon livre n'est toujours pas arrivé.

L'employé Alors… un petit moment, s'il vous plaît. Ah, voilà, Madame Béart. Nous avons expédié un DVD il y a trois jours. Vous l'avez bien reçu ?

La cliente Oui, oui, mais ça fait trois semaines que j'attends mon livre, et c'était dans la même commande. Je vous ai envoyé deux courriels, vous ne m'avez même pas répondu. Je ne suis pas du tout contente.

L'employé Je vous prie de nous excuser madame. Voyons, je vérifie votre commande… Ah, voilà le problème. Nous n'avons plus d'exemplaires de ce livre.

La cliente Mais c'est inadmissible ! Pourquoi ne m'avez-vous pas contactée pour m'expliquer le problème ?

L'employé Nous devons recevoir une livraison. Pouvez-vous attendre encore deux ou trois jours… ?

La cliente Mais vous plaisantez ! Attendre encore ? Ah, ça non. Je veux annuler ma commande immédiatement. Je vous demande de me rembourser dans les plus brefs délais. Je dois vous dire que je ne suis pas du tout contente de votre service. Ça fait dix ans que je suis cliente chez vous et c'est bien la dernière fois que je commande quelque chose !

L'employé Toutes nos excuses, madame. Je vais annuler la commande immédiatement. Alors, euh, référence ACL…

Track 9:17

Question Vous attendez votre remboursement depuis combien de temps ?

(dix jours)

Vous Ça fait dix jours que j'attends mon remboursement.

Question Vous patientez au téléphone depuis combien de temps ?

(quinze minutes)

Vous Ça fait quinze minutes que je patiente au téléphone.

Question Vous faites la queue depuis combien de temps ?

(un quart d'heure)

Vous Ça fait un quart d'heure que je fais la queue.

Question Ils cherchent votre numéro de client depuis combien de temps ?

(une demi-heure)

Vous Ça fait une demi-heure qu'ils cherchent mon numéro de client.

Question Vous attendez sa réponse depuis combien de temps ?

(huit jours)

Vous Ça fait huit jours que j'attends sa réponse.

Track 9:18

L'employé Commande Express, bonjour. Je peux vous aider ?

(Say you placed an order three weeks ago and you still haven't received it.)

Vous J'ai passé une commande il y a trois semaines et je ne l'ai toujours pas reçue.

L'employé Excusez-moi, je pourrais avoir votre numéro de cliente, s'il vous plaît ?

(Say it's HP08M.)

Vous C'est HP08M.

L'employé Merci. Un instant…

(Say you have sent them three emails.)

Vous Je vous ai envoyé trois courriels.

(Say they haven't even replied to you.)

Vous Vous ne m'avez même pas répondu.

(Say that's really unacceptable.)

Vous C'est vraiment inadmissible.

L'employé Je suis vraiment désolé. Vous pouvez attendre encore deux ou trois jours... ?

(Say you must be joking.)

Vous Vous plaisantez !

(Say you have been waiting for three weeks.)

Vous Ça fait trois semaines que j'attends.

(Say no, you want to cancel the order immediately.)

Vous Non, je veux annuler ma commande immédiatement.

(Say: and you ask to have your money back as soon as possible.)

Vous Et je vous demande un remboursement dans les plus brefs délais.

L'employé Bien sûr. Toutes nos excuses.

(Say you are very disappointed.)

Vous Je suis très déçu(e).

Track 9:19

Le client S'il vous plaît, je voudrais acheter une tablette tactile. Vous pouvez me renseigner ?

La vendeuse Oui, vous avez ces modèles avec wifi et Bluetooth, ils font 409 euros. Et vous avez ceux-là qui ont une capacité plus importante, à 489 euros.

Le client Et ceux-ci, pourquoi coûtent-ils 529 euros, ils ont la même capacité ?

La vendeuse Oui, mais ils ont un GPS incorporé.

Le client Vous faites une remise si je paies comptant ?

La vendeuse Ah, non je suis désolée, Monsieur, nous pratiquons la politique des prix bas, et vous ne pouvez pas trouver cet article meilleur marché.

Le client Et si je trouve moins cher dans un autre magasin, vous pouvez baisser le prix ?

La vendeuse Si vous le trouvez moins cher, nous vous remboursons la différence. Nous faisons aussi des remises de 30 à 60 pour cent en période de soldes.

Le client Ah, bien, très bien.

La vendeuse Vous bénéficiez aussi de plusieurs services gratuits compris dans le prix.

Le client Ah, oui, lesquels ?

La vendeuse Livraison gratuite, garantie gratuite pendant un an, assistance téléphonique gratuite et possibilité d'échange ou de remboursement de votre appareil si vous changez d'avis dans les dix jours.

Le client Alors, je vais acheter la tablette à 489 euros en noir.

La vendeuse Ah, je suis désolée, on n'a plus ce modèle en noir dans le magasin mais je peux la commander et nous proposons la livraison gratuite en 48 heures. Ça vous convient ?

Le client Oui, c'est parfait.

Track 9:20

Le vendeur Allô, Koria, services après-ventes, bonjour.

Le client Euh, oui, bonjour. J'ai acheté une tablette tactile il y a une semaine, et j'ai changé d'avis. Je la préfère en blanc. Je voudrais l'échanger.

Le vendeur Oui, vous avez votre numéro de commande ?

Le client Je l'ai achetée en magasin, c'est la tablette tactile TT 32 avec wifi et Bluetooth. Je la voudrais en blanc, mais j'en ai besoin dans une semaine absolument.

Le vendeur Alors, oui, c'est possible. Vous avez 10 jours pour retourner votre achat, et... attendez, je vérifie, oui elle est disponible, je peux l'expédier tout de suite et vous pouvez aller la chercher en magasin dans trois jours.

Le client C'est parfait, merci.

Track 9:21

Question Vous partez à Paris quand ?

(un mois)

Vous Je pars dans un mois.

Question Il commence son travail quand ?

(deux semaines)

Vous Il commence son travail dans deux semaines.

Question Elle est allée visiter l'Italie quand ?

(deux ans)

Vous Elle est allée visiter l'Italie il y a deux ans.

Question Votre mari a acheté sa tablette tactile quand ?

(six semaines)

Vous Il a acheté sa tablette tactile il y a six semaines.

Question Vous avez retourné votre achat quand ?

(trois jours – use *'nous')*

Vous Nous avons retourné notre achat il y a trois jours.

Track 9:22

Le vendeur Bonjour madame, je peux vous renseigner ?

La cliente Oui, je voudrais un appareil photo numérique.

Le vendeur Oui, alors vous avez du choix. Vous avez ceux qui ont un zoom numérique, ceux qui ont un zoom optique, et ceux qui ont un grand angle avec un écran, et celui qu'on solde, c'est un modèle plus vieux.

La cliente Cet appareil rouge là, c'est celui que je préfère. Il a un grand angle ?

Le vendeur Ah, non celui-ci, il a un zoom optique.

La cliente Et, ce noir, là, celui qui se trouve dans la vitrine, il a un grand angle ?

Le vendeur Oui, et si vous voulez un appareil avec un grand angle, c'est celui que je vous conseille.

La cliente Eh, bien je le prends. Ah, et j'ai vu vos offres promotionnelles sur internet. Est-ce que c'est celui qui est livré avec un étui rigide en cuir ?

Le vendeur Oui, tout à fait. Et c'est aussi celui que vous pouvez acheter sur internet. Si vous l'achetez sur internet, vous bénéficiez d'une réduction de 10 pour cent en plus !

Track 9:23

La cliente Bonjour, je voudrais une télévision haute définition, vous pouvez me renseigner ?

(Say: Yes, you have these models here, they cost 789 euros.)

Vous Oui, vous avez ces modèles, ici, ils font 789 euros.

(Say they have free warranty for three years.)

Vous Ils ont une garantie gratuite pendant trois ans.

La cliente Vous avez des modèles moins chers ?

(Say: Yes, this one which is in the window with a smaller screen.)

Vous Oui, celui qui est dans la vitrine avec un écran plus petit.

(Say: And this one which is in the sales. It's an older model.)

Vous Et celui qu'on solde. C'est un modèle plus vieux.

La cliente Et, il y a une garantie gratuite pendant trois ans sur celui-ci ?

(Ask which one.)

Vous Lequel ?

La cliente Sur celui que vous soldez ?

(Say: No, but we offer free delivery.)

Vous Non, mais nous proposons la livraison gratuite.

La cliente J'en ai besoin absolument tout de suite.

(Say: If you buy this TV now, you can receive it in two days' time.)

Vous Si vous achetez cette télévision maintenant, vous pouvez la recevoir dans deux jours.

La cliente Merci. C'est parfait. Je vais prendre celle-ci en solde.

(Ask how she wishes to pay.)

Vous Vous réglez comment ?

La cliente Par carte.

(Say: Oh… you have a further 10% reduction today!)

Vous Oh ! Vous bénéficiez d'une remise de 10 pour cent en plus aujourd'hui.

Unité 10

Track 10:1

Agnès Il faut bien dormir, il faut manger sainement, il faut profiter de la vie au maximum.

Philippe Il faut faire du sport, manger équilibré, et il faut dormir beaucoup.

Pascaline Pour être en forme, il faut bien manger et il faut marcher une heure par jour.

Jean-Claude Il faut bien dormir, il faut avoir un bon métier et il faut penser positivement.

Leïla Oui, je pense que pour être en bonne santé il faut d'abord garder le sourire, puis il faut manger sainement.

Sandrine Pour rester en forme, il faut éviter le stress et se détendre suffisamment.

Ahmed Il faut dormir beaucoup et faire de l'exercice régulièrement.

Céline Pour avoir la pêche, il faut boire deux verres de vin tous les jours et sortir avec ses amis !

Track 10:2

Interviewer Est-ce que vous fumez ?

Nathan

Nathan Je ne fume plus.

Interviewer Pourquoi ?

Nathan Parce que maintenant j'ai des enfants.

Lionel

Lionel Oui, je fume.

Interviewer Depuis longtemps ?

Lionel Oui, ça fait euh… je fume depuis dix ans, quinze ans.

Vanessa

Vanessa Je ne fume plus, mais j'ai fumé.

Interviewer Pourquoi avez-vous arrêté ?

Vanessa Alors, moi, je n'avais aucun problème quand je fumais, mais je pense que c'est tout à fait nocif pour la santé.

Marine

Marine Non, je ne fume pas.

Interviewer Vous n'avez jamais fumé ?

Marine Si, quand j'étais adolescente, j'ai fumé.

Interviewer Combien de cigarettes ?

Marine Oh, à l'époque je fumais environ dix cigarettes par jour.

Interviewer Et pourquoi vous vous êtes arrêtée ?

Marine Je me suis arrêtée de fumer quand je suis tombée enceinte de ma première fille.

Mehdi

Mehdi Moi, je n'ai jamais fumé. Je n'ai jamais aimé cela, et je trouve que c'est très mauvais pour la santé. Je voudrais interdire les cigarettes aux terrasses des restaurants ! Je déteste manger dans la fumée, c'est très désagréable.

Véronique

Véronique Moi, je veux arrêter mais c'est difficile.

Interviewer Et vous avez essayé un traitement pour arrêter ?

Véronique Non, je n'ai rien essayé pour l'instant, et je n'ai consulté personne mais je vais peut-être acheter des patchs ou alors aller voir un tabacologue.

Track 10:3

Interviewer Vous fumez ?

(Say no, you no longer smoke.)

Vous Non, je ne fume plus.

Interviewer Vous avez fumé pendant longtemps ?

(Say for about ten years when you were a teenager.)

Vous Pendant une dizaine d'années, quand j'étais adolescente.

Interviewer Pourquoi est-ce que vous avez arrêté ?

(Say you think it's very bad for one's health.)

Vous Je pense que c'est très mauvais pour la santé.

Interviewer Vous avez pris quelque chose pour vous aider ?

(Say, no, you took nothing.)

Vous Non, je n'ai rien pris.

Interviewer Vous avez vu un tabacologue ?

(Say no, you have never seen a therapist.)

Vous Non je n'ai jamais vu de tabacologue.

Track 10:4

Dialogue 1

Jennifer Décobureau, Jennifer à l'appareil.

Sandra Allô Jennifer, oui, bonjour. C'est Sandra. Je ne me sens pas très bien, donc, je ne vais pas venir au bureau aujourd'hui.

Jennifer Oh, mais qu'est-ce qui ne va pas ?

Sandra J'ai mal à la tête. J'ai chaud et froid. Enfin, ce n'est vraiment pas la forme, quoi… Je vais rester au lit.

Jennifer C'est la grippe ?

Sandra Non, je crois que j'ai attrapé un mauvais rhume.

Dialogue 2

Marc Ah, bonjour Nathalie, ton père, ça va mieux ?

Nathalie Non, pas vraiment. Il est toujours aussi fatigué et il dort beaucoup. Il a des vertiges et il a mal au ventre et ne mange presque plus, et en plus maintenant, il souffre de rhumatismes.

Marc Ta mère doit être inquiète.

Nathalie Oui, et comme, elle, elle ne dort part, elle est vraiment crevée.

Dialogue 3

Laurent Salut, ça va, toi ?

Nadja Oui, en pleine forme ! Et toi ?

Laurent Oh moi, bof, ça va sans plus.

Nadja Qu'est-ce qu'il y a ?

Laurent Je suis un peu déprimé. Je viens de perdre mon emploi.

Nadja Et ben dis donc. Oui, en effet, ce n'est pas marrant. Et ton frère, il travaillait dans la même boîte que toi, n'est-ce-pas ?

Laurent Oh mon frère, il est toujours stressé mais lui, ça va, il vient d'avoir une promotion !

Track 10:5

Amie Salut ! Comment ça va ?

(Say so-so.)

Vous Bof, ça va, sans plus.

Amie Qu'est-ce qui ne va pas ?

(Say you are not feeling too good, you are very tired.)

Vous Je ne me sens pas bien, je suis très fatiguée.

Amie Ah bon et pourquoi ?

(Say you have a very bad toothache.)

Vous J'ai très mal aux dents.

(Say you're not sleeping well.)

Vous Je ne dors pas bien.

Track 10:6

Amie Alors comment ça va aujourd'hui ?

(Say you are on top form.)

Vous Je suis en pleine forme !

Amie Alors tu n'as plus mal aux dents ?

(Say no. You're feeling much better.)

Vous Non, ça va beaucoup mieux.

Track 10:7

moi
oui
poids
loin
doigt
noir
bois
ouest
Guadeloupe
louer

Track 10:8

lui
nuit
pluie
fruit
bruit
huit
puis
suis

Track 10:9

1 froid
2 cuisine
3 rien
4 huile
5 pourquoi
6 vois
7 aujourd'hui
8 gallois
9 cuit
10 produit
11 oie
12 Guyane
13 rhume
14 jouais
15 juin
16 juillet
17 lundi
18 minuit
19 vitamines
20 huître

Track 10:10

1 Tu as eu froid aujourd'hui ?
2 Oui, c'est une oie.
3 Ce bruit, je crois que c'est la pluie.
4 Moi, je suis arrivé(e) à l'heure.
5 C'est le huit juin à minuit.
6 C'est chez toi ou c'est chez lui ?
7 Tu as pris un fruit, toi aussi ?
8 Je dois manger des produits frais.

Track 10:11

Question Vous faites du sport pour rester en forme ?

(Say yes, you play tennis.)

Vous Oui, moi, je joue au tennis.

Question Et vos enfants ? Qu'est-ce qu'ils font ?

(Say your daughter does a lot of sport.)

Vous Ma fille, elle, elle fait beaucoup de sport.

Question Et votre fils, il est sportif ?

(Say your son is not fit, he goes out and goes to bed after midnight every day.)

Vous Mon fils, lui, il n'est pas en forme. Il sort et se couche tous les jours après minuit.

Question Et votre femme, qu'est-ce qu'elle fait, elle, pour rester en forme ?

(Say your wife watches her weight. She eats a lot of fruit.)

Vous Ma femme, elle, elle surveille son poids. Elle mange beaucoup de fruits.

Question Et elle fait du sport ?

(Say no, your wife spends time in the kitchen cooking healthy meals.)

Vous Ah, non, ma femme, elle, elle passe son temps dans la cuisine pour préparer des repas équilibrés.

Track 10:12

Jacques

Interviewer Jacques, est-ce que vous avez déjà eu un accident ?

Jacques Oui, j'ai eu un accident de moto très grave il y a environ vingt ans.

Interviewer Qu'est-ce qui vous est arrivé ?

Jacques Je me suis cassé une jambe et un bras et je me suis fracturé le bassin. J'ai passé deux mois à l'hôpital et puis j'ai fait de la rééducation.

Interviewer Et maintenant, vous êtes tout à fait rétabli ?

Jacques Ma jambe me fait mal de temps en temps, je boite un peu, je ne roule plus en moto !

Guillaume

Interviewer Et vous Guillaume, vous avez déjà eu un accident ?

Guillaume Oui, je me suis cassé le nez et déboîté une épaule.

Interviewer Vous faisiez de la boxe ?

Guillaume Non, je jouais au rugby. J'ai dû arrêter de jouer pendant un an et j'ai eu des séances de kiné pendant six mois. J'ai beaucoup grossi.

Interviewer Et maintenant, ça va ?

Guillaume Ah oui, tout à fait, mais peut-être un peu moins beau qu'avant ! Mais je joue toujours au rugby !

Margaux

Interviewer Margaux, vous avez déjà eu un accident ?

Margaux Oui, l'année dernière j'ai glissé dans la neige et je me suis fracturé une cheville. J'ai eu un plâtre pendant six semaines.

Interviewer Et vous êtes complètement remise aujourd'hui ?

Margaux Oui ça va, mais ma cheville me fait mal de temps en temps. Mais j'ai un bon souvenir, j'ai gardé le plâtre, avec toutes les signatures de mes amis !

Annie

Interviewer Annie, vous avez déjà eu un accident ?

Annie Oui, quand j'étais petite je me suis gravement brûlé la main gauche.

Interviewer Qu'est-ce qui s'est passé ?

Annie Je jouais avec des allumettes, comme beaucoup d'enfants. J'ai passé trois semaines à l'hôpital, j'ai dû avoir une greffe. Ma mère s'est beaucoup inquiétée !

Interviewer Et aujourd'hui, tout va bien ?

Annie Oui, tout à fait, je n'ai pas de problème mais je n'ai pas oublié cet accident, j'ai eu très peur !

Raoul

Interviewer Et vous Raoul, vous avez déjà eu un accident ?

Raoul Oui, j'ai eu un accident de travail assez sérieux.

Interviewer Qu'est-ce que vous avez fait ?

Raoul Je me suis coupé le doigt avec un cutter. J'ai eu une opération. Je n'ai pas travaillé pendant six mois.

Interviewer Et vous êtes complètement remis maintenant ?

Raoul Oui, à peu près. Mais, j'ai changé de travail. Je ne travaille plus avec des objets coupants.

Track 10:13

1 **Question** Qu'est-ce qui vous est arrivé ?

(Say you broke your nose.)

Vous Je me suis cassé le nez.

Question Comment ?

(Say you were playing rugby.)

Vous Je jouais au rugby.

Question Et maintenant, ça va ?

(Say, yes you are feeling better but you have a crooked nose.)

Vous Oui, je vais mieux mais j'ai le nez tordu.

2 **Question** Vous avez déjà eu un accident ?

(Say yes, you fell down the stairs two months ago and hurt your back.)

Vous Je suis tombée dans les escaliers il y a deux mois et je me suis fait mal au dos.

Question Vous êtes allée à l'hôpital ?

(Say, no but your back hurt for six months, you stopped sports and you put on a lot of weight.)

Vous Non, mais j'ai eu mal au dos pendant six mois, j'ai arrêté le sport, j'ai beaucoup grossi.

Question Et, vous êtes complètement remise ?

(Say you feel better but your back still hurts from time to time.)

Vous Ça va mieux mais mon dos me fait toujours mal de temps en temps.

3 **Question** Vous avez eu un accident ?

(Say yes, you had an accident at work, you fell off a ladder and fractured your pelvis.)

Vous Oui, j'ai eu un accident de travail. Je suis tombé d'une échelle et je me suis fracturé le bassin.

Question Et vous êtes allé à l'hôpital ?

(Say yes, you stayed there for two months. You had a cast and you had physiotherapy for six months.)

Vous Oui, j'y suis resté pendant deux mois. J'ai eu un plâtre et j'ai fait de la rééducation pendant six mois.

Question Et maintenant, vous êtes complètement rétabli ?

(Say yes, you're on top form.)

Vous Oui, je suis en pleine forme.

Track 10:14

Interviewer Bonjour Lucia. Vous êtes de quelle nationalité ?

(Say you are Italian.)

Lucia Je suis italienne.

Interviewer Et vous allez finir vos études dans quel pays ?

(Say you are going to finish your studies in France.)

Lucia Je vais finir mes études en France.

Interviewer Et vous êtes enceinte ?

(Say yes, you will give birth in France in two months' time.)

Lucia Oui, j'accoucherai en France dans deux mois.

Interviewer Vous êtes couverte par la Sécurité sociale ?

(Say yes, but you will have to request a European medical card in Italy.)

Lucia Oui, mais je devrai demander une carte européenne d'assurance maladie en Italie.

Interviewer Et comment ça marche, vous serez couverte intégralement ?

(Say you will be entitled to the necessary treatment and say you will be treated as if you were insured in France.)

Lucia J'aurai droit aux soins médicaux nécessaires. Je serai traitée comme si j'étais assurée en France.

Interviewer Vous devrez payer ?

(Say yes, you will pay the medical expenses and then you will have to claim the money back.)

Lucia Oui, je paierai les frais d'accouchement et je devrai ensuite demander le remboursement.

Track 10:15

Comment s'appelle le système de santé dans votre pays ?

Comment ça marche ?

Est-ce que l'équivalent de la carte vitale existe dans votre pays ?

Devez-vous payer les consultations chez le médecin traitant, ou chez les spécialistes comme les dentistes, les ophtalmologistes, les gynécologues par exemple ?

Est-ce que le système des mutuelles existe ?

Faut-il payer les médicaments chez le pharmacien et les frais à l'hôpital ?

Track 10:16

Interviewer Comment s'appelle le système de santé dans votre pays ?

Suzanne Alors, au Québec, le système s'appelle la RAMQ, c'est-à-dire la Régie de l'assurance maladie du Québec.

Daniel En Belgique, ce sont des caisses privées. Pour pouvoir bénéficier des soins de santé et indemnités, il faut obligatoirement avoir une mutuelle, une partie de votre salaire est utilisé pour payer les cotisations.

Interviewer Et comment ça marche ?

Suzanne La RAMQ est un programme universel gratuit et toute personne qui habite légalement au Québec a droit à tous soins dans le cadre de ce programme. Les soins médicaux couverts par le régime d'assurance maladie sont ceux qui sont nécessaires sur le plan médical et rendus par un médecin omnipraticien (appelé aussi « médecin de famille » ou « médecin généraliste ») ou par un médecin spécialiste. Ces services sont couverts, donc gratuits, peu importe l'endroit où ils sont rendus : cabinet privé, centre hospitalier, centre d'hébergement et de soins de longue durée, centre de réadaptation ou domicile du patient.

Daniel Aujourd'hui, le système des soins de santé belge est accessible à la majeure partie de la population. Si on est malade, on s'adresse le plus généralement à son médecin généraliste (aussi appelé « médecin traitant ») qui assure les soins de première ligne. Tous les professionnels de la santé sont contrôlés par les autorités publiques fédérales pour vous dispenser les meilleurs soins.

Interviewer Est-ce que l'équivalent de la carte vitale existe dans votre pays ?

Suzanne Oui, tous les résidents ont une carte d'assurance maladie qui donne accès aux services de santé couverts dans le cadre du régime.

Daniel Non, pas en Belgique.

Interviewer Devez-vous payer les consultations chez le médecin traitant, ou chez les spécialistes comme les dentistes, les ophtalmologistes, les gynécologues par exemple ?

Suzanne Non, si vous avez une carte d'assurance maladie, la plupart des médecins l'accepte comme paiement de leurs honoraires. On les appelle des médecins participants. Ils sont payés par la Régie de l'assurance maladie du Québec. Mais, certains médecins ne participent pas au régime d'assurance maladie. Ce sont des médecins non participants. Ils n'acceptent pas la carte d'assurance maladie comme paiement de leurs honoraires et ils déterminent eux-mêmes leurs tarifs. Dans ces cas-là, le patient doit payer la consultation.

Daniel Oui, en Belgique, on doit payer les consultations.

Interviewer Est-ce que le système des mutuelles existe ?

Suzanne La plupart des gens qui travaillent au Québec ont une mutuelle qui est payée par leur employeur.

Daniel Alors, en Belgique, la mutuelle est obligatoire et l'assurance privée est facultative. La mutuelle rembourse les consultations, par exemple.

Interviewer Faut-il payer les médicaments chez le pharmacien et les frais à l'hôpital ?

Suzanne Non, les médicaments et les frais hospitaliers sont gratuits avec la carte d'assurance maladie.

Daniel Oui, il faut payer et la mutuelle vous rembourse ensuite, mais pas intégralement pour l'hôpital. Si vous avez une assurance privée, c'est elle qui paiera la différence. Si vous n'en avez pas, c'est à votre charge. Si vous êtes à la retraite, vous êtes couverts à cent pour cent.

Track 10:17

Dialogue 1

Le patient Bonjour, docteur. Je ne vais pas bien en ce moment. J'ai chaud, j'ai froid, j'ai des douleurs dans les jambes et je suis très, très fatigué.

Le docteur Ah ! C'est la grippe, il y a une épidémie en ce moment. Prenez du paracétamol ou de l'ibuprofène. Buvez beaucoup et reposez-vous.

Le patient Je ne peux pas prendre de l'ibuprofène, j'ai de l'asthme.

Le docteur Alors je vais vous donner du paracétamol. Prenez-le trois fois par jour après manger, mais ne le prenez pas pendant plus d'une semaine et revenez dans quelques jours si ça ne va pas mieux.

Dialogue 2

Le docteur Alors, qu'est-ce qui vous arrive, Madame Delors ?

La patiente Je ne sais pas docteur. J'ai très mal à la gorge, et je ne mange pas beaucoup. Je crois que j'ai un peu de fièvre et je ne peux rien faire. Je suis épuisée.

Le docteur Alors, je vais vous ausculter... Oui, c'est une angine aigüe. Je vais vous prescrire des antibiotiques. Vous n'êtes pas allergique à la pénicilline ?

La patiente Non, je ne crois pas.

Le docteur Prenez deux comprimés matin et soir pendant sept jours. Prenez-les au moment des repas. En cas d'allergie, arrêtez le traitement immédiatement. Vous avez votre carte vitale ?

La patiente Oui, la voilà.

Le docteur Bon, j'espère que ça ira mieux. Ne vous fatiguez pas trop et finissez vos antibiotiques, une angine mal soignée, c'est mauvais.

Dialogue 3

La pharmacienne Bonjour, Odile. Qu'est-ce qui ne va pas ?

La cliente Bonjour, Amélie. Je ne me sens pas bien depuis hier. J'ai une rougeur là, dans le cou et j'ai mal au cœur, j'ai des vertiges et j'ai un peu mal à la tête. Tu peux me donner un conseil ?

La pharmacienne C'est peut-être quelque chose que tu as mangé. Qu'est-ce que tu as mangé hier ?

La cliente Hier soir je suis allée au restaurant avec des amis, nous avons partagé une pizza aux tomates, aux poivrons et au fromage.

La pharmacienne C'est probablement une réaction allergique aux tomates et aux poivrons. Je vais te donner des comprimés antihistaminiques. Prends-les pendant deux jours mais ne les prends pas à jeun. Ne mange pas de nourriture épicée et ne bois pas d'alcool. Ne t'inquiète pas, ça va passer, mais repose-toi et va voir le médecin si ça ne va pas mieux d'ici deux jours !

La cliente D'accord. Merci.

Track 10:18

Marie-Claude Salut. Puh, ce n'est pas la forme aujourd'hui.

(Ask Marie-Claude what's wrong with her.)

Vous Qu'est-ce qui ne va pas ?

Marie-Claude J'ai très très mal à la tête.

(Tell her to take some ibuprofen and go to bed.)

Vous Prends de l'ibuprofen et couche-toi.

Marie-Claude J'ai pris deux comprimés il y a deux heures. J'ai toujours très mal et maintenant j'ai des vertiges.

(Tell her to rest for a while and ring the doctor.)

Vous Repose-toi un moment et téléphone au médecin.

Marie-Claude Je pense que c'est tout simplement un rhume.

(Tell her to call him this evening if she doesn't feel any better.)

Vous Appelle-le ce soir si ça ne va pas mieux.

(Ask Marie-Claude how her back is.)

Vous Et ton dos, comment ça va ?

Marie-Claude Bof, ça va, sans plus. Je prends des anti-inflammatoires mais ils me donnent mal à l'estomac.

(Tell her to take them with meals, not to take them on an empty stomach.)

Vous Prends-les pendant les repas. Ne les prends pas à jeun.

Marie-Claude Oui, tu as raison. Je dois les prendre avec les repas, mais je les oublie toujours.

(Tell her to exercise a bit and eat healthily.)

Vous Fais un peu d'exercice et mange sainement.

(And tell her not to worry, it will get better in a few days' time.)

Vous Et ne t'inquiète pas, ça ira mieux dans quelques jours.

Marie-Claude Oui, j'espère. Merci de tes conseils.

Track 10:19

Interviewer Qu'est-ce que vous avez dans votre armoire à pharmacie ?

Pierre

Pierre Alors, moi, j'ai de l'aspirine, des gélules d'ibuprofen, j'ai du bicarbonate de soude et des pastilles pour le mal de gorge.

Interviewer Le bicarbonate de soude, c'est pour quoi ?

Pierre C'est pour aider la digestion. Oui, le bicarbonate de soude, j'en prends régulièrement, parce que j'ai souvent des brûlures d'estomac.

Interviewer Et ça se prend comment ?

Pierre Ça se vend en comprimés effervescents. Il faut diluer un ou deux comprimés dans un verre d'eau.

Julien

Julien J'ai des sachets de paracétamol, de l'alcool à quatre-vingt-dix degrés et des sparadraps. J'ai aussi des somnifères. Comme soixante-deux pour cent des Français, apparemment, j'ai des troubles du sommeil. J'en prends un tous les soirs. Et ma femme, elle a de l'aspirine pour les maux de tête et de l'eau oxygénée pour désinfecter les plaies et soigner les petits bobos.

Interviewer Et c'est tout ?

Julien Euh, on a aussi une crème pour les piqûres d'insectes et de la pommade à l'arnica pour les coups. On en utilise beaucoup quand les petits-enfants sont à la maison !

Marie

Marie Alors, moi j'ai surtout des médicaments homéopathiques. J'en prends pour tout un tas de choses.

Interviewer Par exemple ?

Marie J'utilise de la crème au propolis. J'ai la peau très sèche, j'en passe tous les matins.

Interviewer Et puis ?

Marie J'ai du magnésium. J'en fait des cures deux fois par mois, c'est bon pour lutter contre le stress.

Interviewer Et vous avez des médicaments pour les douleurs, de l'aspirine ?

Marie Non, j'en utilise très peu. Je préfère me soigner avec des méthodes naturelles.

Track 10:20

Dialogue 1

Amélie Je ne dors pas avant trois heures du matin. Je pense au travail... Je suis fatiguée toute la journée. J'ai besoin de décompresser.

Samantha Vous devriez essayer le yoga. C'est excellent pour se détendre. Et, je vous conseille aussi de faire une cure de magnésium, c'est très bon pour le stress. Et, rassurez-vous, moi aussi je pense toujours au travail !

Dialogue 2

Thierry Je ne suis pas en forme en ce moment. J'ai souvent des migraines.

Annie Alors, pour les migraines, je te recommande la camomille. Fais-en bouillir six à huit feuilles pour faire une tisane, et bois-en un verre tous les matins. Tu verras, ça ira mieux.

Dialogue 3

Thomas Ah, docteur, j'ai toujours des brûlures d'estomac après manger. Je suis souvent en déplacement d'affaires, je mange régulièrement au restaurant.

Le docteur Et bien vous devriez manger plus lentement, il faudrait aussi éviter les nourritures trop grasses et trop épicées. Et buvez, buvez beaucoup entre les repas. Et je vous suggère aussi de boire des tisanes à la menthe, c'est bon pour la digestion. Allez, ne vous inquiétez pas, ce n'est pas grave, ça devrait passer.

Track 10:21

Anna Je dors mal la nuit parce que je pense à mon travail. Je suis stressée et très fatiguée.

(Talking to your boss.)

Pierre J'ai pris cinq kilos en trois mois.

(Talking to your brother.)

Sandrine J'ai une migraine.

(Talking to a friend.)

Matthieu J'ai une rage de dents terrible !

(Talking to your neighbour.)

Luc Je me suis cassé le poignet au squash et foulé la cheville en montagne. Sans parler de mon genou tordu au ski !

(Talking to your colleague.)

Track 10:22

Anna Je dors mal la nuit parce que je pense à mon travail. Je suis stressée et très fatiguée.

Vous Vous devriez aller au lit à la même heure tous les soirs. Et faites du yoga, ça détend ! Et je vous recommande de prendre du magnésium, c'est bon pour le stress !

Pierre J'ai pris cinq kilos en trois mois.

Vous Tu devrais faire du sport et puis il faudrait faire un régime aussi, enfin, il faudrait manger plus équilibré.

Sandrine J'ai une migraine.

Vous Pour soigner la migraine, je te recommande la camomille. Bois-en une tisane et couche-toi.

Matthieu J'ai une rage de dents terrible !

Vous Prenez vite un rendez-vous chez le dentiste. En attendant, faites des bains de bouche.

Luc Je me suis cassé le poignet au squash et foulé la cheville en montagne. Sans parler de mon genou tordu au ski !

Vous Vous devriez arrêter de faire du sport, et je vous conseille d'utiliser de la pommade à l'arnica pour les coups !

Track 10:23

Présentatrice Alors, nous avons voulu savoir ce que les Français pensaient des médecines douces. Pour débattre de cette question, nous avons invité aujourd'hui Nicolas, père de famille.

Nicolas Bonjour, merci de m'avoir invité.

Présentatrice Alice, retraitée.

Alice Bonjour.

Présentatrice Isabelle, chef d'entreprise.

Isabelle Bonjour à tous.

Présentatrice Martin, médecin généraliste.

Martin Bonjour.

Présentatrice Et Philippe, exploitant agricole.

Philippe Bonjour.

Présentatrice Alors, vous Nicolas, par exemple, vous utilisez des médecines douces ?

Nicolas Moi, oui, j'utilise l'homéopathie essentiellement, pour soigner mes enfants et je fais aussi quelques séances de réflexologie de temps en temps.

Isabelle Eh bien moi, je suis tout à fait contre, franchement. Je trouve que les médecines douces exploitent la naïveté des gens. L'homéopathie ou l'acupuncture, qu'est-ce qui prouve que ça marche vraiment ? Non, pour moi c'est du pipeau tout ça.

Nicolas Non, au contraire je ne suis pas d'accord avec vous. Tenez, prenez la pommade à l'arnica, par exemple, c'est très efficace pour les bleus.

Isabelle Oui, c'est vrai, mais vous parlez de soigner des petits bobos, pas des maladies graves.

Présentatrice Et vous Alice, qu'est-ce que vous en pensez ?

Alice Moi, comme Isabelle, je suis contre. Il y a cinq ans, j'ai voulu arrêter de fumer. J'ai fait de l'acupuncture et ça n'a pas du tout marché.

Martin Moi, je suis plutôt pour. Je pense que si on peut se soigner de manière plus naturelle, c'est mieux. Tenez, prenez l'ostéopathie par exemple. J'avais des douleurs de dos et dans les épaules, j'ai fait des séances chez un ostéopathe, et il m'a complètement guéri, et je n'ai pris ni anti-inflammatoires, ni autres médicaments nocifs.

Nicolas Je suis tout à fait d'accord avec vous, Martin. Ma mère a fait des cures pour soigner un psoriasis. Elle est allée dans le Massif Central pendant deux ou trois ans pendant ses vacances pour se faire soigner par les eaux de source et elle ne souffre plus du tout maintenant.

Isabelle Et elle a été remboursée par la Sécurité sociale, j'imagine. Moi, je trouve que c'est scandaleux !

Nicolas Oui, mais vous savez, elle n'est pas allée à La Roche-Posay pendant ses vacances pour faire une cure de jouvence, mais pour soigner une grave maladie de la peau, et dans son cas, ça a marché.

Présentatrice Et vous Philippe, qu'est-ce que vous en pensez ?

Philippe Moi, je ne sais pas. Je n'utilise pas les médecines douces tout simplement parce que quand je suis malade, je vais chez le médecin, il me prescrit des médicaments, et voilà. Je suis ni pour, ni contre. Je n'ai pas d'exemples pour dire si ça marche, mais je n'ai rien qui prouve le contraire. Je ne les utilise pas, c'est pas pour ça non plus que je n'y crois pas. Par contre, je sais que la médecine conventionnelle est efficace.

Alice À mon avis, c'est psychologique. Si on y croit, ça marche, et si on n'y croit pas, ça ne marche pas !

Présentatrice Et bien, je vous remercie tous.

Invités Merci. Merci. Merci, au revoir.

Track 10:24

Question Vous êtes pour ou contre l'homéopathie ?

(Say you are against it.)

Vous Je suis contre.

Question Pourquoi ?

(Say you don't know if it really works.)

Vous Je ne sais pas si ça marche vraiment.

Question Qu'est-ce que vous pensez des cures thermales ?

(Say you're rather in favour.)

Vous Je suis plutôt pour.

Question Pourquoi ?

(Say your wife went to a treatment centre for skin problems and now she is completely cured.)

Vous Ma femme a fait une cure pour des problèmes de peau et maintenant elle est complètement guérie.

Question Et l'acupuncture, qu'en pensez-vous ?

(Say you are neither for nor against.)

Vous Je ne suis ni pour ni contre.

Question Et la sophrologie ?

(Say you think it's no great shakes.)

Vous Je pense que c'est du pipeau.

Question Alors en fait vous êtes plutôt contre les médecines douces ?

(Say it's very controversial, and say in your opinion, it's all in your mind.)

Vous C'est très contesté, mais à mon avis c'est psychologique.

Track 10:25

Dialogue 1

L'herboriste Bonjour Madame, je peux vous aider ?

La cliente Eh, oui, j'ai des insomnies. Mon médecin m'a prescrit des somnifères mais je ne me sens pas bien le matin. Vous avez quelque chose pour traiter les insomnies ?

L'herboriste Alors, oui, bien sûr, la valériane. Ses tiges et racines agissent sur le cerveau, c'est très efficace, vous dormez bien et le matin vous êtes en pleine forme. Prenez-la en tisane, une tasse le soir avant d'aller au lit.

Dialogue 2

L'herboriste Bonjour Monsieur, je peux vous renseigner ?

Le client Oui, je suis toujours fatigué, je manque d'énergie. Qu'est-ce que vous pouvez me conseiller ?

L'herboriste Essayez le ginseng. C'est une plante incroyable qui augmente votre performance intellectuelle et votre résistance au stress. Prenez-le en poudre. Diluez une cuillère dans du thé ou du café tous les matins.

Dialogue 3

L'herboriste Bonjour Madame, vous désirez ?

La cliente Bonjour. Je suis un peu déprimée. Vous pouvez me recommander un remède efficace ?

L'herboriste Alors, pour les dépressions légères, prenez du millepertuis. Sa substance a le même effet sur le cerveau que les antidépresseurs mais avec moins d'effets secondaires. Mais si ça ne marche pas, allez consulter votre médecin.

Unité 11

Track 11:1

Agnès

Question Est-ce que Grenoble a beaucoup changé ?

Agnès Oui, la ville de Grenoble a beaucoup changé. Par exemple, il y a un peu moins de circulation et plus de transports en commun grâce au tramway. Et avec la création de plus de pistes cyclables, les gens prennent moins leur voiture et se déplacent plus en vélo.

Question La ville est plus verte ?

Agnès C'est ça ! On a aussi construit plus de bâtiments écologiques. Par exemple il y a un éco-quartier qui a reçu un prix. Bref, il y a moins de pollution qu'avant.

Question Et la population ?

Agnès L'université est dynamique et donc il y a toujours autant d'étudiants à Grenoble. Il y a aussi beaucoup d'entreprises liées aux technologies de pointe, qui attirent des chercheurs. Il n'y avait pas autant de cadres internationaux autrefois.

Philippe

Question La Rochelle est très différente maintenant ?

Philippe Oui, elle est beaucoup plus grande. Il y a beaucoup plus de jeunes que dans le passé puisqu'il y a une université depuis 1993. Mais certaines choses ne changent pas : la mer est magnifique, le climat est agréable, les bâtiments historiques sont exceptionnels. Il y a autant d'avantages à vivre à La Rochelle qu'autrefois, et de moins en moins d'inconvénients !

Question Est-ce qu'il y beaucoup de circulation ?

Philippe Avant, il y avait de plus en plus de problèmes de circulation, et donc plus de pollution. Il était aussi très difficile de se garer et de circuler dans les petites rues du centre-ville. Mais maintenant il y a moins de voitures, plus de piétons et plus de vélos dans le centre : la Rochelle a une des premières zones piétonnes de France, et il y a aussi de plus en plus de cyclistes. Ça c'est beaucoup mieux.

Question Alors vous appréciez cette ville ?

Philippe Beaucoup. Je l'aime de plus en plus !

Track 11:2

1881 (mille huit cent quatre-vingt-un)

1950 (mille neuf cent cinquante)

1999 (mille neuf cent quatre-vingt-dix-neuf)

1974 (mille neuf cent soixante-quatorze)

1945 (mille neuf cent quarante-cinq)

1967 (mille neuf cent soixante-sept)

1936 (mille neuf cent trente-six)

Track 11:3

1881 (mille huit cent huitante-et-un)

1999 (mille neuf cent nonante-neuf)

1974 (mille neuf cent septante-quatre)

Track 11:4

Avant 1642, la calculatrice n'existait pas.

Avant 1688, on ne buvait pas de champagne.

Avant 1816, on ne pouvait pas faire de photos.

Avant 1829, l'alphabet Braille n'existait pas.

Avant 1865, on ne pratiquait pas la pasteurisation.

Avant 1884, il n'y avait pas de poubelles à Paris.

Avant 1894, on n'avait pas inventé le cinéma.

Avant 1974, les cartes à puce n'existaient pas.

Avant 1980, on ne prenait pas le TGV.

Avant 2002, on ne payait pas en euros.

Track 11:5

Personnellement, je trouve que le passé, ce n'était pas exactement le « bon vieux temps » comme certains le disent. Je vais expliquer pourquoi en vous parlant de trois domaines : le travail, la technologie et la santé.

Tout d'abord, à mon avis, autrefois on travaillait plus assidûment et on se reposait moins souvent. Par exemple, ma pauvre grand-mère passait tout son temps dans la cuisine parce que toute la famille rentrait manger à la maison à midi. Et mon grand-père faisait les trois-huit dans une usine. Les « trente-cinq heures » n'existaient pas, les congés payés non plus ! Les gens avaient plus fréquemment des emplois manuels, moi je n'aimerais pas ça, je préfère mon emploi de bureau.

Ensuite, on n'avait pas autant d'appareils ou de technologies pour nous aider. Par exemple, ma grand-mère, qui s'occupait de sa maison et de sa famille, n'avait pas de machine à laver le linge, de lave-vaisselle ou d'aspirateur. Et les usines étaient moins automatisées. Toutes ces machines ont complètement transformé notre vie. Et aujourd'hui, avec le portable et l'internet, on communique aussi plus rapidement.

Enfin n'oublions pas non plus les progrès de la médecine. Autrefois, quand on tombait malade, on guérissait moins rapidement sans les traitements modernes. De nos jours, grâce aux transports on peut voir un médecin ou aller à l'hôpital et se faire soigner plus vite. Et grâce à la sécurité sociale, tout le monde a accès aux soins médicaux. Du temps de mes grands-parents, ça ne se faisait pas aussi facilement.

Ainsi je pense qu'il ne faut pas considérer le présent et l'avenir avec pessimisme : tout n'était pas rose autrefois, le passé avait bien des inconvénients.

Track 11:6

(a) On n'a plus de temps.

(b) On a plus de temps.

Track 11:7

1 Elle appréciait plus la nature.
2 On communique plus rapidement.
3 Grenoble est une ville plus animée.
4 On n'a plus de temps.
5 Il y a plus de grandes surfaces.
6 On possède plus de voitures qu'avant.
7 Ils n'habitent plus en ville.
8 La Rochelle est beaucoup plus polluée.
9 Je voyage plus que mon arrière-grand-mère.
10 Elle s'habille plus élégamment.

Track 11:8

1 On n'a plus de grandes surfaces dans ma ville.
2 On n'a plus de temps pour se détendre.
3 On utilise plus de téléphones portables.
4 On appréciait plus la nature.
5 On n'aime plus les vacances à l'étranger.

Track 11:9

1 (a) On a plus de grandes surfaces dans ma ville.
  (b) On n'a plus de grandes surfaces dans ma ville.

2 (a) On a plus de temps pour se détendre.
  (b) On n'a plus de temps pour se détendre.

3 (a) On utilise plus de téléphones portables.
  (b) On n'utilise plus de téléphones portables.

4 (a) On appréciait plus la nature.
  (b) On n'appréciait plus la nature.

5 (a) On aime plus les vacances à l'étranger.
  (b) On n'aime plus les vacances à l'étranger.

Track 11:10

Ma famille est originaire de Suisse : mon grand-père Camille est né en 1912 dans un petit hameau du Jura suisse. Mon frère jumeau et moi sommes nés en Suisse en 1966 et nous avons passé notre enfance en Suisse et notre adolescence en Belgique. Mes frères Jacques et Félix habitent en Suisse. Moi je me suis marié et je me suis installé en Angleterre en 1991. J'y habite toujours. Cette année, au mois de septembre, le grand-père a eu 100 ans. On a fait une de ces viguétzes !

Track 11:11

Question Daniel est né en quelle année ?

(Say he was born in 1966)

Answer Il est né en 1966.

Question Il est né dans quel pays ? Et dans quelle ville ?

(Say he was born in Switzerland, near Geneva.)

Answer Il est né en Suisse, près de Genève.

Question Il a passé sa jeunesse où ?

(Say he spent his childhood in Switzerland and his teenage years in Belgium.)

Answer Il a passé son enfance en Suisse et son adolescence en Belgique.

Question Il est marié ?

(Say yes, he got married in 1991.)

Answer Oui, il s'est marié en 1991.

Question Et il vit toujours en Belgique ?

(Say no, he lives in England now.)

Answer Non, maintenant il habite en Angleterre.

Track 11:12

Je suis née en 1971, en France, à Lyon. Ma famille est originaire de la région lyonnaise. En 1972 mes parents ont déménagé, ils se sont installés à Paris. J'ai deux frères qui sont nés à Paris. Nous avons grandi à Paris. Maintenant je suis mariée et je vis en Allemagne.

Track 11:13

Bonjour, je m'appelle Toan, et je viens du Viêtnam. Mes grands-parents étaient en vie à l'époque coloniale, quand le Viêtnam était français. Mon grand-père parlait donc un peu français. Aujourd'hui nous sommes une grande famille – mon père, ma mère et mes trois sœurs et frères. Quand j'étais petit, on vivait tous à la campagne. Mes parents étaient tous les deux agriculteurs. Le travail dans les champs était très dur. Ils sont à la retraite maintenant.

Mes deux sœurs, mon grand frère et moi, nous avons quitté le village et nous nous sommes installés dans une grande ville pour y chercher du travail et une meilleure vie. Mon grand frère est devenu donc coiffeur et mes deux sœurs commerçantes. Moi, j'ai fait des études universitaires ; je suis le seul dans la famille. Et je travaille maintenant comme enseignant de français. La fête de fin d'année est souvent la seule occasion où la famille se réunit. On se retrouve autour d'un repas et on passe de bons moments ensemble à la campagne.

Track 11:14

Suzanne

Mes parents se sont connus dans une gare de Montréal. Mon père, Jacques, était policier et revenait d'Australie où il a participé à la Seconde Guerre mondiale. Ma mère, Thérèse, était institutrice. Ensuite, ils se sont mariés ; c'était en 1950, à Vaudreuil, le village natal de ma mère, un bel endroit près d'un énorme lac. Après quelques années, papa s'est acheté une belle auto américaine et est devenu chauffeur de taxi à son compte. C'était l'époque de la Révolution Tranquille au Québec (en 1960–70), où beaucoup de choses ont changé dans « La Belle Province ».

Au bout de cinq ans, je suis née à Beaurepaire, une municipalité de l'île de Montréal où se trouvait la maison de mes parents. Un peu plus tard, mon frère Denis est arrivé.

Roxana

Je suis née en Roumanie dans les années 40, et j'ai grandi à Bucarest. Mon père était professeur de physique à l'université, et ma mère était institutrice. Je me suis mariée dans les années 60, puis j'ai eu deux filles dans les années 70. En Roumanie, nous vivions sous une dictature ; la vie y était difficile et la population était persécutée. En 1979, nous avons décidé de quitter la Roumanie pour la France car nous parlions tous français couramment. Mon frère et ma sœur, eux, ont préféré émigrer aux États-Unis. Nous avons fui le pays clandestinement et nous sommes arrivés en France en 1980. Aujourd'hui je suis professeur de littérature française à Paris.

Xavière

Je suis née dans une famille française juive d'Afrique du Nord, originaire de la ville d'Oran, en Algérie. Mes parents y sont nés. Mon frère et ma sœur sont aussi nés dans ce port situé au bord de la Méditerranée. À cette époque, l'Algérie était un département français. C'était avant 1962, avant l'indépendance de l'Algérie. En 1962, les populations qui habitaient en Algérie mais qui n'étaient pas d'origine algérienne ont dû quitter l'Algérie brusquement à cause de la guerre. C'est pour cela que moi, je suis née dans le sud de la France. Par contre, mes deux grand-mères, maternelle et paternelle, sont nées au Maroc, l'une à Casablanca, l'autre à Tétouan, au Maroc espagnol. Puis, elles ont quitté le Maroc et se sont installées en Algérie au début du vingtième siècle. Dans leur famille on parlait couramment le français, l'arabe et l'espagnol. L'une parlait le Castillan, l'autre parlait le Valencien, deux variantes de la langue espagnole. Leurs ancêtres lointains venaient sûrement d'Espagne, avant l'Inquisition et l'expulsion des juifs en 1492.

Track 11:15

1 La station est ouverte toute l'année et le domaine skiable est ouvert du 18 décembre au 17 avril.
2 Moi, je n'ai jamais fumé. Je n'ai jamais aimé cela, et je trouve que c'est très mauvais pour la santé.
3 Les médicaments et les frais hospitaliers sont gratuits avec la carte d'assurance maladie.
4 Vous devez normalement payer les médicaments prescrits par le docteur. Les médicaments sur ordonnance ont un prix fixe.
5 Pour pouvoir bénéficier des soins de santé et indemnités, il faut obligatoirement avoir une mutuelle, une partie de votre salaire est utilisé pour payer les cotisations.

Track 11:16

Mes parents se sont connus dans une gare de Montréal. Mon père, Jacques, était policier et revenait d'Australie où il a participé à la Seconde Guerre mondiale. Ma mère, Thérèse, était institutrice. Ensuite, ils se sont mariés ; c'était en 1950, à Vaudreuil, le village natal de ma mère, un bel endroit près d'un énorme lac. Après quelques années, papa s'est acheté une belle auto américaine et est devenu chauffeur de taxi à son compte. C'était l'époque de la Révolution Tranquille au Québec (en 1960–70), où beaucoup de choses ont changé dans « La Belle Province ».

Au bout de cinq ans, je suis née à Beaurepaire, une municipalité de l'île de Montréal où se trouvait la maison de mes parents. Un peu plus tard, mon frère Denis est arrivé.

Track 11:17

Je suis née en Roumanie dans les années 40, et j'ai grandi à Bucarest. Mon père était professeur de physique à l'université, et ma mère était institutrice. Je me suis mariée dans les années 60, puis j'ai eu deux filles dans les années 70. En Roumanie, nous vivions sous une dictature ; la vie y était difficile et la population était persécutée. En 1979, nous avons décidé de quitter la Roumanie pour la France car nous parlions tous français couramment. Mon frère et ma sœur, eux, ont préféré émigrer aux États-Unis. Nous avons fui le pays clandestinement et nous sommes arrivés en France en 1980. Aujourd'hui je suis professeur de littérature française à Paris.

Track 11:18

Je suis née dans une famille française juive d'Afrique du Nord, originaire de la ville d'Oran, en Algérie. Mes parents y sont nés. Mon frère et ma sœur sont aussi nés dans ce port situé au bord de la Méditerranée. À cette époque, l'Algérie était un département français. C'était avant 1962, avant l'indépendance de l'Algérie. En 1962, les populations qui habitaient en Algérie mais qui n'étaient pas d'origine algérienne ont dû quitter l'Algérie brusquement à cause de la guerre. C'est pour cela que moi, je suis née dans le sud de la France. Par contre, mes deux grand-mères, maternelle et paternelle, sont nées au Maroc, l'une à Casablanca, l'autre à Tétouan, au Maroc espagnol. Puis, elles ont quitté le Maroc et se sont installées en Algérie au début du vingtième siècle. Dans leur famille on parlait couramment le français, l'arabe et l'espagnol. L'une parlait le Castillan, l'autre parlait le Valencien, deux variantes de la langue espagnole. Leurs ancêtres lointains venaient sûrement d'Espagne, avant l'Inquisition et l'expulsion des juifs en 1492.

Track 11:19

1 Autrefois, les gens n'avaient pas le téléphone du tout. Moi, quand j'étais petite, on n'avait qu'un seul téléphone à la maison, un gros appareil gris. On ne s'en servait pas beaucoup parce que téléphoner coûtait cher. Je me souviens qu'on appelait mes grands-parents, qui habitaient loin et qu'on ne voyait pas souvent, tous les dimanches. Maintenant les choses ont changé. Presque tout le monde a un téléphone portable, et je connais même

des gens qui en ont deux. On passe des coups de fil fréquemment et on communique aussi par textos et par email. On est connectés à nos amis et à notre famille en permanence.

2 Dans ma petite enfance, lorsqu'on avait besoin d'une information, on la cherchait dans l'annuaire ou dans une encyclopédie, ou bien on se déplaçait pour trouver le renseignement à la mairie ou à la bibliothèque par exemple. Mais dans les années 80, il y a eu une petite révolution en France : l'apparition du minitel. On avait un mini-ordinateur à côté du téléphone, et on pouvait ainsi obtenir des renseignements et accéder à des services (comme consulter l'annuaire, vérifier la météo, acheter des billets de train...) immédiatement, chez soi. C'était l'ancêtre de l'internet. Maintenant le minitel a disparu, à la place on a l'internet sur nos ordinateurs, nos portables et nos tablettes tactiles.

3 Autrefois, mon grand-père achetait le journal tous les jours. Il prenait *Le Progrès de Lyon* qui publiait des nouvelles nationales et surtout régionales. Mon père a continué cette habitude et aujourd'hui encore il achète le journal tous les jours, mais il préfère un quotidien national, *Le Monde*. Moi je n'achète pas le journal papier. En revanche, je consulte des journaux en ligne presque tous les jours ; je lis les gros titres et je consulte seulement les articles qui m'intéressent. Souvent je les lis sur ma liseuse. Ça me permet de lire aussi les journaux internationaux. J'aime bien comparer les points de vue de pays différents sur les mêmes événements.

Acknowledgements

Grateful acknowledgement is made to the following sources:

Images

Book cover: © View Pictures Ltd/Alamy.

Page 5: © Hélène Pulker; *page 7 (1)*: © Hélène Pulker; *(2)*: © Hélène Pulker; *(3)*: © Hélène Pulker; *(4)*: © Hélène Pulker; *(5)*: © Élodie Vialleton; *(6)*: © Hélène Pulker; *(7)*: © Christine Sadler; *(8)*: © istock.com/JurgaR; *page 8 (1)*: © Hélène Pulker; *(2)*: © MJ Reilly/Flickr; *(3)*: © Jeffrey Blackler/Alamy; *(4)*: © Hélène Pulker; *(5)*: © Hélène Pulker; *(6)*: © Hélène Pulker; *page* 9: © Hélène Pulker; *page 10*: © Kevin George/Dreamstime.com; *page 17*: © Hélène Pulker; *page 18*: © Ian Shaw/Alamy; *page 20 (a)*: © Christine Sadler; *(b)*: © Colibri–Fotolia.com; *(c)*: © Dave Penman/Alamy; *(d)*: © Hélène Pulker; *page 21 (left)*: © Hélène Pulker; *(right)*: © Hélène Pulker; *page 22*: © Hélène Pulker; *page 24 (a)*: © Business/Alamy; *(b)*: © Hélène Pulker; *(c)*: © Hélène Pulker; *(d)*: Flickr © jmvnoos in Paris; *page 30*: © Hélène Pulker; *pages 32–3*: Bagieu, P., reproduced with kind permission from J.C. Gawsewitch; *page 34 (a)*: © Directphoto.org/Alamy; *(b)*: © International Photobank/Alamy; *(c)*: © Directphoto.org/Alamy; *(d)*: © Per Karlsson, BKWine 2/Alamy; *page 44*: © NetPhotos/Alamy; *page 45 (top)*: © Peter Stone/Alamy; *(bottom)*: © Hélène Pulker; *page 46 (top left)*: © Hélène Pulker; *(bottom left)*: © Hélène Pulker; *(top middle)*: © Kumar Sriskandan/Alamy; *(bottom middle)*: © Hélène Pulker; *(top right)*: © Pontino/Alamy; *(bottom right)*: © Elisabeth Hammerschmid/Dreamstime.com; *page 47*: © Hélène Pulker; *page 49*: © Julien Rousset/Fotolia; *page 66 (top left)*: © Robert Fried/ Alamy; *(bottom left)*: © Ekaterina Pokrovsky/Dreamstime.com; *(top right)*: © Dmitriy Shironosov/Dreamstime.com; *(bottom right)*: © Business/Alamy; *page 76 (1)* © Hélène Pulker; *(2)*: © Hélène Pulker; *(3)*: © Hélène Pulker; *(4)*: © Hélène Pulker; *page 80* © Sarah Heiser; *page 81*: © BSIP SA/Alamy; *page 83*: © Jaileybug/Alamy; *page 89*: © Hélène Pulker; *page 93 (top left)*: © Image Source/Alamy; *(top right)*: © Directphoto.org/Alamy; *(bottom left)*: © Rolf Adlercreutz/Alamy; *(bottom right)*: © Stockfolio/Alamy; *page 94*: © istockphoto.com/Xavier Arnau; *page 114*: © Sophie Giscard; *page 119*: © Jessica Podd; *page 123*: © Phovior/Alamy; *page 127*: © Hélène Pulker; *page 129*: © Hélène Pulker; *page 132*: © Hélène Pulker; *page 138*: © Yannick Saint-Andre/Fotolia; *page 141*: © Nik Wheeler/Alamy; *page 142*: © Photononstop/Alamy; *page 143*: © Alain Vialleton; *page 145 (top left)*: © Alain Vialleton; *(top right)*: © Alain Vialleton; *(bottom left)*: © Alain Vialleton; *(bottom right)*: © Alain Vialleton; *page 148*: © Alain Vialleton; *page 150*: © World History Archive/Alamy; *page 151 (left)*: © Alain Vialleton; *(right)*: © Élodie Vialleton; *page 153*: © Man vyi; *page 155 (left)* : © Hemis/Alamy; *(right)*: © Dave Penman/Alamy; *page 158*: © Elizabeth Whiting & Associates/Alamy; *page 164*: Éditions Albin Michel, 2007; *page 165*: Éditions Albin Michel, 2007; *page 166 (top)*: © Élodie Vialleton; *(bottom left)* © Daniel Bosmans; *(bottom right)*: © Exinocactus /Dreamstime.com; *page 169 (left)*: © Toan Nguyen; *(right)*: © Toan Nguyen; *page 173*